YOU'VE GOT TO BE KIDDING ME

A memoir of my Life and Times in Insurance Claims

By Trevor Cottington

Dedicated to:
Karon, Hayley and Josh

You've Got to be Kidding Me
A memoir of the Life and Times in Insurance Claims

© Trevor Cottington 2024

First published in UK in 2024 by Trevor Cottington Books

Cover design and layout by Trevor Cottington

CONTENTS

Prologue

MY LIFE AND TIMES IN INSURANCE CLAIMS

It probably goes without saying, but I will say it anyway, that one person's humour can be another's pain and suffering. We may laugh at someone slipping over on a banana skin, but if the person ends up with a fractured skull and a brain injury, it becomes somewhat less funny. In my many examples in this narrative, I have avoided using anyone's surname, except maybe once or twice. First names may be true, or maybe not. I will let you decide. I intend no offence to anyone – honestly.

I have also avoided using the company names but where I have mentioned a company name, it is generally false.

I have tried not to make light of the pain and suffering side, but sometimes how someone has injured themselves simply beggar's belief. A great many of the claims I have dealt with involve horrible injuries and fatalities. I am not including those except where other interesting points arise.

When I have relayed some of these stories over a beer with a friend or two, they often say 'you have got to be kidding me'. I'm not.

I must emphasise that this is a personal memoir and my memory may fail me, so please forgive any errors. The places are real, the people are generally real, the incidents true, but the chronology of events has by necessity been truncated and sometimes back-dated. Many claims take years to resolve which for the sake of brevity I have had to condense into a few paragraphs.

I thank my family for proofy-reading this – all mistakes in speling, syntax and punctuation; are theirs and theres alone.

Chapter One

HOW IT STARTED

I'm not sure how or why I ended up in insurance. Well, that's not entirely true... I do know and it's all because of my impatience. But before I dwell on that, a little background might help.

In the immortal words of The Who's Pete Townshend, I was born with a plastic spoon in my mouth. My parents were both divorcees with children of their own (a son for Mum and a daughter and son for Dad) and they met at a holiday camp which was all the rage in the 1950s. Foreign holidays or 'going abroad' were unheard of, not that there were many places to go, what with Europe still recovering from the ravages of WW2 and flying was only for the super-rich, which my parents certainly were not. Indeed, Mum never set foot outside of the country until her 60th birthday when I took her on a booze cruise to France. After that, the travel bug bit deep and she was often on cruises and travels. She even went to Australia in her mid-60s, on her own. Dad, on the other hand, had served overseas during the war and had been to Malta and South Africa and had no desire, or indeed the money, to even consider foreign holidays. It was not until I was in senior school that I heard that one of my classmates had spent his summer in, of all places, Jersey, traveling by overnight ferry, which was considered very exotic.

Although there was a 14-year age difference between Mum and Dad they were well-suited and married in 1953 or 1954. By the time wartime rationing had ended, I came along as a child of the Harold MacMillan 'You've never had it so good era'. Mum had, according to her, gone to the doctor complaining of stomach cramps to be told that she was pregnant with me. Dad was 47 years old when I arrived on the scene and there was around an 11-year age gap between my two half-brothers and, I think 16 or 17 years between me and my half-sister. My half-sister, Judith, was quite young when she married a much older man called Ivan. I don't think they had children though and they were probably divorced by the time Dad died, but I never saw her again after his funeral.

My two half-brothers were Mark and Norman. I resembled Mark (Dad's son) far more than Norman but both left home very young at the ages of 13 or so to go into military cadet school when I was about 2 or 3. Mark went into the Air Force and Norman into the Navy. Both had left the Forces around the age of 18 or so. Consequently, from a very young age, I was very much an only child. Mum married four times and I am one of eleven – all steps and halves – and I haven't seen or spoken to any of them for decades...we are not a close family by any stretch of the imagination.

We lived in a house that my parents had rented, but it was one of only 2 semi-detached pairs of houses on the estate which to my 13-year-old mind made us somehow superior to everyone else. Actually, it did to my mother too, who was always trying to be rather grand, putting on a fur coat to go to a restaurant...which they did maybe once a year, birthdays probably, and as their birthdays were only a week apart in March doubtless a double celebration. Not that they ever really mentioned ages or as far as I can remember exchanged gifts or cards. I did give them presents, paid for by Dad for Mum and Mum for Dad, and nearly always the same – a pack of 100 cigarettes, which you could get in those days. Unfiltered Players Navy Cut for Dad and Mayfair or Gold Leaf for Mum.

I did OK at school, gaining a liberal sprinkling of 'O' and 'A' levels, but due to home circumstances, the prospect of a university education was never an option. My parents were, what I now realise was, working class. Dad was the manager of a butcher's shop in Sutton and Mum had worked in a sweet factory and in various clerical roles until she ended up dealing with customer complaints in what was then the local Gas Company – SEGAS. Both were heavy smokers and in 1971 at the age of 61, my father succumbed to the inevitable lung cancer. Strangely, Mum carried on smoking, if anything more than before. She never believed that smoking had caused her husband's illness, always saying that he had died of 'rapid cancer', like that was something different, even though he went through agonies in the hospital for months before passing away in May. Hardly 'rapid'.

So, with Dad passing we were down to just one income. I believed that Mum did earn more than Dad (but free meat was a bonus) but he had died leaving nothing at all. I don't think he even had a bank account. Apparently, according to Mum, he did leave enough to buy me my first 26" 5-speed racing bike, but I am sure she bought it as a way of some kind of grief counseling. I remember having a day off school for his funeral, but that was it. At the time I

13

don't recall much in the way of grief, some sadness of course, but he had been in hospital for months and my visits became less frequent as I could see this man who could lift a half carcass of beef and transport it from lorry to shop with seemingly no effort, gradually waste away to skin and bones to the point where he could not talk without causing pain. It was not a pleasant sight and so I distanced myself from it on the pretext of homework.

We muddled through for a few months and then the summer holidays were upon us. Luckily, I was a resourceful lad and through my scouting, which I enjoyed immensely, I was a reasonable cook. I also enjoyed my own company and was quite content playing in the garden on my own. I recall throwing the javelin...ok it was a garden fork... as far as I could down the lawn repelling the invading Roman army. All went well until my strength grew and the fork went further than the lawn and bent its prongs on a small wall that separated the lawn from a flower bed. Indoors I was an extremely keen model maker and had probably constructed every kit Airfix made, but my favourites were aeroplanes (German WWII for preference) and tanks as well as model soldiers. The soldiers, all 1/48th scale, were all carefully painted and employed in the many battles on a large board I had crafted with hills and scenery all made from plaster of Paris and painted in muted greens and browns. So good was the camouflage that from time to time I found pockets of the enemy still lurking under a lichen bush waiting to ambush passing troops.

That August Mum had booked a week's stay at a holiday camp. Warner's almost certainly, but where I cannot recall. We must have gone by train because mum didn't drive... and never did learn, so I guess somewhere on the South Coast – Littlehampton probably. Mum always believed that Warner's holidays were far superior to Butlins where only 'common people' went. I don't remember much about that holiday except that Mum met Harry.

Now, Harry lived in South Norwood, so pretty close to where we were in Croydon. He drove a car and was widowed with two daughters. Marilyn was at university and Jan was a year younger than me. Within days of getting back home Mum was being 'courted' by Harry and within weeks announced a sort of engagement and by that November they were married. They were well matched, both heavy smokers and Labour supporters. My nose was seriously out of joint because I was unceremoniously booted out of my bedroom to the box room as the two girls were supposed to be sharing my old room. That would have been difficult as I recall that there was only one single bed in it and the Marilyn rarely came home. In fact, she married someone she met at uni and moved to Telford and we hardly ever saw them. I liked her though.

Meantime, the tensions back at home were many. You see, I was not the 'son' that Harry had expected. I was not particularly sporty at all (unlike his daughter who did everything – hockey, lacrosse, and rugby probably) I didn't follow football (well, I did... I had been a Chelsea supporter but he keenly followed Arsenal and when I heard that, I decided not to overtly follow any team, at least at home) and every meal time was unbelievably tiresome. Harry was fixated on his experiences as a radio operator 'during the

15

war'. My dad had been 'in the war' but didn't talk much about it. He had been involved in the convoys to Malta and had been on a ship that was torpedoed and he nearly drowned when some other poor soul jumped from the ship and injured Dad's back when he landed on him. Dad was sent to South Africa for convalescence and his uniform shows that he was in the Royal Artillery and as we have concluded he was a gunner on armed merchant ships as Dad had said he had been in the merchant navy. Anyway, Dad was a corporal or a sergeant and had boasted once that he had put a bloke on a charge because he'd pissed in a fire bucket. Harry's stories were often repeated and I accept the experience must have left its mark because he never stopped repeating them, ever. I had turned off listening a long time before but he did mention also being on a ship that was sunk, so he and Dad might have been on the same one. I have always hoped that it was Harry whom Dad put on a charge for the fire bucket incident.

Anyway, Harry was also argumentative and provocative. Not so skilled at arguing at the time I decided silence was the best policy and so I clammed up. I don't think I spoke more than half a dozen words to him over the next 5 years. I tried never to be in the same room and the only time I had to face him was Sunday lunch. Always a big deal with my mother who cooked a roast dinner every Sunday and it was compulsory to attend. Being a teenager who frequently slept in until noon on Sundays, and by the time of 16+ often with a hangover too, the first thing to pass my lips on Sunday after a toothbrush was a roast dinner, eaten in silence, at least by me.

And so it was Harry's revenge to make it abundantly clear that there would never, ever be enough money to fund my university education. Even though my grades were sufficient at A level to get me into one of the lower colleges, the thought had been erased from my career path and so I knew I would have to get a job. Strangely exactly a year later my step-sister with only 2 A levels to my 3 (Geography, Biology, and Economics in case you were wondering – an eclectic mix) went off to Liverpool Uni on a full grant + frequent top-ups from Harry! She did not get on with Mum in the same way I didn't get on with Harry. She never really came back 'home' either.

In June 1974 (much to the surprise of my mother who had bet me £1 a pass), I passed all 7 of my O levels (at my school sitting 7 subjects was normal, and only those additionally sitting French might do 8) and indicated that I would stay on for A levels. So, from June to September, I had the better part of three months to either mooch about playing cards with my friends or I could do 'something'...but what?

My half-brother Norman was working at a solicitor's office in Strand, London and he got me a job as an 'outdoor clerk' (whatever that was) on the princely sum of £50 a week. My fares were over £10 per week and the journey was a pain too – a bus into Croydon, a walk to East Croydon train station, a train to Victoria, and then a tube to Temple and a short walk, up Arundel Street to 199 Strand, which was pretty much opposite the Royal Courts of Justice (RCJ). My office was on the 5th floor, in the attic and I shared the tiny space with two permanent outdoor clerks, Stephen and Paul. They were both dressed in sombre black or dark grey suits. Mum had bought me a pair of aubergine-coloured trousers and a matching blazer, assuring me that this combination would be fine for a summer job and also for 'going out in' ... not that I went anywhere that could remotely have required such attire. As for shirts, my school ones would do along with my school tie. Perhaps because of my strange sartorial ensemble, Stephen was very offhand with me but Paul and I got on OK. Stephen eventually became the senior partner of the firm.

My role, such as it was, was basically to collect and deliver 'briefs' to counsels' chambers in the adjacent Temple. The briefs were all on foolscap paper (slightly longer and narrower than A4 size), folded lengthwise, and bound with red tape, which I learned meant litigation. I soon became very knowledgeable of the various Inns of Court and their layouts, chambers names, and suchlike. I can still find my way around to this day.

One of the things we had to do was to appear before a Master in the High Court and pass over a bundle of papers and say a few words, the Master would look at the documents, issue an order by scribbling something on the papers and then hand them back to us. Paul had asked me to watch what he said and did and copy him – it seemed easy enough, even though I had not the faintest idea about what I was doing. Paul explained all the clerks from other firms would all arrive at court at 10.30 am and proceed to the Master's Chambers, which were in the rabbit warren of the RCJ. All hearings were at the same time, so there could be ten or more cases to be heard and you would sit on a bench and wait patiently until the clerk or the Master called out the case – Smith and Jones for example. They never said 'versus', it was always 'and'. The Master would sit behind a desk and depending on whether you were the plaintiff or defendant (we were generally the plaintiff) you then approached the desk and placing the papers on the desk facing the Master you would rest your hands on the table leaning on your fists, thumbs inwards and say something like 'good-morning Master. I represent the plaintiff in the action, Smith, and my colleague here on my left (the other outdoor clerk) the defendant Jones, and here are the pleadings.' At that point, you would pass the bundle to the Master who would untie the mysterious pleadings, read them in silence, and then ask the other clerk if he had any objection to what we were asking for and depending on the answer scribble his Order. This all seemed frightfully simple and I could not wait to have a go.

According to Paul and Stephen, the most feared Master was Master Ritchie. I do not know why he was feared but apparently, he could ask awkward questions and had a habit of tossing papers that were improperly presented (such as having staples in the papers not covered with a paper tab or tape, lest the good Master should snag a finger on an errant staple) back at the offending clerk with stern words not to repeat the offence and come back another day. My first appearance before Master Ritchie came soon enough.

Stephen was on holiday and Paul and I were quite

literally run off our feet delivering briefs and Paul asked me to take an urgent bunch of pleadings to the Court to appear before a Master that morning. Off I went and to my surprise, the Master sitting that day was none other than the feared Ritchie. Paul had told me that in our case the defendant in the action had failed to supply photographs or documents by a certain time and was in breach of a prior Order of the court. It would be simple enough he said.

I was quaking in my shoes when our case was called and I walked nervously up to Master Ritchie's huge desk and, placing the papers in front of me and leaning on my fists, began my prepared speech:

'Good morning Master. Here are the pleadings and I represent in the case the plaintiff in the action and my colleague on my left the defendant.' The other clerk was even more nervous than me. Ritchie opened the slim pleading bundle and quickly read the text. Looking up at the defendant clerk said to him in a menacing tone 'It says here that you were Ordered to supply the plaintiff photographs and a statement by last Friday and you haven't. Is that true?'

'Er, yes Master. Due to the holiday season, I'm afraid...' At that point Ritchie interjected.

'I don't want your excuses, I didn't ask for an excuse, I just asked if it was true. You have had plenty of time to send these documents to the plaintiff and you have failed. You have until this Friday to comply or there will be judgment in default and the costs of this hearing to be costs in the case.' And turning to me said pleasantly enough 'Does that suit you?' Guessing I had 'won' I gave my thanks and gathering up the papers again, I went back to the office feeling rather smug with myself. I showed Paul the Order and rather cockily said that 'me and Master Ritchie, are like that' (holding up two entwined fingers). 'OK then' Paul answered with a smile, 'any more matters before old Ritchie you can have them!'

It wasn't long before another matter arose. This time a solicitor at the firm asked me to go over to the Court and ask for 'Interlocutory Judgement'. 'What's that?' I asked innocently. 'It doesn't matter and I haven't time to explain it – it's simple enough – just ask for interlocutory judgment. The other side won't oppose you. Off you go now.' And with that, I was dismissed from his office. Neither Paul nor Stephen was about, so repeating the mantra to myself about interlocutory judgment I trotted over to the RCJ found the appropriate court, and noted that my old mate Ritchie was sitting. I smiled to myself and sat in the row of hard chairs awaiting the case. Only one other person was sitting on the chairs so I guessed he was my opponent. I moved next to him and whispered 'Are you here for Smith and Jones?' 'Yes,' he answered. I whispered again, 'I'm asking for interlocutory judgment. Are you going to oppose?' 'No' he replied. That's good I thought, this was going to be a doddle.

It was a hot day and my shirt was sticking to my back as the case was called. I sauntered over to the Masters table and going through the familiar routine began:

'Good morning Master, I represent the plaintiff in the case, Smith, and my colleague here on my left for the defendant Jones. I am asking for interlocutory judgment.'

Ritchie looked up at me raised an eyebrow and growled: 'Do you know what that means young man?' What? I guessed he hadn't heard me? Maybe he was getting a bit deaf? This wasn't going according to my script. I decided to repeat myself.

'Er, good morning Master, I represent the plaintiff in the case, Smith, and my colleague here on my left for the defendant Jones. I am asking for interlocutory judgement'.

'Yes, I heard that. I'm asking you do you know what interlocutory judgement means? Well, do you?'

'Er... no Master, I do not. I was just asked to appear and ask for interlocutory judgment.' The chap on my left was sniggering at this point.

'Well, go away and don't come back until you know what you are talking about' he thundered. And with that, he flung the pleadings at me and waved me away. The other clerk fairly skipped out of the courtroom as I meekly followed him with my tail between my legs. I guessed my love affair with Master Ritchie was over before it had really begun. It was a very valuable lesson though and although I did not fully appreciate it at the time, in business there is no point in bullshitting or bluffing – it rarely works and you need to know what you are talking about, and if you don't know or understand something: ask.

One of the more boring jobs we had to do was to go to Companies House near Old Street tube station and look up in dusty old ledgers the registered offices of companies the firm was intending to sue. The registers were just being transferred to microfiche and sometimes the details were on the blue fiches, sometimes in the books. We needed photocopies of some of the pages and these were procured for 6p a page (which the firm then charged the other side 10p a page) and I would return with pages and pages of irrelevant drivel when all that was needed was an address. Anyway, it made for a morning out.

I had just asked the clerk at the desk for a fair number of pages and paid the fee with cash from my pocket (I was generally repaid when I got back to the office from petty cash for my travel cost and the photocopying), when to my horror I realised that I had only a few coppers left in my pocket. I had insufficient funds to buy a return tube ticket and had no real idea of where I was in relation to the office, except it was a fairly long tube journey that involved one change of line. Luckily, I had on me my new chequebook. The firm was not paying my wages in cash, but monthly in arrears into my bank account (which made the travel to work fares a problem for the first month).

Opening a bank account back then was easy enough and my account was held at NatWest, Temple Bar which sounded very grand to me. The thing was that although I had a chequebook, I had never written a cheque and did not know if my account actually had any money in it. I couldn't phone the office as I didn't have the 10p coin needed at a pay-phone. The tube fare I needed was only 25p.

I began to walk back to the Old Street tube station and on the way, I saw a NatWest bank. I went in there and taking out my chequebook asked the teller how I could get cash out of my account? She told me to write the cheque out for 'cash'. I did so and tearing out the cheque, handed the piece of paper to her. She looked at it and raising an eyebrow, said that as my account was not at that branch, she would have to phone my bank to make sure that I had sufficient funds for the cheque to clear. Turning on her heels she went away and a few minutes later returned and said that it was fine, stamped my cheque with a big round marker, reached into the till, and slid a 50p coin under the glass. Yes, I had written out a cheque for just 50p! I later found out that the bloody bank charged me £1 to make the phone call. Anyway, now flush with fifty pence in my pocket I was able to get back to the office.

One sunny day I was asked to help a client at a hearing at Kingston Crown Court. It was explained that I only had to sit behind our barrister, take a note of what was said, then tell the client that all was well and shake his hand. I would not be required to speak at all. Again, it seemed easy enough.

This time I made sure I got a 'float' from petty cash as I had no idea how much it would cost to get to Kingston. I found the court easily enough and later in the barrister's robing room, met the barrister. He could tell that I was very junior (the aubergine outfit might have been telling) and assured me that all I had to do was take a note of what he said. I met the client who was a taxi driver who had been caught drunk driving and this was a hearing to see whether he could appeal the sentence of the court – a year ban and a fine.

At 2 pm we went into the court. The client was in the 'dock' and the barrister sat in the front row behind his lectern on which he had several books and papers. I sat immediately behind him. A voice boomed "The court will rise" and in came the judge, all bewigged and in a red gown with ermine on the collar, and as he took his seat at the enormous leather chair that was set much higher than the rest of us, he bowed. We were standing and nodded back and retook our seats. Apart from me, our barrister, the client, the judge, and the clerk of the court, the massive courtroom was empty. This was my first time in a 'real' court and I was just taking in the surroundings when my barrister stood up and began his well-prepared speech. I was jotting down as best I could what he was saying, basically that as a taxi driver losing his licence for a year was unduly harsh and would cause great hardship to his wife and family. The judge asked something or other because at that point I heard my barrister say 'Oh, I'll just take instructions on that point your honour from my instructing solicitors'...and turning 180 degrees he turned to me! My eyes must have been like a deer caught in the headlights because I hadn't really been paying attention to what I had been writing, well, not enough to answer any question and could barely read my own scribbled notes, when the barrister whispered 'rhubarb, rhubarb, rhubarb... don't worry old boy, just playing for time...and thank you' then turned back to the judge and carried on. My hand was so sweaty at this point I could barely hold my pen, let alone write with it. But I needn't have bothered as the judge simply said "Leave to appeal is refused", stood up and left and that was that. We were in and out of the court in about 15 minutes flat. Outside the court, the client shrugged his shoulders, thanked our barrister and me for doing our best, called the judge a bastard and left to get a bus to go home.

It was 1976, the year of the heatwave and getting a job was easy. But which one? I had four firm offers, subject to A-level results. British Rail wanted me as a 'traffic controller' but never really explained what that actually meant or entailed. The perks were laid out though - a lot of holidays, free rail travel and effectively a job for life as BR never laid off anyone, the unions were just too powerful. The other three jobs were with Croydon Council. One was in Weights and Measures/Environmental Heath, another in Building Control and the last in the Legal Dept.

I wasn't keen on the job in Building Control (my friend Nigel got that one) but Weights and Measures/ Environmental Heath looked great. They would pay for me to attend college to get a qualification (5 years apparently) and the office was literally a stone's throw from home. Then disaster struck.

A pre-requisite of W&M/EH was O-level physics. I'd got Chemistry and Biology O Levels but had given up physics because I hated the teacher and there was far too much maths. Besides, I never understood electricity (and I still don't, but more of that later). There was an option at school of taking GCSE Physics but I had to get a grade A... and I had to cram 2 years of study into 4 weeks before the exam... so W&M/EH's loss turned into Legal's gain, assuming I got 3 A levels that is.

That summer I worked all the hours I could at Sainsbury's. I stacked shelves, filled polystyrene trays with meat joints before they went on a conveyor through a machine that weighed, labelled and priced them, swept floors, collected trolleys from the car park, in fact, working very long hours. As I didn't reach the basic tax threshold, I was being paid more money than full-timers (which ticked them off mightily). I needed the cash so I could buy myself a couple of suits and get some business shirts and ties. I hadn't a clue of course. My shirts came from C&A and were all highly patterned (it was the fashion at the time, OK?), ties from a market stall and my two suits from the old man's outfitters, Owens – one coloured brown the other aubergine. I know, I know, I am a fashion victim. Oh, and a new haircut. At the time my hair was down to my shoulders and pretty unkempt to be honest, but again at school that was the fashion. No one ever had their hair cut, not unless you wanted serious ridicule. I must have impressed someone at Sainsbury (perhaps the new haircut?) as they offered me a position as a trainee manager, but I declined.

I had dreams of doing something 'in the law'.

Chapter Two

THE PEOPLE'S DEMOCRATIC REPUBLIC OF CROYDON

And so, in September 1976 I started my career in the legal dept (actually called the Town Clerks Dept) of The London Borough of Croydon (LBC), on the princely salary of £2,250 p.a. and boy did I feel important, dressed as I was in my brown suit and flowery shirt and tie!

The legal dept was split into various sections and I was expected to rotate between each after a few months. The departments were Contract, Conveyancing, Housing, Litigation and, strangely, Parking Enforcement. I was to be sent on day release to get a qualification – to become an Associate of the Institute of Legal Executives no less, which would give me letters after my name – at the terribly grand sounding institution of Kingsway-Princeton College, High Holborn in London.

I began in Contract. My manager, Margaret, was an elderly lady (well, she seemed old to me, but I guess was in her 50s) and she smoked constantly using a cigarette holder and her whole demeanour gave her the look of Disney's Cruella De Vil. She had a smoker's cough and I soon realised had undergone more surgeries than a chap of 18 years needed to know about, but that did not stop her telling me in every gory and intimate detail. Her health was poor and so she was frequently off sick leaving me to more-or-less my own devices. She had a crazy system of filing and in her absence one week I reorganised the lot. I'm not sure she ever noticed as before long I seemed to be doing just about everything there was to do.

Margaret was keen to let everyone know that her grade (everyone in LBC was obsessed with grading) entitled her to an office, a small square of threadbare carpet and, get this, a coat and umbrella stand as well as a trainee - me. I was christened 'Gofer' as I was always being asked to 'gofer' coffee, 'gofer' stationery etc. I didn't mind as it gave me quite literally breathing space from that tiny office.

Next door was a combined office of the Litigation, Housing and Parking Enforcement Depts. Housing and Parking consisted of just one person each, both ladies. Litigation consisted of three. Two ex-coppers and another trainee, a few years older than me – Malcolm. The ex-Policemen were also retirees who had done 25 or 30 years 'on the job' and were now on a full pension and were also getting full pay from the Council. Across the corridor was the Conveyancing Dept where there were four chaps all doing, well, conveyancing.

Housing disputes didn't interest me much and Parking Enforcement even less, but Litigation held out a bit of promise. These were the people who commenced proceedings against people who had transgressed the myriad of rules of Weights and Measures/Environmental Health – filthy restaurants and shops, people selling sub-standard and misrepresented goods etc. They also evicted trespassers – Travellers in the main, even though Croydon did boast of having a permanent Travellers Campsite. OK, it was next to the municipal sewage works and in the shadow of the power station, but a site nonetheless. The ambience could not have been good though, as the Dept was always trying to evict Travellers from parkland and cricket and football pitches.

Evicting trespassing travellers was always a challenge. To evict anyone, the Bailiffs needed to try and get the names of the parties, in this case, itinerant travellers who had invaded the rather lovely Lloyd Park. When asked for names were they likely to give honest answers? The Bailiff returned to LBC with the names they had obtained. Three that I recall were Donald Duck, Michael Mouse and the exotic-sounding Rose Alligator. The court papers were therefore completed with 'person or persons unknown' residing at such and such.

At the Magistrate's hearing three people turned up all clutching their Deed Poll papers signifying that they were indeed Mr Duck, Mr Mouse and Mrs Alligator so they said they had not been properly served. The magistrates agreed and the case was dismissed on this seeming technicality so we went back to the office and sent out the Bailiffs to once again get the names.

Undeterred and taking no chances on technical dismissals, the next set of court papers had included Messrs Duck, Mouse and Mrs Alligator, along with Arthur King and his wife Guinevere, Henry Eight and his partner Ann Boleyn and a host of other celebrity names past and present.

This time the eviction notice was secured, all the Bailiffs now needed to do was enforce it. Off the tow trucks went, along with a Police escort and upon arrival at the site it was soon realised that the caravans all had the type of hitch that needed a metal pin to secure and all the tow trucks had the standard ball and socket type. The mission was aborted and the team returned the following day, this time with the right tow hitches. The moment the tow trucks stopped several shabbily dressed small children surrounded the trucks all hurling abuse while others went to the rear of the trucks, then swiftly relieved them of the hitch pins... and ran away. The Police stood idly by putting the theft of the pins down to 'high jinks' and remained leaning on their patrol car doing nothing.

Finally, more hitch pins were obtained but moments before action could be taken the whole group of travellers hitched up their caravans to their smoky transit vans and other untaxed trucks that would never pass an MOT and went back onto the road to go and invade some other council's land (Bromley we hoped). The next thing was to send in the council dustcarts and several binmen to collect and remove the accumulated rubbish that had been left behind. It took two days apparently.

Malcolm became a firm friend and I ended up assisting him and his wife in renovating their house every Saturday for the next 3 years or so. The skills I learned in doing electrics, plumbing, plastering, bricklaying, wallpapering etc set me up for when I had my own property. Malcolm always said that when the time came, he would return the favours. In the event sadly that didn't happen.

Meantime back at work, I ended up remaining in the Contracts dept as Margaret was forever off sick and there was no one else prepared to do her work. So, I was left to draft up contracts. It was not difficult, nearly all the contracts the Council prepared were standard documents and all I had to do was find the right one for the contract. At the tender age of 18-19 there I was preparing contracts valued at hundreds of thousands of pounds for the supply of food for the council schools and canteens, as well as the more frequent contracts for the renovation of council houses along with more modest supply of cleaning materials and window cleaning to council offices. Each contract had to be bound or tied in green ribbon and we had a special hole punch that drilled three holes in the thicker documents. The thinner ones were stapled at the long edge and then covered in a green sticky cloth tape. Each department had different colours for their documents. Red for litigation, green for contract and conveyancing and white for family (such as adoption papers) and I was the best sewing person in the legal department... or the only one who was prepared to do it, but I didn't mind. I was learning.

Now councils are very rigid about who can and cannot send out letters in the Council's name. In fact, no one could sign off anything, apart from the Town Clerk, a nice chap called Mr Dixon. All letters were submitted to Mr Dixon's formidable secretary all separated in a large book ready for him to sign. The letters had to be initialled by the drafter and supplied in quadruplicate. One copy went to the dept archive, one to the council archive, one copy back to the drafter (me) to file and the original went to the post room for sending to the addressee. No letter or internal memo could have spelling errors or smudges and if they did, they would be struck through and returned for retyping.

In my office (I always considered the office to be 'mine' as Margaret was hardly ever there) there were two telephones on the desk. One made normal calls in and out, but the other was initially a mystery to me. It looked like a normal telephone except that the dial only had, I think, the '1' and '0' available. It turned out that this was the Dictaphone. What you did was pick up the phone and wait until the head of the typing pool (another formidable lady) answered and you said 'New disk please' and she would place a re-recordable gramophone disc into a machine and then you began dictating. If you wished to pause the disk, to enable you to think what you are going to say, you dialled '1' and at the end of the letter you dialled '0' although saying 'yours faithfully' seemed to me to be pretty obvious that the letter had come to an end. But woe betide you if you mumbled or said the wrong word because the ladies in the pool typed exactly what they heard.

I recall one day a letter was returned to me, original and three copies all with the word 'doughnut' in the middle of a sentence about where the recipient was to sign and witness the enclosed contract. I ventured back to the pool and asked the typist, who had a twinkle in her eye, about the erroneous word. 'Doughnut is what I heard young man and doughnut is what I typed. You need to improve your diction and don't mumble so much'. Bearing in mind this was in the days pre-computers and the ladies all had manual electric typewriters so retyping the doughnut letter was a chore for her but a valuable lesson to me. A lesson I soon learned and never forgot. Indeed, my dictation was thereafter often used as the test tape for typist and secretary interviewees. I felt rather proud about that.

One day a rather aged solicitor, Mr Abbott, came bursting into my office indignantly waving a letter about. I asked what was the problem? He furiously waved the letter, then spluttered:

'Do you use the word "ultimo" in your letters?'

I had to confess I didn't (in truth, I wasn't entirely sure what it meant. I knew it was Latin and meant either this month or last month and was often abbreviated to just ult, but I never used it. There was 'proximo' too but that too was a linguistic mystery. But Mr Abbott was very much old-school and even signed off his letters with 'your obedient servant', something that as a public servant he felt obliged to use, but he was alone in that regard). It turned out that he had written to a firm of solicitors and had used the word ultimo in the letter and in response the person had written a post-script on the bottom which said 'P.S. Ultimo went out with the Ark'. Old Mr Abbott was utterly speechless and turning in a cloud of dust and smelling of mothballs he slunk off back to his office to carry on doing what? Not sure I ever knew.

Back in the main office and chit-chatting with Malcolm, I asked what was with the piles and piles of papers stacked all along one wall? These piles of papers must have been over 3ft high and went all along one wall and the piles never seemed to move. It turned out that these were all the parking tickets that needed summonses served on errant motorists. There was only one lady, Mandy, overseeing the process and she was a lazy so-and-so. Parking ticket summonses had to be issued within three months of the ticket being issued otherwise they were void. Glancing at the stacks it was clear that some of these were long overdue, and thus void, and the council was losing thousands of pounds in uncollected revenue. From time to time there was a blitz on the backlog where we all mucked in, but within days Mandy had let the piles grow again.

I once said to Mr Dixon that I'd assist in the backlog in my own time, not for overtime, but for 50% of the revenue I collected. Given the number of voided tickets and the difficulty in tracking the right addresses of motorists (you had to write to the DVLA to get the details and it took weeks), you'd have thought it was a win/win for the Council but Mr Dixon said it was an interesting thought, but I ought to concentrate on my studies instead. Years later the council did outsource parking ticket collections to Capita who made millions in the process, but I thought of it first.

Working for a council meant that apart from our normal annual holidays, 20 days at that time, we could earn another 12 days by doing extra hours as flexitime. There was a machine where you had to clock in and out every day and remove your plastic 'biscuit' from the machine when you were out of the office and not expected back (such as when you went to court) or at lunch. Of course, we all abused the system. Whoever was back first from lunch clocked everyone in and each week we filled in a form where we added a few extra minutes and hours travelling/waiting in court just so that at the end of the month you had gained an extra 8 hours. We were careful not to overdo it as that would rouse suspicion, but as far as I can recall everyone got one extra flexi day a month. So, what with council holidays for the Queen's Birthday and bank holidays, 20 days annual leave, and 12 flexi days my holiday entitlement was around 40 days. Not bad at 18/19 years old. No wonder councils are inefficient.

One evening, whilst 'working' late – it was probably 5.30pm and Malcolm and I were chatting about Saturday's DIY project, the telephone in my office rang. This was most unusual as we hardly got calls at all, and certainly not after the golden hour of 5pm when the office was exited en-masse by the staff, but my phone extension number was close to a number in the main Housing Dept and I sometimes got their calls in error. I answered warily but politely and was met with a stream of invective.

The conversation went something like this:

'Hello, hello, this is Mr Smith, I'm sick and tired of phoning you, you do nothing about my leaking bath you're fucking useless you are...'

'Mr Smith I'm sorry but...'

'Don't you interrupt me! Sorry isn't good enough. What are you going to do about it eh? I pay my rates...'

'I'm sure you do, but you've come through to the wrong...'

'I said don't interrupt me!! So, what are you going to do about it eh? Eh? I've waited weeks and weeks I have, and all I get are excuses and excuses and delays and delays. I pay my rates and I demand you do something about it or I'll come down there and smash someone's face in. Well, what are you going to do about it?'

I paused for a moment and then thundered:

'DO YOU KNOW WHO THE HELL YOU ARE SPEAKING TO??'

Rather meekly Mr Smith replied 'nooo'.

'Good,' I said, 'fuck off!!' and hung up!

One day I heard laughter and merriment coming from the Conveyancing dept. Curiosity aroused, and I went off to investigate. The chaps were all huddled around a telephone, hand over the mouthpiece, listening to someone. What's going on I asked? They told me to listen in and dialled the number again. The number was a firm of solicitors who had an arguably embarrassing name, but it wasn't the name so much as the voice of the person, the switchboard operator I presumed, who was causing the ribaldry because she had such a sexy, dreamy voice:

'Good morning, Knockers and Fishnets, sorry about the name, how can I direct your call?'

The chaps were right, it was a gorgeous voice oozing sexuality and they were dying to know if the face lived up to the voice. I suggested that there was only one way to find out and that was to pay them a visit. I'd walked right into that one, as they then said they had a frightfully urgent package to deliver to them, it was vital that it got there today (all lies of course) and as K&F were a short train ride away, I could take the package and find out if their mental image of the voice lived up to the actual vision. I thought of the extra flexi hours and off I went with the package that was so vital that it had to be hand-delivered to the actual solicitor in the office. The conveyancers had thought that the longer I was in the office there was more chance of hearing and seeing the owner of 'the voice'. On arrival later that day at the solicitor's office, I was greeted by a nice young lady behind the reception desk and I explained I needed to hand deliver the packet to Mr So and So. She seemed somewhat bemused by this request and said she would get the solicitor to come down to reception. But clearly, she wasn't the 'voice'. As I stood there in the reception waiting for Mr So and So, behind the reception, I could see that there was a tiny room where sat in front of a large board of wires and cables and wearing a telephone headset with a mouthpiece, was an extremely large lady of indeterminate years. She can't be? Surely not? Not her?? At that moment a light flashed on the reception board, she poked in a cable and said:

'Good morning, Knockers and Fishnets, sorry about the name, how can I direct your call?'

Oh my god – it was HER! She was the 'voice'. What could I tell the chaps back at the office?

The following morning a deputation from the conveyancers came into my office. Leaning on the doorframe one of them asked breathlessly – 'well did you see her?'

'Oh yes', I casually replied, 'she looked like Lesley-Ann Down' (a very slim and attractive actress who was in the popular series 'Upstairs, Downstairs' and I had the hots for her myself). 'Told you so' said one of the chaps slapping another on the shoulder and off they went, happy with beaming smiles, back to their office. I never did have the heart to tell them the truth.

Day release got me out of the office during term time and my fares and lunch allowance were paid by the Council, which was good. Princeton-Kingsway College was close to Old Street tube station in London and despite its grandiose name was in fact a rather shabby Polytechnic. (It has since been demolished). My classroom was right next to another where the class was being taught the fundamentals of scaffolding or some such activity. We felt rather superior doing law.

Our tutors were all barristers and our terms were split between Tort, Contract, Constitutional Law and Conveyancing. Criminal law was to be next year. I loved tort and was pretty good on contract as that was what I was doing daily at work. I hated conveyancing as I thought it was tediously dull. The rest of my classmates were all employed at solicitor offices as trainee legal execs. I was the only one who worked for a Local Authority.

On day one I was fairly early and sat at a two-seater desk and before long the desks filled up as the students entered, ignoring me, leaving me all alone at my two-seater desk. Must have been the aubergine-coloured suit putting them off? Anyway, the tutor began and after a few minutes a rather flustered and attractive young lady entered the class, apologised for her late arrival and giving me a beaming smile sat next to me, being the only available seat in the classroom. I felt so smug. And Lucy smelt heavenly.

At lunchtime four of us went to the nearby pub for lunch. It was always the same – pie and mash and a pint. The other two were Adrian and David who had latched onto to Lucy like bees to honey... but she sat next to me lads, don't forget it. Of course, typically Lucy was engaged and any romantic intentions on my, David's or Adrian's part were soon crushed.

The conveyancing tutor was a young barrister who admitted to only knowing one joke and this made his lectures even more dull than the subject. In the last lesson pre-exam, he asked us to consider the next year (criminal) and we were asked to split into groups of four and answer the following question: what is the difference between unlawful and illegal? We were given twenty minutes.

There was a shuffling of chairs and one in our group started writing furiously. I thought the answer was that there was no difference... they are the same in the same way that flammable and inflammable are the same, but the one with the pen scribbled away.

After twenty minutes the groups began to give their convoluted answers – I think we had concluded that they were indeed the same.

'No', said the tutor rather smugly, 'unlawful means it is against the law and illegal is a sick bird of prey'. That was the 'joke' and to be honest it must be quite a good one as forty-five years later I can still remember it!

The year wore on and exams came and went. I passed and gained distinctions in the Tort paper and back in the real world at LBC I swung by the Personnel dept and proudly showed them my pass certificates. The crusty Personnel chap (this was long before the politically correct, but daft title, of Human Resources) congratulated me and asked if I was carrying on for next year? I confirmed I would be, but asked about a pay review? 'Of course', he said, 'you will get an 'increment'.' 'What's that', I asked, somewhat puzzled? £50 apparently. 'What a month?' I hoped. 'No, a year'. I said I'd worked my butt off, carrying Margaret, passed exams with distinctions and was getting less than £1 a week in reward? In fact, a paltry 75p per week after tax. I felt insulted, so I turned on my heels and stormed out of his office in a blur of brown suit, floral shirt and tie. Malcolm tried to put a spin on things and said that it was only my first year and I should not be impatient, but I was.

At that time, I was going out with Julie. I had been going out with her since the Lower 6th at school and we were an 'item'. Three steady years or so with your first girlfriend was unheard of, but we seemed OK. Now Julie worked for an insurance company called American International Underwriters or AIU. Some American company I had never heard of. She was doing clerical work of some kind and she said it was not only a fun place to work, but they were recruiting in the motor claims dept. The pay was likely to be better than the Council and if I wanted to, she'd get details. I wanted.

So, sometime in July 1977, I went off for an interview at AIU. John T interviewed me for the motor claims position who immediately noted that I didn't drive nor did I have even a provisional driving licence, so he surmised that I wouldn't be much use to him, but he knew AIU was looking for someone in their construction claims dept and that was all about contracts and suchlike, so I might be more suited for that. Did I want to try? I wanted.

A few days went by and then Mike interviewed me for the position of claims adjuster dealing with construction and engineering claims. I must have made an impression (the brown suit perhaps?) or they were desperate, but he offered me the job on the spot. A couple of days later I got the formal offer of £2,750 pa. I was thrilled. I immediately resigned from LBC and accepted the AIU job which meant I was due to start at the beginning of September 1977.

Most of that August was spent on holiday (two weeks at Scout Camp – I was a leader by this time) and using up my accumulated flexi-days so there was not much of a 'goodbye' at LBC. I think they gave me a pen as a leaving gift.

Lying in bed with Julie in late August she casually mentioned that they had a new starter next week in her dept, the same day as I was starting apparently. Oh no, I thought with my eyes widening and my heart sinking, it's surely just a coincidence, yes? But it wasn't...

Chapter Three

AIU

As a new starter, I was not expected to begin on day 1 until 10.00am to allow the others to get in and get themselves organised. I was on time, looking eager in my new grey suit but still wearing the floral shirt and gaudy tie. Mike quickly introduced me to the rest of his team. Tim was to be my immediate supervisor. He was in his 30s and seemed pleasant enough. Tim was responsible for UK construction claims and a couple of desks away sat Roger, who was in charge of international ones. Roger was an interesting character. I guessed he too was in his 30s; he wore thick-rimmed glasses and was enveloped most of the day in a fog of cigarette smoke. He had a mop of unruly hair and a droopy moustache rather like the TV detective Magnum or a 70s porn star (apparently). He had a slight Northern accent but I couldn't place from where, Newcastle perhaps?

Bearing in mind that in those days everything was paper and there were files piled high on most desks, including mine. Tim told me to sit and read the files, write notes and give a view as to what should be undertaken next. At LBC I had seen some potential insurance claims before, particularly involving motorists who had crashed into road signs and lamp-posts (or street furniture as they were known) or pedestrians who had fallen over road works and uneven paving, who would write to the council threatening all manner of dire consequences. I had attempted to try to answer some of the letters myself but Margaret had said that all such letters had to be unanswered and sent to the council's insurers, a company called Municipal Mutual, who would deal with them. So that is what I did and I never heard anything more. To my mind dealing with those claims seemed a damned sight more interesting than sending out a contract for soap for public lavatories and here I was about to deal with exactly those sorts of claims. I was quite excited.

As I read through the files it became clear that nearly all of the claims were for theft of contractor's equipment (or 'plant' as they call it) from building sites. Generators and transformers seemed frightfully popular targets as was scaffolding and a mysterious piece of kit called a whacker vibrator plate.

Some of the papers on my desk were simply letters advising new claims from brokers. I had heard of these middlemen but was never entirely sure what they did. I asked Tim what is it that brokers do and he said 'Buy me lunch, that's what!' The new claims needed to be handed over to a processing clerk who would put them into a new pink folder and allocate each a claim number all copied and cross-referenced from a very large ledger and index card system. The clerk would also find the policy from somewhere else and slot that into the pink folder so I could read what sort of policy the contractor had purchased. There were two main ones – a Contractors All Risks policy (known confusingly as CAR as I thought that meant car insurance. Apparently not, car insurance was called 'Auto', this was an American firm after all). The other sort was

EAR, or Erection All Risks which must have made everyone smile with the obvious double entendre. As to the distinction between the two I knew not. I asked which processing clerk I needed to hand the letters to and was taken down the office to the filing cabinets and there at a desk was Julie. She looked up, all tight-lipped and with a look that could turn milk sour, but Tim seemed not to notice. Apparently, any processing matters or minor queries had to be referred and given to Julie and Tim would deal with technical queries. I handed the new matters to Julie and she took them without a word. This was going to be tricky.

During those first few weeks, relations between Julie and me were becoming strained as she could not accept that I could give her work, and totally unbeknown to me she had resigned without having another job to go to. She got another job easily enough, at a company that supplied spare parts for vacuum cleaners, but the writing was on the wall and before I was 20, we had split up for good.

I got my head down as I had a great deal to learn about construction and the terminology. What was piling? What was the difference between sheet piling and contiguous piling? What was a 'set point' too? All these things were mysteries to be learned and solved.

One of the nicer things I found was that all I had to do was put my post into one tray and files I had finished with into another. A nice elderly lady called Doris would wander the office a few times each day and find the files for each item of post and deliver them back to you with the post item sticking out the top and she would re-file the others in the huge filing room at the side of the open-plan office that was her domain. Unless Doris was off sick or on holiday only a brave soul ventured into her filing room. Doris had a desk at the entrance where she sat guarding her territory and she knew where everything was and if anything was found out of place, she would track down the likely culprit and give them a stern talking to. At LBC I had to do my own filing so this was a step up. When Doris retired about a year or two later, she wasn't replaced and we all had to do our own filing, which was a pity.

Apart from lunches with brokers Tim was no stranger to the local pubs at lunchtimes and would disappear for hours at a time for mysterious 'meetings' and returned louder and worse for wear. I soon learned that for good reason Tim was called a 'legend in his own lunchtime'.

After a couple of weeks, another new chap arrived. A trainee for Roger. The new chap was called Martin and he turned out to be a year older than me and rode a motorbike. He had previously worked at another insurance company, Eagle Star. We became firm friends (and we still are some 40+ years later) and lunchtime drinking buddies and we both played a mean game of bar billiards. Sometime later I let slip details of my salary only to find out that Martin was on £250 less than me... and I never let him forget it.

One morning sometime in early December I was looking at a new claim for the loss of newly planted hydroseeding for a sea defence contract in Scotland. There was a storm apparently and the whole beach which had been graded and planted with marram grass had all been washed away. The claim was well more than £100,000. I was puzzled and asked Tim why would our policy pay for that?

His answer was that storm damage was covered. I pressed on and said whilst I understood that 'storm' was a covered peril (as was a tempest, though I couldn't really understand the difference between that and storm, I suppose there must have been a distinction) why did we pay for what I considered 'inevitable' damage? After all I said, storms can hardly be unexpected in November in Scotland and to be planting hydroseeding that late in the year must have meant that either the contract had run massively over time, or the project had been mistimed in the first place. If the project had been mistimed that made it a Professional Indemnity claim (so not us) and if the project had overrun then there was a chance that the loss was indeed inevitable. Tim raised his not-inconsiderable eyebrows and asked what did I know about such things? I said that I had A level geography and knew about sea defences (true) and had A level Biology too and taken a special interest in marine biology (partly true...ok a very small part) and that at that latitude at that time of year, marram grass would simply not have germinated in time to form sufficient root structure to stabilise the sandy dunes. I guessed that marram grass needed to be planted months before, probably in the Spring. Tim was unimpressed but agreed I should appoint a loss adjuster to investigate and retain an expert at Glasgow University to provide a report on the hydroseeding itself.

Loss adjusters are a peculiar breed. They act as the eyes and ears of the insurer and physically go and see the policyholder, look at the damage and provide the insurer with an estimate of the loss so they can put money aside to pay for the claim. This is called the reserve. At that time loss adjusters charged the insurer a fee calculated on a percent of the final agreed loss. This was called 'scale fee' and it seemed a daft system to me. It could encourage the adjuster to inflate the claim so he could get more in fees and on the smaller claims not do a proper job as his fee would be tiny. But that was the system and I knew no different.

A few weeks went by and the loss adjuster's report on the seeding claim landed on my desk with a thump. The report was huge, but the conclusions were that the project was indeed 6-8 months behind schedule and the seeding had indeed been planted very late in the year, in fact during a frost. Glasgow University also agreed that there was no prospect whatsoever of marram grass germinating at that time of year, let alone growing a root structure to stabilise the dunes. The loss was considered to be foreseeable at best or inevitable at worst.

Tim was rather surprised but agreed with me that we could deny the claim, which when explained to the brokers and contractor was a position they reluctantly accepted. I of course was cock-a-hoop; my misgivings had been vindicated and I had saved a £100,000+ claim.

AIU was a major player in the UK and International construction market and we were always busy with new claims and projects. A few projects particularly stick in my mind not just because of their size or the terrible accidents that resulted, though some were, admittedly, unbelievable.

The Thames Barrier was a massive project designed to prevent London from flooding and total devastation should there be a spring surge tide at the same time as a high tide combined with heavy rain. I can't quite remember the precise sequence, but you get my drift. At this time (late 1970s) the project was typically running late. As insurers, we never minded projects running late as the premium was calculated on time + the value of the project and this was a time of quite high inflation so there were always premium adjustments to fill up the coffers for the losses. At that time insurers worked on the basis that even if all premiums equalled the sum of all claims (known as a 100% loss ratio) they would still make money on the investment income. Premiums come in first and claims are paid out gradually. Some insurers even went as far as a 105% loss ratio and were unconcerned, they were still technically solvent.

It is worth mentioning that most major projects are written in the insurance market by several carriers to spread the risk. The first person to sign up for a risk on the 'slip'* is considered the lead insurer and those that sign up afterwards are the 'follow' or coinsurers.

[*simply, a slip of paper with the basic risk details that are passed by brokers to several insurance carriers. The full terms and policy wordings are delivered later, but as most policies were considered fairly standard, they were, and are, designated as abbreviations on the slip as were the additional add-on terms and exclusions. The insurance market had been like that for 100s of years and it seems to work.]

The Thames Barrier was a significant project costing many millions of pounds and AIU was supposed to be the lead insurer of the risk, but the 'top brass' in the GLC and in Whitehall were loath to allow this prestigious British project to be 'led' by an American company, so instead Commercial Union were designated the lead insurer, a good sound British company. So, although AIU were 'follow' we had agreed with CU that if we wanted to go to the site and look at a claim ourselves, we could.

At this time the Barrier was still in the fairly early stages of construction. A pier had been constructed out into the Thames so that cranes could drive twin rings of interlocking sheet piles into the river bedrock and when those were finished the water that was within the rings could be pumped out and the void between the two rings filled with concrete. This is called a cofferdam. Once set and cured the middle part of the ring, still full of water is also pumped out leaving a huge concrete tube sticking out of the water. The sheet piles are then pulled out of the river bed for reuse. The middle of the ring is where all the machinery will be installed once the dry bottom of the void has been concreted over.

The construction of the temporary piers from each bank of the Thames was such that the piers only went partway across the river, there had to be a gap between them to allow ships and boats to pass. That meant that the central cofferdam had to be constructed from floating barges with massive piling cranes on them. This was difficult as the steel piles needed to be inserted not only vertically, but interlocked with its neighbour to ensure it was completely watertight. The Thames is tidal at this point so not only was the floating crane going up and down with the tide, but it was also at the mercy of the flow of the river in both directions. Tricky engineering indeed... and the middle pier was leaking.

It was suggested that I go and have a look at the problem and report back. There were very experienced loss adjusters and engineers dealing with the matter and I was unsure as to what I could say or do that might assist, but I was inquisitive and this was a once-in-a-lifetime moment. So 'booted and suited' off I set to see for myself. It was a freezing cold day and our trip to the central pier had to be timed to coincide with a high tide (although I didn't know why) and that gave me time to chat with the project engineers and look at the fantastic models of the barrier and the drawings.

There was a film show that explained all the engineering and safety instructions. I had to change my office shoes for some safety boots and donned a hard hat and fluorescent jacket, but decided I needed to keep my briefcase and camera with me. The camera was my own and I didn't want to risk it getting wet, so it was shut firmly in the briefcase.

The film show over I asked the chief engineer whether the barrier would actually work if and when the time came? Given that the project had overrun by a year or more there was a thought that the barrier would not be finished before the next danger time, something to do with

51

tidal changes, the gravitational pull of the moon etc. The chief paused for a moment as if in thought, shrugged his shoulders and said 'hope so' and that was that.

The central pier had been a problem from the start. Physically getting floating cranes there, ensuring that they were stable in a fast-flowing river, whilst driving massively long interlocking sheet piles was a tall order, but it had been done. The problem was that the outer ring was leaking and divers had been sent down to try and weld up the holes. The Thames of course is not crystal-clear water and was described as like swimming in oxtail soup with practically zero visibility. So, although the water in between the two rings was being pumped out, water was still getting in. The engineers had explained that as concrete was denser than water, if they began filling the ring between the piles with specialist quick-curing concrete this would displace the water and all would be well. That was the theory at least.

The time had come for me to have a look for myself. There was a tiny launch boat waiting for me at the dockside. The skipper looked at my briefcase, then at me, and said rather incredulously:

'You taking that (meaning the briefcase) with you?'

'Yes,' I said 'it's got my camera in it' as if that explained everything, and as nimbly as I could and clutching my briefcase, I hopped in.

The skipper said that it would take just 5 minutes to get to the cofferdam but said that as the water was choppy and moving with a big swell, I needed to stand at the prow. I wasn't entirely sure why. A few minutes later the cofferdam loomed in front of me. It was about 5-6ft proud of the water level. Suddenly there was a big wave and the skipper revved the tiny craft and up the wave we went until the fender on the prow popped over the sheet piles of the cofferdam and the boat levelled out. Almost as quickly the swell began to reduce, the boat began to tip backwards and hanging from the fender the skipper yelled 'Jump!' and out I jumped, tightly gripping my briefcase in one hand, onto a small platform just inside the cofferdam where there was a handrail that I grabbed as if my life depended on it, which in a way it did. I was safe. The next wave dislodged the boat and the skipper turned the launch away, presumably to collect the next poor soul to risk life and limb.

The inside of the cofferdam was a maze of scaffolding and from the top of the sheet piles to the depths of the cofferdam, there were sheets of thick polythene flapping in the cold air and being buffeted by jets of water that were streaming in from the Thames. I had clambered down the ladders (still clutching my briefcase) until I was nearly at the bottom. I was getting soaked and in truth could not see anything of interest. The foreman tried to explain to me where the problem was, but the noise from the water gushing onto the polythene was like a constant drum and I could hear almost nothing, so I just kept nodding in apparent understanding. I could not wait to get out of there. It had just occurred to me that all that was separating me from a very watery grave was a ½ inch thick row of sheet piles, and they were leaking! I feigned interest for about 30 minutes and thought that that was long enough.

The foreman radioed for the launch and back the skipper came, accelerated up a wave and landed the little boat on the cofferdam once more. Onto the launch I hopped and cold and wet we went back to the shore. It was not until I was safely back inside the warmth of the site office that I realised I had not taken a single photograph and so had nothing to show for my trip. I'd gone to the very bottom of the Thames and not many people can say that, but I had nothing to prove that I had!

Back in the even safer confines of my office in Croydon I made my report and explained the possible and only solution so far to the leaky cofferdam problem. Concreting underwater.

The next thing I heard was that the contractors (a partnership of some of the country's leading civil engineering contractors) had contacted a concrete company, such as Readymix, to have 20 concrete trucks arrive in ten-minute intervals to allow them to pour their mix into a hopper which would then be pumped out to the ailing cofferdam. They had calculated that 20 lorry loads should be enough but the pour needed to be undertaken as a continuous flow, there could be no join in the concrete as that might possibly be a point of weakness. Well, after 15 lorry loads the concrete didn't seem to be reaching anywhere close to the top of the cofferdam. The engineers went over their calculations again and still thought 20 was sufficient, but to ensure safety they ordered another 10. An hour later another 10. By this time Readymix had run out of the specialist concrete that was critical to the pour, so the contractors contacted Blue Circle and to be on the safe side, Tarmac as well. In the end close to 50 lorry loads were used and the engineers were baffled. Where had all the concrete gone?

Divers were sent down and they reported that a huge plug of concrete was being squeezed out from the bottom of the cofferdam into the Thames, another massive plug had detached itself from the cofferdam and had wrapped itself to the bottom of the pier and a third was a huge blob in the middle of the Thames. The Port of London Authority came on the scene and considered the second two plugs were potential shipping hazards and had to be removed 'somehow'.

The detached plugs were removed by a floating crane, but the plug attached to the pier was a different and trickier problem. The proposed solution was to send divers down to drill holes in it and then blow the plug into fragments with underwater dynamite. Well, they must have used a tad too much dynamite because on the day the explosion successfully blew the plug to pieces but in so doing demolished a huge section of the pier too. The damage was spectacular. Overall, the costs went into the millions of pounds.

I was also dealing with claims for personal injury, ones that either happened on building sites or to members of the public who tripped and fell over roadworks and suchlike.

Quite how anyone assessed the value of a broken wrist on one person as opposed to another seemed to me to be another dark art. There was little or no guidance and to be honest we took a 'punt' at a number and sometimes it was accepted, sometimes not.

It is probably at this time I ought to say that I accept

that no one sets out to injure themselves deliberately in the hope of getting compensation from someone as the process is long and tedious. Furthermore, whilst some of the accidents I have dealt with have their funny side I do not mean to belittle the fact that one person has been hurt and, in some cases, fatally so. However, all claim handlers were told not to get emotionally involved in any case and treat each injured person as just another name on a file. Whilst I remember some of the names of injured people, I will only use generic names.

Two major tramways were being built in the UK, one in Newcastle and the other in Glasgow. Once again, the top brass in Whitehall had decreed that such prestigious projects had to be insured with British companies even though AIU had come up with the most economical premium proposals. A deal was done behind the scenes and Municipal Mutual would lead the risks with 10% and AIU would write the remaining 90% and retain claims control handling. So, on paper MM were leaders and AIU followers, whereas in practical handling terms, we were in charge.

Two peculiar cases in Newcastle come to mind. One for Mrs A who was standing on the pavement when a Newcastle City bus went past and its wheel kicked up a stone and struck her, blinding her in one eye. It was alleged that the stone had come from the building works and the contractors had failed to ensure that the roads were swept clean of debris.

The other was Mr B who was a workman on the project. He had stood on a piece of wood that had a nail sticking up and this had penetrated the sole of his shoe and had gone into the bones between his toes in the middle of his foot. He said he went home, had a hot bath, dabbed the wound in Dettol and went to bed. In the middle of the night, he was awoken by an extreme pain in his now hugely swollen foot that had taken on a greenish/blackish hue and so he took himself off to the nearest A&E dept. At the hospital, he had the wound once again cleaned, this time properly, but was admitted. X-ray had shown that the nail had penetrated a bone in the foot and bacteria had caused anaerobic gangrene. He had his foot amputated the following day.

Both of those accidents were tragic, but were the contractors to blame? The stone could have come from anywhere and there was simply no evidence that it came from the building site, and all timber should be de-nailed as a matter of routine (all carpenters are supposed to do that) and how come he was walking on wood anyway – why didn't he pick it up and put it in a skip? Furthermore, why was he wearing shoes on a building site instead of safety boots that have a steel inner sole? Both cases were very arguable.

At this time any injured person was entitled to Legal Aid so pursuing an action cost them nothing; should they win their legal fees were met by the defendants and should they lose, their solicitor's fees were again paid by the Legal Aid Board but only a tiny proportion of costs was reimbursed for the successful defendant, usually an insurer. As insurers, we seemed to be on a hiding to nothing and besides, in most cases, the injured party won.

I took the view that there were risks of losing in both cases so I called the claimant's solicitors and explained my arguments. They listened but still felt that at court they would win, but if I had any sensible proposal, they would take their client's instructions.

Mrs A's case had risks that hers was simply an accident that no one was to blame for.

Mr B's case was more of a challenge. He was a workman who should have been wearing safety boots (even though Personal Protective Equipment (PPE) was not compulsory at that time – it became law a few years later) as wearing PPE on this project site was mandatory so he was, in the parlance, contributorily negligent – or 'con neg' as we called it. But for how much? The failure to wear a seat belt in a car was and currently remains, a reduction of 25% as it is believed that even when wearing a seatbelt there will still be some injury. But a safety boot would have completely prevented the injury, so was he 100% contributory negligent? I got a deal on Mrs A for 50% of what an eye was 'worth' and secured a deal with Mr B with a reduction of 75% of his claim.

In 1977 London Bridge station was being extensively refurbished and I recall an amusing incident of a chap with a large pneumatic hammer drilling into the floor when suddenly he and the drill disappeared into a void at his feet.

Astonishingly he had his fall broken by landing on a wax-works figure in the London Dungeons who occupied the vaults under the station. The vaults and the configuration of the area were largely unknown to anyone as the plans and drawings had all been lost during the bombing of London in WWII.

Of course, we got a claim for the damage and also from the Dungeons for the water dripping through the roofs/ceilings 'spoiling the atmosphere' for visitors. The damage to the waxworks was paid but the water ingress was likely to be a much more significant claim. I decided to pay a visit, purchased a ticket (on expenses of course) and went in like any other visitor. I declined the claim on the basis that the dripping water enhanced the experience giving it the real feel of dank and dingy dungeons and besides, once the station was completed the water would dry up anyway. I heard no more from them.

Close to The Tower of London another project involved excavation work. A JCB driver was scraping away soil when he uncovered a skull and other bones. Horrified that he had uncovered a plague pit (it was possible) he jumped out of the cab of the excavator, ran up the embankment, slipped and fell back into the 'grave' fracturing his ankle in the process. I could not accept that the contractors were responsible for the accident so I defended it (successfully). Meanwhile, the Coroner and Police had to be involved to identify, if they could, who the bones belonged to. Amazingly the archivists at the Tower eventually found records. It turned out that there were three corpses – three unnamed Scottish soldiers beheaded at Tower Hill after the Battle of Culloden Moor. Obviously, back in 1746, their corpses had been simply flung unceremoniously into an unmarked grave. We had them re-interred at Camden Cemetery in a simple Christian ceremony.

It was around this time that Mike, head of the department, resigned. I cannot recall where he said he was off to, but there was an internal power struggle to get his old job. There were two contenders. Tim was one, the other Chris who was in a similar position to Tim but handling property claims. Both departments were of similar size.

Chris was qualified whereas Tim was older and with more experience and seemed to be 'in' with the head of claims, a chap called Craig. Tim was a bullshitter to a degree level whereas Chris wasn't. Tim got the job.

The offices we were in were rather shabby and so we were moved to brand new offices just opposite East Croydon Station. We were on the 5th floor. The layout was different too. Instead of ranks of desks, we now had 'pods' or cubicles and surrounding these were colourful walls or dividers about 5 feet high. This gave some privacy but also made it difficult to see who was in at a glance and if you called out someone's name, we were like meerkats popping up to see who was calling. There was a maze of narrow pathways to get from one end of the office to another and each floor seemed to have a different configuration.

Managers still had offices though and Tim's was on a corner giving him two aspects overlooking the station platforms. Craig had the opposite one but much larger although he only overlooked the company car park.

As with all new buildings, there were teething problems. The lifts were in a single rank of 4 in the centre of the building and come 5pm the queues were huge. The lifts were always seemingly out of service too, so some of us habitually worked late to avoid the rush. I say 'worked' but in fact, three of us, Roger, Chris and I, had taken to playing chess after work often for hours at a time. We were fairly evenly matched too. Roger though could be infuriating. I recall playing with him and after half an hour waiting for his move I said "for god's sake Rog, move something!" He looked up and said "Oh, is it my go then? I was waiting for you!" ...and so, another twenty minutes would pass before he made his move.

I was coming up to 21 years of age and had just passed my driving test (2nd attempt) when the very next day Malcolm asked if I would drive him to Hendon Police College where he was going to train to become a policeman during a twelve-week residential course. Although I was keen to practice my driving skills, the thought of driving through the centre of London (and back) during rush hour to boot, filled me with a sense of dread and a good deal of adrenalin. Malcolm said he knew the way, Streatham through Brixton, Elephant and Castle, over a bridge and round Hyde Park Corner and straight up the North Road to Hendon. 'Piece of piss' apparently. So off we went.

I'd been loaned a car – a blue Ford Escort Estate - which was now filled with all of Malcolm's gear for his residential course. Naturally, I'd torn up my 'L' plates, well, it's the first thing you do after passing your driving test. The journey was fraught, my palms were sweaty and I'd taken to wearing driving gloves to enable a good grip on the steering wheel as we approached the notorious Hyde Park Corner. I had been warned about this. Back then there were no road markings and certainly no traffic lights – you saw a gap and you put your foot down on the accelerator and went, praying that the other cars would avoid you. Of course, I hesitated and at that point learned the definition of a millisecond. A millisecond is the time it takes to hesitate there for the car behind to honk its horn… and that is exactly what happened. 'Go, go, go!' yelled Malcolm and spotting a gap in the traffic, I went. How I missed hitting anything that morning I will never know, but we arrived in Hendon, unscathed and in good time.

Exchanging goodbyes, I began the journey back. It should have been easy, but somehow or other I ended up on the south circular road which I recalled went somewhere near Croydon (it doesn't). Just outside Crystal Palace, the car began to splutter and looking at the fuel gauge I could see the car was running on fumes. Patting my trouser pocket, I could feel only loose change and maybe a pound note or two and pulled into a handy petrol station.

Fuel was fairly cheap back then, but reaching into my pocket the pound notes turned out to be scraps of paper with the directions to Hendon scribbled on them and the change was about 75p. Credit cards were practically unknown and I didn't have one anyway, so gently pressing the fuel nozzle I dribbled in as much four-star as I could without going over the magic 75p. I think I got to 70p and stopped. This was about three litres and provided I didn't get lost again, should be enough to get me home. The cashier raised an eyebrow when I handed over the change, all in coppers plus a few ten pence coins, but I said it was all I had with me, oh and could he please direct me back to Croydon?

By now I had moved out of home into an extremely large, but unfurnished, attic flat a short walk from the office. I could not afford the rent on my own and Roger offered to share with me. I quite liked Roger, even though he was 'strange' in his ways and apart from the ribbing we would inevitably receive about 'two single blokes called Trevor and Roger sharing a flat' (emulating some of the sitcoms at the time of the gay next-door neighbours one of whom was almost always a 'Roger' or a 'Trevor') we decided it made financial sense, so he moved in.

Friends and family donated a lot of rickety furniture and spare kitchen utensils and I bought a second-hand double bed (much to my mother's puzzlement. 'Why on earth do you need a double bed?' 'In case I get lucky mum') and splashed a bit of paint about to make the place habitable. Curtains came a lot later...well, it got dark and we were high up and the window in the bedroom was tiny, so I figured curtains could wait.

We were also 50 yds from a pub and a very short walk to a snooker hall so what more could I need? The walk to the office took me past Croydon market and if I got the timings right, I could buy fruit and veg very cheaply. Running a car, paying rent, feeding myself and going to the pub meant there was little or no spare cash. I couldn't go on any holiday (apart from Scout camp) for years.

I mentioned that Roger was 'strange', perhaps a 'bit of a character' would be a better description. He had some odd ways about him, and on the whole, we got on fine, but at work, he was terribly disorganised.

We still had paper files and computers were a rarity. We even had a department handwriting cheques.

Some claims went on for years and the files got huge in size, often in many folders. The more complicated and controversial claims often involved a meeting between all of the insurers and brokers, frequently with lawyers present too. These were known as 'Market Meetings' and were considered a chore as everyone who attended always had something to say and the meeting could last hours, sometimes all day. One such case involved Roger as 'lead' and due to the importance and value of the claim, Craig was involved too.

The meeting was apparently at 9 am in London. According to what I heard Roger arrived 15 minutes late (blaming a missed rail connection), sweaty and carrying a large holdall. Plonking the holdall on the desk and getting a 'daggers look' from Craig about being late, he unzipped the holdall and reached in to retrieve the papers. His face froze, then calmly removing a tennis racquet from the depths, announced to the gathered attendees that he'd picked up the wrong holdall, this was actually his tennis gear, and the one with the file in was still at the office...could we all perhaps reconvene tomorrow? Apparently, Craig was furious and left without a word and was on the next train back to Croydon.

On arrival at his office his secretary said she was surprised to see him back so soon, did the meeting go well? 'No, it fucking didn't!' he thundered and kicked a waste paper basket across the office. The basket rose in a graceful arc into the air and sailed out of a window (5 storeys up remember) and down into the car park below, leaving a trail of paper blowing in the wind and thankfully missing anyone underneath and any parked cars.

'Thank goodness that window was open,' his secretary said, somewhat relieved.

'I didn't know it fucking was', he angrily replied, slamming his office door. Everyone had heard the commotion and there were stifled laughs and grins all around.

Roger turned up about 30 minutes later and sat at his desk, with his head down, and lit a cigarette.

'Everything OK Rog?' someone innocently asked him.

He didn't reply.

Chapter Four

PROMOTION!

With Tim now in his element telling all and sundry that he was 'Worldwide Property and Construction Claims Supervisor for AIU' he had a vacancy to fill. His old one. Even Tim could see that even though I had only been handling claims for just over 2 years, I was turning over a huge volume and was getting some great results. Brokers thought I was 'tough but fair' and I was pleased about that. Without even asking, he promoted me to his old position. I got a pay rise and it was timely as I had just totalled my car in a head-on crash in a country lane. 50/50.

I was now in a cubicle on my own and a trainee called Ray was recruited. Martin had left to go into loss adjusting and Roger was, understandably, looking elsewhere too.

Meantime I was stuck into a problem involving bird shit, or guano, to give it its proper name.

We were insuring the Humber Bridge. At the time it was going to be on completion the largest single-span suspension bridge in the Northern Hemisphere. It was a prestigious project and although not 'lead' we had a significant share so I was involved in all the claims, and there were dozens.

Such was the size of the risk that there were probably 10 or more insurers writing the project. One of the greatest problems with the bridge was the spiralling costs and delays in getting materials, especially the steel wire that was to form the main supporting cables of the bridge which were going to be about 1.5 miles long.

Such was the rising cost of steel that the consortia building the bridge decided that it would be economic to buy the galvanised steel wire from British Steel in advance and store the massive reels of cable in a purpose-built warehouse, but unheated and unlit, close to the 'spinning' area. The reels were massive, each weighing tons, and required a forklift truck to move them. The theft risk was considered negligible and there was no fire risk – steel cables in a steel shed with nothing flammable meant there was nothing to burn, but the steel could be affected by water, so it was decided that each reel would be wrapped tightly in polythene on the quayside before storage.

The storage risk was placed with the top four insurers on the main bridge project, each taking 25% all for a princely premium of £1000 p.a. with an excess of £250 for each claim. It was considered to be money for old rope (or new wire?). So, the storage began, and the years rolled by.

Eventually, the time came when the wire was needed to begin the spinning of the main cables. Two huge towers had been constructed and between them and the ground anchors at each end of the bridge, the cables had to be installed. To do this a wheeled pulley was suspended from another small wire and it was pulled over the length of the span dragging yet another wire with it from a huge spool. As soon as the pulley reached the other end of the bridge it was pulled back in the opposite direction dragging another wire. Eventually, enough wires were in place to be tied or spun to form a rope... and in the meantime, backward and forward the pulleys would go, day and night and so the supporting cables would grow in diameter. And then it was noticed that some of the stored wire was damaged. The wire was pitted in places and nobody could figure out how and why this had happened.

Examination of the wire by forensic scientists revealed that the pits had been caused by acid attack. But from where had acid come, how did it get onto the reels and not damage the polythene that was there to protect it? The answer was found by detective work going back to the time that the wire had been transported to the bridge site by road from British Steel. The reels of wire had been placed on the quayside in stacks before being wrapped in polythene and placed in the warehouse. It was whilst the reels were on the quayside that seagulls had deposited faeces in quite liberal quantities onto the bare wire. Once wrapped, the acid from the seagull's gut attacked the steel wire, causing the pitting. If there was any defect in the wire it could not be used as its structural strength was compromised and so had to be scrapped.

Then the claim came in. The cost of the replacement wire was put in the hundreds of thousands of pounds. But was this a claim under the project cover or on the warehouse cover?

The project insurers said that the warehouse cover was applicable as the damage had been caused whilst in storage. As I mentioned the four warehouse insurers were the same top four insurers as those covering the bridge, but the bottom 6 or so on the project all naturally wanted to pay nothing and so blamed the warehouse insurers. As there was a clear conflict of interest it was agreed that AIU would deal with the warehouse claim (so me!) and as the dispute was simply one between insurers we would try and resolve the matter amicably.

We called all the insurers together, along with the brokers, into a room and debated the issues. I argued that whilst there was a case that the damage got worse in storage, the thing or incident (called the proximate cause) that started the chain of events happened before the reels were even in the warehouse, namely the seagulls crapping on the wire outside – and that was at the risk of the project.

The converse argument was that a drop of poo by itself would not cause damage, it was the time it took for the damage to occur and wrapping exacerbated the significant problem. After all, the wire on the bridge now would be the target of the seagulls' bowels and that wasn't causing damage. I said that if the wrapping was a factor, it was undertaken outside, not inside the warehouse, so again back to the project policy.

Nevertheless, it was clear enough that the top four insurers were financially implicated come what may, as they were on both policies, so it was how to persuade the bottom 6 on the project that they were saving money. The cost of litigating the points would be significant and the outcome uncertain.

Finally, a deal was struck with each policy contributing 50% to the loss, but then the question was how many policy excesses were under the warehouse policy? At £250 a pop, it would not be a great deal. The brokers argued that as it was one claim it should be one excess of £250. At worst, they argued one per year of cover, so four or £1000. I was arguing for 1 per reel and said that each deposit was one lot of damage, so arguably many per reel. In the event, I accepted that if one 'deposit' was enough to make the reel a total loss, then one excess per reel seemed right.

The brokers finally agreed and as there were something like 500 reels affected, I made a saving of £125,000.

I had to go to North London a few times to settle some trip-and-fall cases for members of the public who had tripped over pavement works that one of our more negligent contractors had created. I suggested that Ray cut his teeth on a case for Mrs Goldstein who had twisted an ankle on uneven paving, or something like that. The Jewish community in that part of North London was very friendly when I went to see them, but my visits were overly long due to the endless cups of tea and cake I was offered and irrelevant discussions about life and family that seemed to take hours. 'Go and see Mrs G and see if you can get a deal up to £2,500', I suggested to Ray, 'but don't settle' I added with a chuckle, 'unless you get a cup of tea and a slice of chocolate cake.' Off he went. The following morning, he was back and said his settlement discussion had taken well over three hours. 'Why so long?' I said, raising an eyebrow. 'Oh, I told Mrs G that my boss told me I couldn't settle unless I got a slice of chocolate cake. She hadn't any in, so she sent Mr G down to the shops to get one. He was on a Zimmer frame and he took simply ages!' I was starting to worry about Ray...

Back at the office, Roger and Martin had both left and so no one was overseeing the international claims, so Tim decided that I should look at both UK and International aspects and form a team. Several junior replacements were coming and going, but we needed someone else.

Without ever mentioning it to me, Tim then recruited Jeff.

Chapter Five

JEFF

Over the previous years, I had met with several brokers. At that time there were 100s of them around the country. Even in London, there were probably 20 or so with whom we built up connections. As the years rolled by a lot of them merged and became the behemoths that they are today.

Each broking house had in effect two teams: a 'placing' team who dealt with our underwriters by placing and writing a risk and a claims team that, of course, dealt with us. Some were better than others. Some would add value to a claim, others merely acted as post-boxes and added nothing, just waiting for our response to the claim. As our only methods of communication were post and telephone from time to time we would save up several files for one broker and then plan a visit. There was always the chance of lunch and a few beers too.

Jeff headed a team in Woking at a fairly large company and he had two female colleagues, Carole and Jo. I would sometimes arrange to go and see them as for my part Jeff added nothing to any debate, he was the proverbial post-box, and Carole and Jo were nice luncheon companions being both chatty and 'easy on the eye'. We had a lot of business together and so would meet every six months or so either at their office or ours.

Now, Jeff was a tall chap, well over 6ft and looked like the cartoon character Desperate Dan. Jeff too always had a permanent '5 o'clock shadow'. He had a Tommy Cooper-type laugh and would mimic the old comedian at any opportunity. His complete repertoire consisted of impersonations of Tommy Cooper and 'Rigsby' from the TV show 'Rising Damp' and seemed to be best buddies with just about everyone in the market. He was well known, had a reputation as being a bit 'blokeish' and even though I regarded him as a pushover, I did like the chap. He was full of stories too and was a great joke teller. He drove an old Ford Anglia which he named 'Silver' as when accelerating it left a cloud of white exhaust fumes in its wake and he would yell 'Hi Ho Silver, away' after the horse in the B&W 'Lone Ranger' TV series. He was also 12 years older than me. It therefore came as somewhat of a surprise to be told by Tim that my new 'junior' was to be Jeff. For once I was struck dumb.

I immediately decided to grow a beard to make myself look older. Beards were not common then, so I thought it would make me 'stand out' and I bought myself a three-piece suit as well.

Jeff busied himself getting to know our practices and procedures and given his age and background experience I thought he would soon be able to take on a portfolio of work. He took the files but was he able to deal with them? Yes, and No.

One of the peculiar aspects of working in a claims department at an insurance company is that if you tread carefully, you may never have to make a decision that you are truly responsible for. Despite his size, Jeff was a master at tip-toe. We passed out almost every claim to loss adjusters and solicitors to investigate and handle (we had a lot of complex litigation both in the UK and Internationally) and the adjusters and lawyers provided "advice and opinions" that was our option to either accept or reject. Jeff found it easiest to accept every recommendation and if it was found later to be incorrect, or open to another interpretation, he could quite legitimately say he was simply following the advice given by someone else more knowledgeable than him. Well, that was certainly true. I never came across anyone who had less knowledge than Jeff.

Tim of course was unable to see through the façade, indeed he wasn't far behind Jeff in the tip-toe stakes either, and he had employed him. He could hardly admit to making a mistake.

Jeff's skill in avoiding doing anything was brought home when a few months after he arrived, I went on holiday, expecting him as my de facto #2, to look after the incoming post and deal with anything urgent. When I got back, he explained that he was swamped with other things during my two weeks and besides, he didn't want to interfere with 'my' files. I did say that these were the company files and if I had got knocked down by a bus, he'd have to deal with them, wouldn't he?

Next year I went away for another 2-week holiday (another Scout camp – I never did anything else) and when I got back Jeff was as pleased as punch when he said, pointing to stacks of neatly arranged files, that he had dealt with everything for me in my absence. I was amazed.

On opening the first file, which I knew was a complex matter, I could see a letter on the top which said:

'Thank you for your letter of 1st August, Mr Cottington is away at present and will deal with your correspondence immediately on his return to the office.'

OK, I thought, maybe that's not too outrageous, he's given me a bit of breathing time.

The next file was a pretty simple matter, well the file was skinny so I guessed it was not too complicated, even for Jeff:

'Thank you for your letter of 3rd August, Mr Cottington is away at present and will deal with your correspondence immediately on his return to the office.'

And so, it went on, every file was the same! He'd done nothing at all on any of them. In consequence, as I allocated the new claims to the team, I kept him away from anything remotely difficult. Whether he cottoned on or not I never found out, nor did I care.

Not handling a file properly, or at least as I felt they should be handled, left Jeff free to do something that he was good at – arranging social events. He arranged 5 and 12-a-side football matches between AIU and loss adjusters and brokers and even designed a hideous strip for the AIU team. There were cricket matches too and for once I was asked to participate.

I was not, as I mentioned previously, particularly sporty. I had been a very average club swimmer and once represented Croydon or Surrey and came in at a very spectacular last place in a competition swimming backstroke. The reason was that at the age of 13, I was now in an age group of 13-17 and I hadn't had a 'growth spurt' and was at the poolside waiting for the starting pistol with swimmers who were muscular and looked capable of shaving. I think they had got out and were dressed by the time I had finished my two lengths of the pool. I never swam competitively again. Anyway, I digress.

At school, if we played cricket at all I was not chosen to play in any team. I was an OK fielder but as a batsman, I was, frankly, rubbish. I had what I considered to be a very justifiable fear that a very hard ball hurtling towards me at 80mph striking me anywhere on my torso was likely to be extremely painful. However, I put my name forward and it came as no surprise that Jeff put me into bat last.

We were playing a firm of loss adjusters and I was allowed to bowl at least one 8 ball over. I think they scored 20 runs off it. I wasn't asked to bowl again.

When it was my turn to bat, I walked out to the crease and I suppose I must have looked a bit odd-looking. I was wearing white shorts and a T-shirt (also white) a red sweatband around my head (partly to keep my spectacles from falling off) a cricket pad just on one leg (the left one) and white squash shoes. I was a keen squash player and this was all the sporting gear I had. I took my stance with the bat and Jeff said to me 'Why are you holding the bat like that?' I was standing right-handed but with a left-handed grip. I explained that this was the way I held every two-handed sports stick – hockey and cricket came to mind – and no one had ever questioned it before. He sighed and returned to whatever he was doing, umpiring, I guess.

The first bowler began his run up and the ball flew past me like a bullet. I am not sure I even saw it. I hadn't moved. I looked up and shouted, 'When you're ready then!'. The next ball came a bit slower but to my left, so whilst the ball was in mid-air, I turned my body and thrashed wildly at it left-handed. I missed of course, but the fielders were perplexed and immediately moved positions to reflect that I was now playing left-handed.

Back at the crease I was again playing both left and right-handed and managed to prod and poke at a couple of balls much to the bemusement of the fielders who were unsure where they needed to stand, but were reasonably assured that I would not be troubling them wherever they stood.

Finally, I actually hit a ball. I had no idea which direction it was going in and neither did the fielders, but it soared away in a high arc and trickled over the boundary for four runs. The next over saw my fellow batsman out first ball, so that was the end of the game. I was 'Not Out for 4'. According to Jeff, my performance remained something of a record for several years and I don't recall ever being asked to play again.

Tim had boasted that a year or two before I joined, he and some loss adjusters had been bragging about who had gone into the office with the worst hangover. Tim probably, I thought. Anyway, to try and demonstrate the point he and a few others had gone out on a Thursday evening, drunk 10 pints, went for a curry, and the following morning called each other at 9 a.m. to see who had survived. This became an annual event and was now a fixture in the diary for the first Thursday of each December.

I was keen to become involved in the annual event. By the time I first participated, it was 1978 or 1979. What started as a drink with just a few people had grown to something like 50 people. About 6 or so from AIU with the rest all loss adjusters and we were keen to relieve them of as much of their expense accounts as possible.

We planned the route carefully as the idea was to drink a different pint of real ale in 10 different pubs, the survivors of that ending the evening in a curry house to participate in a 'who can eat the hottest curry?' contest. Look, it was the late 70s and that is what we did, ok?

The crawl took a bit of organising as we had to test each pub first (to check out the quality of the ale naturally) and get the landlord's ok to put something like 20 pints on the bar at a certain time as we only had 30 minutes between each pub and 15 minutes of that was walking time so it didn't allow for much drinking time. For the first 4 pubs we paid for the beer in advance, the rest were just 'warned' we were coming as was the curry house.

I distinctly remember my second year. At the curry house, the heady and lethal mix of ten pints and bravado got the better of me. 'They don't make a curry hot enough for me,' I boasted. Someone tipped the wink to the waiter and very soon I was presented with something called 'Bangalore Phal Chicken', a crimson red concoction that steamed and sizzled ominously. I should have noticed that it was served on an asbestos plate and came with a side order of a fire extinguisher but egged on by the crowd I gamely spooned a large portion into my mouth.

To say that it was 'hot' was, and remains, a massive understatement. I think it was the first and last time that I saw the insides of my nostrils. My mouth was alternatively on fire and numb. However, I bravely carried on, each mouthful washed down with ice-cold lager. How I staggered home is a mystery, but I managed to get myself to bed and as the bedroom was swimming in circles, I needed to hold onto the sides for fear of being spun out of bed.

Sleep must have come at some point and the following morning my insides felt like I had swallowed nails and broken glass. That feeling lasted all day and most of the next night too.

Our dealings with loss adjusters, and presumably having something to do with the considerable amount of fees we were paying them, often resulted in lunches – long and boozy. Some were in local restaurants in Croydon, others were in London, but some of the more memorable were frequently held in the offices of the adjusters themselves.

The food at these lunches, which we christened 'school dinners', was usually excellent and the atmosphere very relaxed. Three firms were keen on inviting us, Richards Hogg, International Adjusters Partnership (IAP) and Toplis & Harding.

My first ever such lunch was at Toplis's in Arthur Street close to The Monument and must have been in 1977 or summer 1978 because I recall I was still living at home with Mum and Harry. I did not have any experience eating out so I'd asked Mum's advice about etiquette and so forth. She explained that cutlery would probably be laid out to the sides of the plate (not like at home where the spoon always was across the top of the plate) and I should begin on the outside and work my way in with each course. The bread plate would be on my left and the wine and water glass on my right. BMW – bread, meal, wine. OK, got it.

Tim and I were greeted warmly by our host, Rod, and introduced to his colleagues, Quentin and Rupert. There were almost certainly four or so other guests from other insurers as the table was set for ten.

After a chat, we were seated at the table resplendent with a starched white tablecloth, and I could see that the cutlery setting was exactly as I was expecting. Goody. To my left, working inwards was a small fork, a larger fork then another small fork. On the right was a teaspoon, a knife and finally another teaspoon. A small plate was already set to my left with a bread roll on it and a small knife and a small platter of butter pats were in front presumably for people to share. A white napkin had been folded into a bishop's mitre and sat in between the cutlery.

I unfolded my napkin and laid it over my thighs and at that point, a lady came around with plates bearing a half honeydew melon. I was sure nothing could go wrong with melon. Rod smiled at me and asked whether I would like some port in the melon? I had no idea whether I did or not having never tried it, so not wanting to appear discourteous I said that sounds splendid. Rod approached with a bottle of port and then proceeded to pour in a generous quantity of the fruity red liquid, enough to fill up the well in the half-melon practically to the brim.

Others around the table also signified their acceptance of the port and as Rod was going around the table, he said to me – 'do start, I'll catch up in a moment'. I decided to tackle some of the bread roll first, the melon could wait. Rod had served half the table by this point and again suggested that I begin.

I picked up the spoon and the fork. The melon was not perhaps as ripe as I was expecting or maybe I had dug my spoon in too close to the tough skin, but the melon tipped and a liberal quantity of port overflowed the melon brim and slopped onto the plate. Somewhat embarrassed, I decided I needed to keep the melon from wobbling and so with the fork in my left hand dug the tines straight into the bottom of the melon where I found that the flesh was soft and the skin had been removed presumably to stop the melon from wobbling in the first place.

Using the teaspoon, I scooped out a small quantity of the flesh and popped it into my mouth. Then, withdrawing the fork for a moment, the remaining port began to leak out of the bottom of the melon half and quickly began to fill up the small plate on which the melon was resting, and then overflowed onto the pristine white tablecloth.

As fast as I could scoop up the port with the teaspoon and drink it, the red stain on the tablecloth around where I sat gradually expanded until it nearly encroached on my neighbours. Seeing my predicament, Rod graciously removed my plate bearing the uneaten melon and placed another napkin over the worst of the red stain. However, as the meal wore on the stain began to reappear ominously again, both at the sides and up through the napkin. Replacing the melon with another from the kitchen I sensibly declined the offer of more port.

The main course was steak and some vegetables which I tackled without further mishap. Then we came to dessert. My remaining cutlery was a fork and teaspoon so I guessed a fruit salad of some variety?

A small plate was presented to me adorned with a round mound of lemon sorbet and it was studded like a hedgehog with Cadbury's chocolate biscuit fingers. What could go wrong with that? I picked up the teaspoon and dug out a finger. The blob of sorbet on one end unbalanced it and it dropped onto my plate. The fingers were too long to balance on a teaspoon. So, holding the chocolate finger down with my fork I decided to cut the damn thing in half with the edge of my teaspoon.

The sorbet had obviously caused all the fingers to freeze and become brittle. Suddenly half a chocolate finger shot down the table horizontally and with an audible 'ding' bounced off somebody's wine glass. 'Do you want that back, Trevor?' someone asked. Flushing as red as the stain around where I sat, I demurred and then noticed everyone else was eating the biscuits with their fingers and scoping up the sorbet on the biscuity ends! Oh, good grief. Why didn't anyone tell me?

Whether Rod or anyone else spoke about 'that idiot' from AIU who wrecked a tablecloth, and a napkin and embarrassed himself in front of nine senior people, I will never know. Rod on the other hand must have dismissed it as just 'one of those things' as despite my apparent lack of manners at the dining table, he invited me frequently to the loss adjuster's annual dinner for many years... but more of that later.

Jeff and I attended several school dinner lunches with IAP. As their name suggested they undertook mainly international work. The individuals (Alan, Don and Graeme) were rarely in the country, but when they were, and we were invited to dine with them in the basement of their offices in Artillery Lane, near Liverpool St station, we were always guaranteed a wealth of stories and a very liquid lunch.

On one occasion after the three courses, we were merrily digging into a huge stilton cheese when Jeff espied a massive fruit bowl bearing all manner of exotic fruits. One took his eye and taking it and holding it up asked aloud what it was? The fruit was about the size of a plum, but green and hairy.

'It's a Chinese Gooseberry Jeff,' I casually explained, 'you cut it in half and scoop out the middle with a spoon'.

'Bollocks!' he exclaimed, 'you're making it up,' laughing loudly.

I suggested to Alan and Don that they ask their cook to come out and settle the argument. The cook was duly summoned. She came out to the table and Jeff held up the fruit and asked what it was. The cook replied that it was a Kiwi fruit, to which Jeff turned to me and said 'Ha, you were wrong!' but the cook hadn't finished, 'It's also known as Chinese Gooseberry, they are not very common having only just been imported into the country, but you cut it in half and scoop out the middle with a spoon. They are quite refreshing actually.' Jeff was duly stunned and wide-eyed. I couldn't help but twist the knife a little and casually mentioned that some of the other exotica in the bowl were star fruit, Sharon fruit and physalis... though the last came out as piss-a-lis due to the amount of wine I'd consumed, which made us laugh. My fruity knowledge had been gathered from a TV program I had seen a few nights before, though in truth I had never actually seen, or tried, any of those fruits myself.

Alan and I were due to go to Germany to try and settle a very difficult turbine claim. The facts were dull (during overhaul a spanner had been left in the works – see I said it was dull) but turbines are horribly expensive and the German company was known to be very tough negotiators. Don bet me a bottle of scotch I would not get a deal at the number we were suggesting. To be fair to Don, a smashing chap who sadly died of leukaemia a few years later, the bet was wholly one-way. If I got the deal, I'd get the scotch. If I didn't, he'd get to say 'told you so'. I could cope with those odds. But I'd have to wait a few weeks until the visit to Mannheim to find out who got the bragging rights.

Chapter Six

GOING INTERNATIONAL AND OTHER STORIES

If I have given the impression that claims happen and are settled within a few weeks or months, I apologise. The bird poo claim took probably two or three years. Such timeframes were not uncommon back then, being pre-email and or even fax. We could wait months for a loss adjuster or solicitor report and we would correspond mainly by letter. Although we had a notional service standard of three weeks to answer a letter if anything was answered within a month you were doing pretty well. No one complained either, that's just how the insurance business was undertaken.

I was now looking at 'foreign' claims and thus had to learn practice and procedure in so many countries it was hard to keep up. I didn't deal with anything in the USA though.

My first international trip was to Stockholm, the capital of Sweden. I was going to meet with another insurer, Skanska, and try to resolve several disputes we had.

I arrived at Gatwick airport in plenty of time for my flight. I dislike being late for anything and don't like having to hurry either, so I was probably 2 hrs earlier than I needed to be.

I wandered around the duty-free shops but found I needed nothing at all and could not afford anything either, so I went and sat in a quiet area to read a book. I noticed on an upper level a games area. I went to have a look.

At this time video games were in their infancy and were played at huge machines that looked like one-armed bandits or fruit machines as they were called. I'm not much of a gambler so I avoided the flashing lights of the bandits and had a look at the Space Invaders machine. I had played on that in pubs so was familiar with it and decided to risk a 20p play. Then another and another. I must have popped a couple of pounds worth of 20 pence coins into its greedy slot when I was distracted by the 'bing bong' of the tannoy announcing the gate for the BA flight to Stockholm was now closing and if passenger Mr Cottington is on the concourse would he please make his way to Gate 33 immediately! Grabbing my briefcase, I ran like a scalded cat to Gate 33, waved my ticket and passport to the lady at the desk and was allowed through. I was the last person going through the aircraft door before the stewardess closed it, giving me a 'look'. I had made it, just. I vowed never to do anything daft like that again, and never have.

On taking my seat on the aircraft I put my jacket in the overhead locker and made myself comfy, sweating though I was, for the short flight to Stockholm. We disembarked (or is it deplaned?) and I wandered through to the Customs desk, got to the front of the queue and reached into my pocket for my passport – it wasn't there! I went through every pocket on my jacket and trousers and tipped out the briefcase, but the passport was nowhere to be found.

I knew I had it when I went through Gate 33, but where was it now? My heart sank. It must still be in the overhead locker. Luckily all Swedes speak English and together with a security person we retraced my steps back to the plane. Sure enough, at the back of the overhead locker was the erroneous black passport. I was so relieved.

I must have got a taxi to my hotel as I wasn't comfortable with public transport and had no idea of the geography of Stockholm. I have since been there probably ten times and still am unable to navigate my way around. The city is built on an archipelago of islands all interconnected with bridges, but try as I might I can never find a point of reference.

The all-day meeting with the Swedish insurers was polite enough. They listened to all the points I was making and nodded throughout. I had ordered a taxi for 3 p.m. as my return flight was around 5 p.m. so I needed to be at the airport by 4 p.m. for check-in.

We had enjoyed a lovely lunch in the insurer's canteen – open sandwiches being a particular delicacy – and back to the meeting I started to wrap things up at about 2.30 p.m. and putting my files into my briefcase I said to the assembled team 'So, we are agreed then about such and such?' They looked at one another and their team leader turned to me and calmly said 'No. I am afraid we cannot agree to any of your proposals. Please put them in writing when you return to the UK, but it is most unlikely we will alter our views. Please have a safe trip back to Croydon and thank you for your time.' My jaw fell open. I spluttered 'but I thought you had agreed with me – you were nodding 'yes' throughout our discussions.' 'Mr Cottington you have misunderstood, we were nodding because we understood what you were saying, not that we agreed with what you were saying.'

I had no idea what Tim would say when I got back – in the event, nothing at all. Whatever the issue was with the Swedish insurers, it got resolved at some stage – we probably just paid whatever they were asking for. It's often easier to agree than disagree.

My next trip was to Germany to see the aforementioned turbine manufacturer who had a nasty habit of assembling these gigantic machines in a power station and leaving quite literally, a spanner in the works. Turbines spin extraordinarily fast and the blades in the compressors and generators are so delicate that even dust from unclean air or dirty fuel can cause the edges to wear and thus cause the turbine to go out of balance and shake itself to bits. Given that the rotors on these machines weigh 100s of tons, when one fails it does so spectacularly. Having a spanner or screwdriver get into the machine causes immense and costly damage.

The meeting was in Mannheim, but the nearest airport is Frankfurt. I was travelling with Alan from IAP and he had been to the insured many times in the preceding months but was unable to secure a settlement. Now I was going and, in the parlance, I had the chequebook!

I'd never been to Germany before and was looking forward to the experience. At the airport, we had passed Customs and were seeking the taxi rank. The overhead signage was helpful in dual language, though my eyes widened when I saw the arrowed sign which said: Toilets / Exit / Taxi / Bus and Train Station/Dr. Mullers Sex Shop. A sex shop? In an airport? Only in Germany...

The following morning, we drove to Mannheim and taking in the scenery on the journey I noticed that there were an awful lot of signs to Ausfart, an amusing place name I had never heard of until it dawned on me it meant 'exit'.

The meeting with the Germans was typically efficient. Greetings were exchanged and then a German voice said, 'And now gentlemen, to business.' We went through the huge volume of invoices and tried to unpick aspects of the claim where we did not think the policy would respond. We then came to negotiations and I noticed that whenever the Germans wished to speak in private, they just reverted to their German tongue. Alan and I on the other hand could not say anything privately. Anything we said they immediately understood. As I was going down the various columns I said to Alan:

'If we add a pony to this one, maybe a monkey on that, a pony or two on this one we might be making progress, what do you think?'

Picking up on my drift, he replied 'You'll probably need to go a couple of monkeys there though,' pointing to a number 'maybe a ton on that one and even a grand there.'

We were of course using cockney slang and although a pony is just £25 Alan understood that I meant £25,000. A German voice interrupted us:

'Excuse,' he said 'but what is this talk about farm and zoo animals and weights?'

I didn't answer but said we had a final proposal at some huge number in Deutschmarks and after a lot of debate, in German, they accepted. The deal was done. Oh, and Don now owed me a bottle of Johnnie Walker Black Label.

One particular contractor was a producer of a great number of UK claims as well as the occasional international one. Although UK-based, they had ventured to the other side of the channel into what must have been a very risky business venture. And so it turned out. Their brokers were a large London firm and the two main claim handlers were Henry and his boss Peter.

Henry was very old school. He always wore a dark grey 3-piece pin-stripe suit and was in his late 50s or early 60s. His hobby was caravanning and I knew if I could get him to chat about his caravan adventures, he would be more pliable when we came to talk about the claims.

He was always a tough nut though when looking at claims for 'employee effects'. Our policies covered the tools of trade of employees on building sites with an excess of £50 per person. Employees were always losing tools and clothing in thefts from site cabins and the occasional fire.

Fire losses also involved negotiations with hire companies as our policies were on a written down value basis, whereas the hire companies were entitled under their hire contract to claim 'new for old'. Any fire in a changing room or canteen often involved claims from up to 20 personnel and we had to go through the routine of seeing whether they had home insurance that covered their losses too. It was tiresome and open to fraud. No employee ever seemed to have old tools. All were new (probably as a result of the last claim we paid out on) and were from the same supplier – Snap-Fit – and their clothing losses were all top of the range – Gucci shoes, Pierre Cardin shirts, Levi jeans etc. Of course, those were precisely the kinds of clothing that every British workman wore whilst bricklaying or whatever... well, so they claimed, though I was sceptical.

If I took to Henry 10 claims for 'effects' I may have had one for something more serious, a landslip or something similar. Each effect claim was probably in the £100s of pounds for each employee and I knew if I appeared generous on those, I could be a bit more hard-nosed on the larger claim where there was more opportunity to make a saving. It usually worked too.

Peter always had a novel way of getting his point across. Whatever the claim situation, Peter was able to illustrate his argument by drawing it on a scrap of paper. Lines and squiggles and arrows would be drawn to show how a road collapse happened or how sheet piling had moved, or whatever. These drawings became much sort after trophies and if we returned from a meeting with Peter without one of his masterpieces, we felt short-changed. Back in our office, the team would ask if we had an 'original Peter' and we would proudly show the scribbled sheet and then have to explain what it was supposed to demonstrate. Not sure anyone could understand them, but they went onto the file in pride of place.

The telephone rang. On answering I heard the familiar voice of Alf, a London broker. Alf was a thoroughly nice chap, affable, ex-military and a good drinking buddy, but with an annoying habit of slapping you on the back or grabbing your arm to make a point. I'm not keen on 'touchy-feely' behaviour at the best of times, but with Alf, it was unavoidable as we did loads of business together. He said, 'You know that swimming pool project in Poland?' I groaned...what have they done now? The project had been plagued with thefts and construction errors and I despaired to think what had gone wrong this time.

'You'll never believe it...but they've had a fire'.

'Oh yeah, where?' I wondered, 'in the site cabin complex?'

'Nope', he said rather smugly, 'in the swimming pool itself!'

He went on to explain that the wooden shuttering and formwork of the pool sides had been set alight by someone angle grinding or welding and the heat from that had started a fire in a pile of rubbish that spread to the shuttering. Fire damage to a swimming pool – a new one on me!

The broking house that Alf worked for had their company bespoke policy wordings that, foolishly I thought, our underwriters accepted. The wording was so loose and clauses and phrases so open to interpretation that Alf always referred to these as 'the grey areas' and thus covered them. The rule in insurance law is, and remains, that if a clause in a policy is open to different interpretations, then it is always construed by the courts in favour of the policyholder and against the insurer. It's called 'Contra proferentem' a Latin phrase. This rule is based on the principle that a person behind the framing of such ambiguity is responsible for it. With Alf's broker wording, I knew we were on a hiding to nothing as we had agreed on the wording and so in effect, it was 'ours' and cheekily suggested that his wording should be printed in grey font on grey paper to make those 'grey areas' really stand out! Unsurprisingly Jeff and Alf got on famously and I do not doubt that Alf tore any argument Jeff may have made (but probably didn't) apart in moments. We must have lost a fortune.

The Germans had broken yet another turbine. Another massive loss. Over to Frankfurt, by-passing of course but smiling at the sign of Dr Mueller's shop at the airport, I was once again off to Mannheim after an overnight stay in the city.

This time the German policyholders had calculated the claim somewhat more reasonably and we concluded the deal before lunch, or was it that I was too generous? Anyway, I was invited to lunch at a German restaurant in Mannheim.

Whenever I am in a foreign country, I much prefer eating the 'local' cuisine as although French and Italian restaurants were fairly common in London/Croydon, I never got the opportunity to sample another country's cuisine and I was keen to try. The restaurant was lovely.

We concluded the meal with something that translated as 'wine foam' and was a very light dish made of egg white whisked with sugar and a sweet wine in a large copper bowl heated at the table by the waiter over a small portable stove. Served in a glass with a sweet biscuit it was delicious.

Not being a coffee drinker, my hosts suggested instead a hot chocolate drink made with Amaretto, the almond/marzipan liqueur, all topped with a thick layer of whipped cream.

I was probably on my second of those when my hosts said I ought to be getting to the airport as my flight would be leaving at 4 pm.

I said my BA flight was not until 5.30 p.m. so I had plenty of time. Someone left the table, called their office and hurriedly returned and said that if I got a move on there was a Lufthansa flight at 4 pm and I could change tickets at the airport. A taxi was summoned, I gave my thanks to my hosts and was whisked to the airport at considerable speed. The Mercedes taxi even overtook police cars on the autobahn, there being no speed limits, which despite my intoxicated state, was rather thrilling. Arriving at the airport at about 3.30 pm I hurried to the Lufthansa desk and explained that I needed to change my BA ticket to their 4 pm flight. The clerk said that I was mistaken, there was no flight to Gatwick at 4 pm, but one to Heathrow. That was no good to me.

The journey time from Gatwick to Croydon is about 20 minutes by train. Heathrow to Croydon was a long tube journey, changing lines en route, to Victoria, then a train to East Croydon.

It was as broad as it was long, timewise, and more costly what with the fee for changing tickets, so I decided that I would sit and wait the hour or so until my BA flight was called. I had not long taken my seat and was reading a book when I noticed that someone was standing in front of me. Looking up I saw that it was one of the hosts from the restaurant. I stood up and shook his outstretched hand.

He apologised and said that when he had got back to his office his secretary had realised that she had made a mix-up between Gatwick/Heathrow and, as hosts, they were mortified and wanted to apologise, and handed me a gift-wrapped bottle. He said it was Amaretto from the restaurant – the one I liked so much – please accept it with our apologies. I graciously accepted and said that there was no need, these things happen... and opening my holdall which contained all my overnight things, spare shirt etc, and the paperwork, I popped the bottle in. It landed with a clunk and thanking my host once again, he turned and left. On sitting down, I quickly began to notice a rather strong smell of marzipan. Unzipping the holdall, I could see that the bottle had broken and sticky liqueur was spreading all over my clothes, wash bag and paperwork! I made a quick dash to the toilets where I went into a cubicle to inspect the damage. I picked out as carefully as I could all the glass fragments I could find and dropped them into the toilet bowl and poured out the remains of the liquid into the bowl as well. The sound made by the tinkling glass on the ceramic bowl and the smell of marzipan must have made the occupants of the other cubicles wonder what that guy had been eating, but I was past caring. I dropped the rest of the glass and my washbag and contents into a waste bin and washing my hands of the sticky liquid I went off to the BA Gate.

When I finally got home the marzipan smell was still overpowering and put my clothes into the washing machine. The file and papers had all stuck together though. I peeled apart and dried out what I could and took their still sticky and smelly remains to the office where I photocopied what I could and filed the rest. I was always able to find that file from smell alone.

Alf called cheerily one morning. 'You won't believe this,' he said, 'but they've done it again. That swimming pool project – it's flooded. Torrential rain caused localised flooding which has gone into the site and flooded it too, additionally, they think that the water is contaminated by bugs like cryptosporidium that may have gotten into the grouting of the tiles – so the whole lot will have to come off and be redone'.

OK, that takes the biscuit – first fire damage and now water damage to a swimming pool! You couldn't make it up.

I had received many reports from Toplis & Harding loss adjusters concerning many heavy impact damage losses to dumper trucks on a quarrying project that had just started, I think in Angola. I say 'dumper trucks' but these were huge with wheels so big you needed to climb an external ladder to get to the driving cab. The wheels were probably 10 ft high. The capacity of these trucks was 40 tons of material, so added to the weight and dimensions of the trucks themselves, about 20 tons, any impact would be considerable.

The repairs I was seeing were not small either – anything from $10,000 to $30,000 - hardly 'dented bumpers'. I was puzzled as to how so many accidents could take place in such a short period.

It seems that the quarry was so great that it had a spiral road around the circumference, but the road was only just wide enough to allow two trucks to pass side by side if they were going slowly and carefully. Whoever had the inside route against the rock face was generally the safer one and coming up the road from the quarry floor meant that any contest between a 60-ton load and a 20-ton load resulted in considerable damage to the lighter machine. The drivers were paid by the truckload and so speed became the rule of the day. The more loads they carried the more the drivers were paid. Some of the claims were for total losses too, as the trucks would, due to their speed on the descent, occasionally go over the edge of the quarry or crash head-on with the truck coming up. In either scenario, the driver was likely to jump out of the cab, as staying inside meant almost certain death as the truck tumbled over the edge of the road into the quarry hundreds of feet below. There had been two fatalities already. A total loss of a truck was about $300,000, but I suppose it did mean that there were trucks available for cannibalising spare parts. Although the loss of life was truly regrettable, our policy didn't cover that, but the damage was covered and I thought something needed to be done. The losses could not continue.

The contractors involved happened to have a HQ in Croydon, close to Mitcham and I knew the building well as it was next door to a pub I used to frequent. I contacted the insurance manager, Ian, and gathered up my files and went to visit him.

Ian and I went through the claims and then I broached the tricky subject of loss/risk mitigation. Strictly speaking, this topic was outside of my remit as a claim handler, but I said that these collisions should not keep on happening and either the drivers should go in convoy up and down the quarry road or proceed with greater care by having designated 'passing places' for example. Ian told me that they had a new foreman on the project and he had implemented a new safety system and he had been assured this would reduce the number of accidents to an acceptable low level, maybe the occasional 'bump'. I said has he introduced a convoy system then, or maybe speed limiters on the trucks? 'Neither,' Ian said rather loftily, then continued, 'at the start of every shift he handcuffs the drivers to the steering columns. If they crash head-on then they will probably die and if they go over the edge of the quarry they most certainly will, so they take more care.' I couldn't believe my ears, but it was probably true as we only had a handful of bumps and one fatality over the next few years.

In passing I asked what had happened to the previous foreman? Ian said that the man was an idiot who didn't follow the company rules. The white workers – managers and foremen – all lived in a guarded and gated community about 5 miles from the quarry. The rule was that when driving between the two you didn't stop for anything, certainly not to give anyone a lift, as crime was rife and the area effectively lawless. Apparently, the foreman was driving home on the main road that went through a village, when a kiddie ran out in front of the car and was knocked down. The foreman immediately stopped the car and got out to see what could be done, when he was immediately attacked by angry villagers armed with machetes who hacked him to death. I wisely decided a site visit was not needed.

I have mentioned market meetings and I don't think that any of them were held anywhere other than in London. These meetings were sometimes necessary but the more people present the more views there seemed to be and often the most vocal were the insurers with the smallest share. As an American firm, we tried to avoid even going to market meetings, usually just agreeing to follow the majority view.

Indeed, another American firm called INA (Insurance Co of North America) was of a similar view and they would often call us and ask if we were going to such and such meeting and if so, would pass their authority to us for their percentage of the risk. As INA were based in Maidstone and with poor (and slow) rail connection to the City, whereas AIU were on the doorstep of East Croydon and could get to London in about 15 minutes, we were usually the ones given the authority, but sometimes it was the other way.

The claims manager at INA was a chap called Barry and we met at these meetings and other social events frequently. If the 'lead' on a risk had 30% and AIU and INA each had 20% either firm would then be in the curious position of having a greater say in the handling of a claim than the lead. It happened fairly frequently.

I may have mentioned that I had A-level Geography, so it came as a surprise when I got a claim on the island of Western Samoa and hadn't a clue where in the world Samoa was. Grabbing an atlas, I soon found that it was a Polynesian island in the South Pacific. The claim involved some secrecy as our policyholder was installing a satellite dish as part of the 'Pacific Rim' of the defence for the southern hemisphere of NATO, called SEATO. (As the organisation no longer exists, I guess this is no longer a secret). Anyway, the satellite dish had been fabricated and constructed in the UK and then shipped out of Portsmouth to the island where it was taken by lorry to a mountaintop and then placed into position onto the mounting framework by a crane. The crane operator did something wrong and knocked the dish putting the main support axis out of alignment by about 2 degrees. This is not very much and ordinarily, I suppose would not be a problem with many items, but this meant that the signal from the dish would miss the satellite by a zillion miles.

I appointed a loss adjuster to go to the site and report back. His journey from the UK involved flights from the

UK to New York, NY to Los Angeles and then to Hawaii, then Fiji. From Fiji another flight on a cargo plane to Western Samoa – the whole trip was going to take two days, most of which would be in the air and a lot of waiting time at airports.

I was at my desk when I received a call from the adjuster on the telephone. The line was very crackly and faint but the gist of the call was that the dish was a technical write-off, there was no facility on the island for repair and the cost of shipping the dish back to the UK for repair was more expensive than sending out a replacement. The cost was going to be about $500,000 and the damaged dish was scrap. The adjuster then went on to ask if I minded if he could arrange for the sale of the salvage? I told him to do the best he could.

About a week later, the adjuster was back in the UK and I met with him and he presented me with a report and a cheque for the salvage. It was $250. I was incredulous. A $500,000 satellite dish only fetched $250 as scrap? The adjuster said that there was no facility on the island to deal with scrap metal so he had negotiated a deal with a fisherman who wanted to buy the dish for $250. There were no other offers apparently. I had to ask... why would a fisherman want a satellite dish? Any thoughts?

The answer was that the fisherman was going to drag the dish out into the ocean, knock a few holes in it with a hammer and then chuck some offal into it. Later when the tide came in the dish would fill with water and the offal attract crabs and lobsters, and when the tide went out the water would drain out of the holes, and the fisherman would be left, hopefully, with a big catch of crustaceans for little or no effort on his behalf. He had bought the biggest lobster pot in the world... and all for $250.

Chapter Seven

THE END OF A BEGINNING (PART 1)

One of the nicer things about being a claims handler of significant losses was that loss adjusters were always wishing to 'wine and dine' you and arguably the most prestigious event of the year is the Annual Loss Adjusters Dinner, held at the Royal Lancaster Hotel near Hyde Park. This 'black-tie' event was held in a massive ballroom with dozens of tables. There would be speeches and a guest speaker who, it was hoped, would round off the evening with an amusing speech.

My first invitation was a hand-me-down from Tim who had received a last-minute invite from a senior adjuster, John M, at a firm based in Middlesbrough. Tim had said to John M that he'd already been invited to the 1977 dinner by someone at the dinner in 1976... and he'd already got an invite for 1978 too (the show-off) but he had kindly suggested me as a replacement. It was very last-minute and I suspected that someone else had cried off but I was in no position to be choosy, so I gratefully accepted. I had never met the man before so I had no idea what he looked like, but Tim said that John M was a nice chap, tall, slim and bearded and with a mild Scottish accent. I called John M and he said that he had a room booked for me at the Royal Lancaster, could change there and meet up with him. That sounded perfect.

The Dinner was intended as a get-together of professional loss adjusters and had been an annual event since, I think, the 1920s. As the years went by each firm was able to invite a few special guests, so the event grew in numbers. By the 1970s loss adjusters and their guests were about equal in number - some 600 people.

Tim explained that the Dinner was a 'company approved' event which meant that the hiring of attire was allowed on expenses, so off we went to Moss Bros to get our dinner suits. Tim suggested that it was quite acceptable to wear a black or midnight blue velvet jacket, the obligatory 'frilly-fronted' white or blue shirt and a black bow tie. I opted for a ready-tied bow tie on elastic as I wasn't sure I could tie a bow myself. (I still can't if the truth were known). I declined the hire of a 'cummerbund' on the basis that I didn't know what one was. I could also hire patent black shoes if I wanted to, but I declined. I have never liked wearing someone else's shoes. We were measured up, fitted and a while later left with a large rectangular box containing our chosen items wrapped in tissue paper.

We left the office to go to the dinner at around 2.30 pm, even though the event was due to begin at 5.30 pm for pre-dinner drinks. I thought that three hours was far too long for travelling, but Tim said that there would be time at the hotel (he was staying at the Royal Lanc' too) for a leisurely bath or shower before getting changed. 'Besides', he said with a wink, 'You may have a mini-bar in the room to raid.'

I'd never actually stayed in a hotel before so I allowed Tim to check in first and then just copied whatever he had said. I gave the check-in person my name and he looked in a ledger and said that there was no room in my name. Nervously, I asked him to check again and once more he still said that there was no reservation in my name. Panicking somewhat, I said that maybe my host, John M had booked the room? Then the clerk confirmed, said yes, it was a double room booked and handed me a key on a massive fob chain.

Taking the lift to an upper floor I used the key and in I went. The room was quite large and indeed there was a king-size double bed a mini-bar and a large bathroom with a shower, huge fluffy towels and lots of toiletries to choose from. There was a big TV set and a bowl of fruit on a side table strewn with posh magazines like Horse & Hound and The Lady. I turned on the TV which in 1977 had only 3 or maybe 4 channels to choose from. All that was showing at that time of day was children's TV, so sitting in a comfy armchair munching on an apple, I began watching a cartoon. Time marched on and I had just decided to take a shower when I heard a key in the door lock and in stepped this tall slim bearded chap. He smiled and said in a gentle Scots accent, 'You must be Trevor? I'm John M, pleased to meet you. I've had a hellish journey so do you mind if I shower first? Hope you don't mind sharing a bed as this was all I could get,' and he stepped into the bathroom, shutting the door behind him.

Of course, and I think it goes without saying, but I was somewhat embarrassed. I'd never been in a hotel before, let alone share a room AND a bed with a perfect stranger, but what choice did I have? A few minutes later John M emerged from the bathroom wrapped in a towelling robe and said he would get changed into his 'penguin suit' and then head off to one of the side suites on the lower ground floor where each firm of adjusters had a suite for drinks with their guests. He explained that as a host he had to be there before guests arrived and expected to see me again for a proper chat and introduction just after 5.30. I went into the bathroom and had a long shower followed by a shave. When I came out there was no sign of John M, so I guessed correctly he had already gone down for the pre-dinner drinks.

I opened up my box of clothes and put on my frilly shirt and realised that the buttons were concealed behind a panel of some kind down the front, but the sleeves of the shirt were extraordinarily long – only the tips of my fingers were visible. Then I noticed a crease mark and could see that the cuffs folded back up to form a double cuff. But where were the buttons? There were none, just four holes. Then it dawned on me – cuff links! I hadn't got any and there was nothing I could do about it now. I put on my trousers and bow-tie then held on to the cuffs of the shirt as I put on the jacket. If I pulled the sleeves up so just the edge of the shirt was showing, I'd be fine.

I went to the lift lobby where several other chaps all dressed in DJs were waiting. The lift came and we all went down to the Ballroom floor. There was a handy map indicating the various suites that had been booked by the various firms and I found John M's: Graham Miller Sibilia & Co.

On entering the suite, a waiter handed me a glass of champagne and espying John M I went over to him and quipped that it was nice seeing him with his clothes on for a change. It broke the ice and I was introduced to some of the people standing in the group, a mixture of GMS adjusters and guests. Shaking hands with the guests my right cuff popped out of the sleeve and began flapping about. John noticed and came back a few minutes later with some paper-clips and I pressed and bent them into service. I felt a complete twit, but was making the best of a bad job. I explained I'd forgotten my cufflinks and the others seemed to accept the excuse. The other guests were all middle-aged men and worked for other major insurers such as General Accident, Provincial and Guardian Royal Exchange, all now long gone and merged with other companies. Looking around I noticed that almost all the people in the room were men and middle-aged men at that. By some margin, I appeared to be the youngest there.

On our drinks table were several small booklets and on opening one I saw that it contained the names of all the guests and to the side of each a number, being the table number. My name was nowhere to be seen, I guessed (correctly) that as a last-minute replacement, John M had not got time to get the name altered for the printer run. I found John M's name in the booklet and correctly assumed we would be on the same table, number 35.

Eventually, there was a loud rap of a gavel on a table and a smartly dressed toastmaster in a cherry red frock-coat announced that dinner was served and we all made our way into the ballroom. The room was vast with 60 or more large round tables, each seating 10. Massive chandeliers were hanging from the ceiling and each table was adorned with an ice bucket and probably six or eight bottles of wine, half red, half white. I found table 35 and each setting contained a small card with the name of the guest written in calligraphy. My card had been written in biro and on unfolding it could see that I was supposed to be Gordon McVey – the no-show. I think that it was simply the sign of the times but out of those 600 people, probably only 10 were women. I did notice that they were in massive ballgowns that probably made sitting uncomfortable as the seats were placed very close together.

All of us were standing in front of our seats and then the toastmaster banged his gavel and asked for appreciation for the 'top table'. A slow handclap started and about 10 people came from a side door to take their places at the long straight top table which was set at a higher level than the main floor. The toastmaster then banged his gavel again, requested silence and said 'grace'. We then sat and the meal commenced. No sooner had I taken a sip or two of my wine, than a waiter appeared and refilled my glass which was most acceptable. The person sitting next to me then handed me an envelope stuffed with £5 notes, a biro and one of the menu cards.

Handwritten on the rear of the card were the names of the people at our table and a time. It was explained that every table ran a sweep-stake on how long the speeches would last and whoever got the closest was given the table £50 pot. The sweepstake was supposed to be clandestine, but everyone knew it happened. I wrote my name down and looked at the times the others had put and having no idea about such matters, simply added 5 minutes to whatever time the last person had estimated, and dropping in a £5 note into the envelope I passed the lot to John M.

The speeches were a mixture of the need for further professional education for the rising stars in loss adjusting, thanks to the guests and then finally the guest speaker rose to a huge round of applause. I have no recollection as to who that person was or what they said as by this time the mixture of champagne, white and red wine as well as a glass of port had caused things to become a little blurry. The speeches over (I didn't win the pot) the toastmaster announced, 'Gentlemen if you must, you may,' which was evidently the cue to light up cigars. Before long the room was a heavy fog of cigar smoke, the clinking of glasses and the general hubbub of laughing and talking as the penguins began to wander to other tables to chat with friends and colleagues. I didn't know anyone of course, so downing a final glass of red wine I tottered off back to the bedroom noticing that it was 11.30 pm.

Although this may be considered 'too much information' I was not a pyjama wearer and had not been since the age of 8 or 9. But not only was I about to share a bed with a stranger, and a man at that, but I had no night-time attire. Keeping my underpants on I slipped into the bed and kept close to the side. I must have slept because on waking it was daylight and so I washed and dressed, leaving John M on his side of the bed snoring loudly. I left him a note of thanks for the invite and grabbing my bag went down to breakfast. I was surprised to see Tim there, still in his dinner suit, tucking into an enormous plate of 'the full English'. Joining him at his table he said he had been drinking all night long and having been kicked out of the ballroom around midnight he had then taken a taxi to Soho with his hosts and had spent the rest of the night in some seedy strip joint drinking overpriced 'champagne' and watered-down whiskey at £50 a glass. Being seen at breakfast still in a dinner suit was considered, by some, to give you some kind of 'cache'. I thought it would be more likely to give you cirrhosis of the liver.

John M later moved to a firm in Nairobi, Kenya and we continued to have dealings for many years until his retirement.

I have been extremely fortunate in that I think, except for one or two years, I have been a guest at every Loss Adjusters Annual Dinner (it later became a lunch) for the following 40 years or so. And I have never won the sweepstake on the speech lengths either.

Routine claims are, well, routine and there is nothing remarkable about them, but sometimes a simple comment is made which causes a complete turn of events. Two such cases involved tragic loss of life and both happened within a few miles of each other, oddly within sight of the Humber Bridge.

The first case involved a jack-up barge which was a vessel that had 'stilts' to keep it stationary in the water, in this case on the River Humber. At the end of a very long jetty tankers would moor and dispense their cargo of liquid crude oil down a large diameter pipe or receive refined fuel from a refinery down another pipeline that both ran parallel along one side of the jetty. Both pipelines needed maintenance and the barge could be moved down the side of the pipelines and then fixed in place on the stilts thus allowing the workmen to attend to the repairs under or at the sides of the pipes whilst remaining on a working surface that did not move up and down with the swell of the tidal river. Access to the barge, which had an accommodation cabin and a galley, was obtained via a small bridge from the jetty to a 'catwalk' that ran on the other side of the twin pipelines for the full length of the jetty. If there was a problem for the workmen at all it was that as the bridge was fixed in place, when the barge was moved the men had a long walk sometimes back in the opposite direction to which they had come, basically doing a U-turn.

One winter's evening two workers were returning from town having been in a pub all evening. The jetty was well-lit on the path, but there was no lighting on the pipelines and a string of small lights illuminated the catwalk. The weather was clear and dry but frosty and both men were wearing thick padded great coats to keep out the wind and the cold. As they got closer to the barge the men knew they would need to walk past where the barge could be seen on the other side of the twin pipes, but would need to walk another 100 yards or so before they could cross the bridge and return to the barge along the catwalk. One of the men decided to speed up and told his colleague he was going to be first to the barge and get some coffee so quickened his pace. When he arrived at the barge about 5 or 10 minutes later, he went to the galley, poured himself a fresh mug of coffee and waited for his colleague to arrive. After another 10 minutes, there was still no sign of his colleague so he went out of the galley and looked around for him. After checking the cabins there was still no sign of him so he retraced his steps and went back along the catwalk calling out his colleague's name. He went as far back down the jetty to the place where they had last spoken but there was still no sign of him. Returning to the barge he then phoned the Police, believing that something sinister had happened.

The Police turned up after another 20 or 30 minutes and after relaying the background story, the Police, who had powerful torches with them, discovered that there were scuff marks on the pipelines where the frost looked like it had been rubbed away. The marks were at the point just beside the barge and they concluded that instead of following his colleague the missing party must have climbed over the safety rail and attempted to get to the barge by going across the pipelines in an attempt to beat his colleague to the coffee pot.

However, as the pipes were frosty, and the man was in an intoxicated state, he must have lost his footing and slipped between the pipes and fell the 25 ft or so into the River Humber. As the man was wearing heavy clothing, they presumed he would have sunk like a stone and drowned. At this time the river was in full flow and it was a windy night and even if the man, now presumed deceased, had screamed or shouted out there was almost no prospect of him being heard by anyone. A search was made of the shoreline, but the Humber has one of the fastest flows of British Rivers and there was no sign of a body. Approximately five weeks later a heavily decomposed body was washed up on a beach about 10 miles away and it was postulated that due to the currents the unfortunate soul had been across the Channel to Holland and back.

A letter of claim was sent to the contractor/barge operators and then to me as the apparent insurers. My initial view was that this had to be a 'Marine' claim as the accident involved a barge, but because the barge did not float and was fixed on stilts it was considered construction plant. The allegation of negligence against the contractor was that whilst they accepted that there may be some (some??) contributory negligence by the deceased for hopping over the safety rail and taking a foolish risk, the contractors had not provided a safety boat and by Statute a safety boat was a mandatory requirement and the failure to provide one meant liability attached. I thought all this was nonsense and denied liability on the basis that even if a safety boat had been available (a) no one knew the deceased had even fallen in the water and even if they had (b) he sank like a stone and there was no prospect of rescue and (c) he was wholly the author of his own misfortune (thus he was totally to blame). The solicitors issued proceedings and so I decided I needed to obtain some specialist legal advice.

My appointed solicitors indicated to me the distinctions between construction and maritime law were

113

fine and suggested that we get a definitive view of the case from a barrister in conference.

Meetings, or 'conferences with counsel' (or 'cons' as they were called) always took place at counsel's chambers (the name for their offices) and there are many Inns of Court around the country but the most well-known are in London at Temple, Lincoln's Inn and Gray's Inn. I was very familiar with most counsel's chambers in the Temple and had attended many cons in the preceding years.

My biggest gripe with cons was that they always began at 6 pm. The reason for that is that the courts themselves were in session until 4 pm and the two-hour gap was intended to give the barrister time to return to chambers and re-read the papers in preparation for the con. Given that, there were many cons I attended when it was apparent that the barrister was not familiar with all the facts, the pre-reading time was something I felt that was more honoured in the breach than observance. Further, at that time barristers would only meet with the paying client (me) if instructing solicitors were present and as my solicitor always came along with an assistant and a trainee, there would be five of us to begin with, six if the barrister had a 'junior' with him too. If the brokers, loss adjusters and representatives of the insured were also invited, a con of 8-10 people was not uncommon and this frequently meant that the meeting could last 2-3 hours or more. This would result in a very long day.

At the con on this case however, my barrister gave a clear view that the absence of the safety boat – notwithstanding that, no one knew somebody had gone into the water, and even if they had there was no prospect of rescue (sinking like a stone) still meant that the breach of statutory duty, no matter that it appeared to be a technical breach, resulted in an inescapable conclusion that liability was bound to be found against the contractor... and as the claim for damages was likely to be small, he suggested settling on best terms possible. I was mollified.

Fatal accidents have a fixed value in England and Wales and at that time the amount was £5000 or so plus reasonable funeral expenses. The deceased had no dependency so the claim was fairly low value so I made an offer of around 50% and obtained a settlement.

The second claim was considerably more expensive and involved an oil refinery near Grimsby.

A relatively new style of policy had been developed called a single project policy. The effect was that anyone who was in contract with another party was covered and there was to be no bickering as to who was to blame as not only was everyone covered but you could not cross-claim either. By way of example if a house was being constructed and a plumber caused a water leak that damaged the electrics, the electrical contractor had his claim for damage paid by us and we could not cross-claim or recover from the plumber because he was covered too. The idea was to avoid conflict and make the claims process simpler.

Instead of a house we were covering the extension to an oil refinery and the equipment involved was huge and expensive.

One of the largest vessels in an oil refinery is the 'cat cracker'. This enormous piece of kit is 6-7 storeys tall and weighs about 200 tons. Its function, when heated, is to split crude oil into refined components such as kerosene, petrol, diesel and heavier oils. The cracker had been fabricated elsewhere and came to the site on the bed of an extremely large, multi-wheeled, low-loader lorry. Once on site the cracker needed to be raised to a vertical position by a crane and then gently lowered into its supporting cradle ready for all the pipework to be connected.

The crane used to lift the cracker was in itself an unusual design in that it was made up of two vertical legs, held in position by extremely long guy ropes, and then two other cranes with a lifting capacity of around 50 tons simultaneously lift a crossbeam which is lowered onto the legs. The crossbeam weighed over 50 tons, but as its weight was divided between the two lifting cranes, capacity was not an issue. The crossbeam is capable of lifting well over 250 tons.

All went well with the lift and lowering. The problem came when the four men on the crossbeam (two at each end) had to undo the massive fixing bolts that kept the crossbeam fixed to the legs. With the two cranes supporting the weight of the crossbeam the men at one end undid all of the bolts but at the other end, they failed to undo all the bolts but radioed that they had. As the two cranes began to lift the crossbeam at one end the beam began to rise but at the other, the crane was struggling with the lift, lifting as it was the crossbeam and a leg.

The load began to slew sideways and as it slowly began to tip, in panic two of the workmen jumped into the bucket of yet another crane and survived. But the heavily overloaded crane jib began to buckle under the weight of the crossbeam and leg. There was a loud metallic rendering sound and the jib collapsed, bringing down everything with it and tipping over the 'good' lifting crane too. The whole lot of tangled metal smashed into other expensive machinery on the ground. Sadly, the two other men fell to their deaths.

Understandably the two surviving men, who were Dutch, were shocked and such was the effect on one that his hair had turned white within weeks. The physical damage ran into the millions of pounds. What had piqued my interest though was the contractual chain. Of course, we were covering everyone on site who was in contract. There could not possibly be any recovery...or could there?

I learned that the company undertaking the lift was an English one but they had insufficient equipment or expertise to undertake the lift, so they called upon their Dutch parent company for assistance and they confirmed their capability, so it was, in point of fact, the Dutch company that did the lift, and who screwed up. However, the UK company did not pay or contract with their parent company, so to my mind 'no contract equalled no cover', and whilst we would pay for all the damage to the cranes etc, I figured we could sue the Dutch company for a recovery. The damage was about £2.5m.

But what was not covered was the delay to the refinery coming on-stream and the oil company reckoned that they were losing £1m a DAY in lost revenue and as the repairs were going to cause delays of a year or so the uninsured business interruption loss was thought to be around £300m.

One of the rules in recovery actions is that the uninsured losses rank ahead of insured ones, so if we were only partially successful then the oil company would get their money first and AIU would get nothing. I argued that as AIU were paying the cost of the recovery action the oil company agreed that we would have first 'dibs' of any recovery, but we would split equally all the defendant's costs between us if we lost. I agreed.

We had a con with counsel about the recovery prospects. There were probably 15 of us in a tiny room. Some were standing. Counsel thought that our argument had merit, but believed the policy intended to cover the Dutch company...so figured we would probably lose. Whilst the damage claim was known the business interruption (or consequential loss) was still speculative and he thought that the calculation of it would be not only difficult but require the oil company to possibly disclose sensitive information.

One of the oil company personnel asked 'What sort of sensitive information do you mean?'

I replied 'Well, if I were defending this claim the first thing, I'd be asking is exactly how much profit do you make on a gallon of petrol and how much does it cost you to make in the first place?' The oil execs looked at each other and requested an adjournment whilst they 'had a chat'. A few minutes later they returned and said that as far as the uninsured consequential losses were concerned, they'd accept from the defendant a mere £25m... 'for cash'. My one simple question had caused them to write off £275m!

It was agreed we would proceed to trial if no settlement proposal was made by the 'other side'.

So off to court we went...

Chapter Eight

THE END OF A BEGINNING (PART 2)

Meantime, back in the office, it was realised that a line of business called 'Boiler and Machinery' (or B&M) had their claims dealt with in the liability claims department (which was odd) and I was asked if I would take over the whole portfolio as the claims were very much like the engineering ones I currently handled? I said I would as I felt that after 5 years doing construction, I needed to broaden my experience and there were not many B&M claims anyway. I felt I could cope with the additional workload.

No sooner had I begun handling the claims than the B&M underwriters had decided to sell a new 'scheme' of policy, specifically one for farmers and their milking machinery. I was invited to the Shropshire Agricultural Show to meet with the brokers and learn more about how the cover would work. Cows need milking twice a day (I knew that much) as leaving cows un-milked could cause mastitis and having a motor breakdown meant that any repair had to be completed within the window between the two milking times, day or night. The scheme required an engineer to be on call effectively 24/7/365, not only with the right spare parts readily available but also a new spare motor, in case repair was not possible. The brokers assured us that they had a team of engineers all ready to cover the country and all were fully equipped with vans, spare parts and replacement motors.

In the next few weeks, we sold hundreds of policies as the premiums were low and the potential benefits to the farmer were considerable. The broker was also taking 20% in commission. Underwriters were pleased as within a few months they had received something in the region of £500,000 in premium income. Champagne corks were popped. Then the claims began to come in, first a trickle, then a flood.

It soon became apparent to me that many of the farms, especially in Wales and Yorkshire were very remote and by the time the engineer got to the farm to repair a broken-down motor, there was never enough time to undertake a repair before the next milking was due, the engineer simply installed a new one for the farmer before he needed to return to the depot to pick up the next repair job, and another spare motor. This was all before the days of mobile phones of course.

What underwriters had failed to appreciate was that, unlike normal businesses where maintenance was routine, indeed a statutory requirement in some cases, farmers never seem to do any. Accordingly, dairy farm motors never had any routine maintenance undertaken, so they were almost always driven to destruction.

However, by the time I had collated the necessary information to prove these points, the loss ratios had demonstrated that for every £1 we had taken in premium, we were paying out £100. We were being milked dry. The scheme was cancelled after 6 months and the underwriters who devised the scheme were suddenly asked to leave 'to seek alternative career opportunities elsewhere'.

Before the days of 24-hour television, ITV used to put on documentary 'shorts' during the afternoon and these were frequently repeated. One I recall was called 'Bringing Water to the Desert' or something like that and involved the construction of a twin pipeline crossing the whole of Saudi Arabia with desalination plants at either end, one on the Persian Gulf at Al Khobar, the other at Jeddah on the Red Sea. The film showed how mechanised the process was, with cranes lifting the large diameter steel pipes which were then automatically welded together and wrapped in some material to prevent corrosion, before lowering them into a trench where they were backfilled with sand. Imagine my surprise then when I found that this was the very project AIU were underwriting.

In more or less central Saudi Arabia lies the capital, Riyadh, which sits within a rocky desert that seems to stretch for hundreds of miles in all directions. The capital is also at a higher elevation than the coastal cities so in effect the desalinated water is pumped 'uphill' to Riyadh where it is to be stored in gigantic underground reservoirs.

My local loss adjusters began reporting that the Taiwanese contractors laying the pipeline were behind schedule and seemed to be taking less care with the trenching machines as they were chopping through all utility cables and pipes with abandon. The reason became clear when the cost to the contractor of carefully excavating around a utility was up to $5000 a time, whereas if they chopped up a cable or two, the policy excess was just $1000. So, to them it made economic sense to just blindly dig away – insurers would pay for everything.

To add to the misery, the local telephone company charged not only to repair the lines, even if they were redundant, but also claimed for 'lost revenue' calculated on the number of lines x number of hours x so many riyals per hour. The contractor paid none of the bills, so they were sued by the phone company and the contractor, by offering no defence, allowed the phone company to get the Sharia equivalent of a 'judgement in default' called an Abdel Khader, which was then non-negotiable. Most of the phones in Saudi were transmitted by satellite and the landlines were therefore quite redundant, but that was no excuse or defence in Sharia law.

Apart from all the utility claims, there were other defects in the project and it was suggested that I plan a trip to Saudi Arabia to investigate the claims with the adjusters and discuss solutions with the various contractors involved.

Before I even could go to the Kingdom it was a requirement that I had the necessary jabs to inoculate me against any number of horrible diseases that I didn't want to catch. I also needed a letter from a 'host' (in this case the adjusters) that confirmed my reasons for visiting the Kingdom, where I would be staying, for how long etc and all had to be presented to the Saudi Embassy in London, along with a fee for the Visa. It all went surprisingly smoothly.

My schedule was to fly to Al Khobar where I would meet with an adjuster and go through the various claims and decide how they would be possibly resolved; then I would fly to Riyadh, meet another adjuster and look at problems with the reservoir then meet with the experts to discuss the repair options; and finally, another flight to Jeddah to meet with the 'cable chopping contractors' and try and settle their claims. All of this was to take a week.

Hotels were booked and flights arranged and off I went. The company had never provided me with a credit card, so I asked for a cash float in Riyals and was given a massive bundle of notes (about £500 worth) but I was unable to fully determine the denominations easily as the numbering was in Arabic script.

On arrival at Al Khobar around midnight I stepped out of an air-conditioned aeroplane into what I can only describe as a sauna. The heat and humidity were simply breath taking, indeed I found it difficult to draw breath! Before I reached the bottom of the aircraft steps my suit was soaked with perspiration.

Customs seemed to take forever and when I got to the main concourse, I found a chap with my name on a cardboard notice, my driver I correctly assumed, who took me to my hotel.

I showered and went to bed. Even though it was midnight the noise of the traffic on the road outside was annoying. Cars were tooting their horns all the time, there was no let-up. I must have finally dropped off to sleep with the honking sounds still in my ears. In the morning I enjoyed a very pleasant breakfast and was met by the loss adjuster who took me to see the evidence of some of the claims. I had a camera with me and took it out ready to take a few snaps of the scenery. The adjuster shouted at me 'For God's sake! Put the camera away and don't take it out of your briefcase unless I tell you it's ok!' He went on to explain that anyone caught with a camera in the open was considered by the Police to be a spy and there would be every likelihood that I would be taken to a Police cell, interrogated for hours and would have to pay a substantial fine to be released! I put the camera away immediately.

Later that day after the boring part of looking at the damage the adjuster (who was Dutch) suggested that we spend the evening at their 'compound' where we could relax and have a meal and some refreshments. That sounded better than a night in a hotel restaurant on my own so I gratefully accepted.

Almost all ex-pats live in secure gated compounds, sometimes they are manned with armed guards. I was not sure why as theft is most uncommon in the Kingdom, the penalty (having your left hand cut off) for being caught and convicted is seen as a pretty good deterrent on its own without the risk of being shot as well. It was explained that kidnapping and ransom though was a problem – hence the guards.

I was led into an office-cum-accommodation block and was greeted by several men, some of whom I had been dealing with over the previous months. They handed me a large glass of a clear and fizzy liquid with ice and a slice of lemon, which I was assured was a gin and tonic. Well, it tasted like a G&T but not quite a G&T. Besides, the Kingdom was supposed to be 'dry' so I asked, what was it? I was told that it was a 'Jeddah gin and tonic'. The 'gin' was, in fact, simply raw alcohol, a by-product at the Aramco Oil Refinery and it was sold in very large plastic drums as a raw spirit. You could die if you drank it neat, but if the liquid was cut/diluted with water by two-thirds, then that liquid was about the same proof spirit as normal gin and once lemon, ice and tonic were added, it could... to the thirsty European... be easily mistaken for a real G&T. And after three or four of them, so it proved.

Following dinner and some 'wine' I was getting a little squiffy but before being driven back to my hotel, someone suggested a small glass of a very 'special' wine they had made as an experiment. Even the possession of brewing yeast is considered by the Police an offence, but apparently bread yeast was ok and it was explained that they made wine out of almost anything fruity, even vegetables. I was given a small glass of a liquid that was coloured virulently bright green (lime perhaps? Pea-pod maybe?) and on giving it a sniff the hairs up my nose dissolved. 'Just try it' they chorused and so I did. I have no idea what it tasted of as my senses were overpowered by the sheer heat that came from the vapours of the 'wine'. But I did try a mouthful, much to the merriment of my hosts, who were whooping with joy at my discomfort. Chilli wine! I don't recommend it.

The next day was more of the same boring stuff and my flight to Riyadh was scheduled again to arrive quite late in the evening. I was told that on arrival at the airport, there was a courtesy bus that would take me to the hotel, all I had to do was find it. Stepping off the plane this time I was met with heat, but no humidity, which I found was a bonus. It was just 'hot' and I could cope with that. The flight was late and once again, even though this was an internal flight I still had my bags and documents minutely checked at a security desk. Riyadh airport was simply stunning and huge. Marble of the finest quality was abundant and there was even an indoor waterfall, sculptures and statues and huge pictures of the Saudi Royal Family on every wall.

I had been so delayed that by the time I was on the concourse, there was almost nobody to be seen, and of the courtesy bus, no sign whatsoever. There was a phone though which said 'Hyatt Regency' on a sign so I picked it up and asked where was the bus? I was told that the bus left at 10.30 pm and I had missed it. My heart sank. At that point, ignoring whatever the person was saying on the phone, many scruffy-looking gents all in Arab clothing, headscarves and sandals were surrounding me saying Taxi? Taxi?' I pointed to one and he grabbed my bag and I hurriedly followed him, for he went at quite a pace, down a flight of stairs to an underground car park. There he flung my bag into the back of a very battered Toyota pick-up truck and somewhat fearfully I climbed into the passenger seat. It was filthy and covered in dust and sand. The windscreen was cracked and the driver turned on the engine and we shot out of the car park at great speed. Of course, the driver hadn't asked where I was going and as soon as he was on an open road he pulled to the verge.

'That's it' I thought 'Out will come a large knife and I'll have my throat cut and be a corpse on a dusty highway in the middle of nowhere'.

The driver must have said 'Where to?' but in Arabic. I looked blankly at him and showed him my hotel reservation form. He couldn't read English and shrugged his shoulders. I said rather croakily 'Hyatt Regency?' and he grinned, revealing several missing teeth and exclaimed 'Hyatt, Hyatt'. Then whacking the truck into gear off we sped into the pitch-black night...with no dashboard lights and just one working headlight I noted.

Now Riyadh airport is many miles outside the main city, in the same way Heathrow is from central London, but we seemed to be driving for ages when in the distance I began to see the lights of the city. We got close to a very tall building and I could see from the illuminated sign on the roof that it was indeed the Hyatt Regency. Suddenly the driver pulled over and looked at me. 'It's the large knife time' I thought and the driver held up a hand and rubbed his thumb and forefinger together, the international sign for money. But how much? He said something and guessing what he meant I took out the roll of cash from my pocket. It was dark in the cab and so he turned on the central light under the rear-view mirror which gave a very weak glow as I peeled off a few random notes from the wad and handed them to him. He shook his head and nodded at the wad. I peeled off a thicker amount which he took and counted them and nodded at the wad again. A few more notes were handed over and seemingly satisfied he waved me out the door and as I closed it, with a crunching of gears, he sped away in a cloud of grit and dust. My bag! My bag was still in the back of the truck! The truck then stopped about 25 yards from where I was standing, the driver got out and threw my bag onto the verge, gave a cursory wave, got in the cab again and sped off into the darkness.

Retrieving my bag, I trudged in the darkness to the Hyatt arriving dusty, dishevelled, sweaty and thirsty…but ALIVE! I was so relieved. In my room, I quickly disrobed and took the longest shower of my life.

The following morning, I was met by another adjuster, Richard, and we went in his car to the reservoir where I was to look at the problems with that, which seemed serious and therefore, expensive. During the journey, he naturally asked about my trip and I relayed to him the taxi story. He was horrified and said that firstly the courtesy bus to the hotel ran hourly and I could, and should, have waited for the 11.30 pm one, but secondly, the only taxis in Riyadh were air-conditioned limousines, not beaten-up pick-up trucks! He went on to explain that unlicensed taxi drivers were a scourge at the airport and were known to rip off passengers and that had the driver been stopped by the Police it was likely that we would BOTH be in trouble. He asked how much had I paid the driver? I said, truthfully, I had no idea.

He later said that my hotel overlooked a very notorious square of waste ground and under no circumstances was I to go for a walk there. I wondered why? He went on to explain that that particular square in Riyadh was where public executions were carried out and if one was scheduled, everyone there was forced by the Police to face the spectacle and look on, including any Westerners who happened to be there. It was part of the Sharia law – the punishment had to be witnessed by the public. I said that I had seen a documentary on TV called 'Death of a Princess' about a princess and her lover who were beheaded by sword as she had rejected her parent's choice of husband. He said that it was true and it had happened at that very square in 1977. I went silent for a few minutes contemplating this regime.

By now we were at the reservoir and getting out of the air-conditioned car, Richard leant over his windscreen and lifted the wipers. "The heat causes the rubber to melt and stick to the glass if you don't do that" he explained and slamming the doors we walked away. 'Aren't you locking it?' I asked. 'Nah,' he said with a smile 'no one steals here, at least not twice!' Quite...

We went to the reservoir and there was a burly-looking chap standing by a door. He must have been expecting us and handing me a big torch and using a large key he opened the door. As I stepped in and was about to descend a large flight of steps, I turned and asked Richard if he was coming too? He said he wasn't as he'd seen the problem for himself weeks before. The moment I went in I could see why Richard declined the visit. Going from an outside heat of 114F with zero humidity I stepped into one of the upper layers of Hades. I was standing inside a vast underground reservoir with dozens of concrete columns that went off into the gloomy distance (why illuminate an underground reservoir?) as far as could be seen, even with the torch. The reservoir was half-full of water and coupled with the heat I believed you could cut the humidity with a knife and spread it on a slice of bread. I could barely breathe. The man with me (who was from the contractors who built the reservoir) explained that the water was desalinated, basically seawater with the salts removed, but you couldn't drink it as it still had some salts in it, but it was fine for irrigating salt tolerant crops. However, the humidity and the high sodium content of the water had reacted with the concrete on the columns causing them to spall, or crumble, thereby exposing the steel of the columns which were now rusting. If the columns failed the roof would collapse and the whole reservoir would be a total loss.

I had seen all I needed and although I had only been there 10 minutes or so, that was enough – I was drenched. Perspiration was pouring off me, my suit trousers were sticking to my skin and my open-necked shirt was clinging to my back. We came up the steps and out through the door into the bright sunshine. I thanked the contractor for his time and returned to Richard and his car. Oddly, by the time I had walked there, maybe 50 yards, I was completely dry again. Weird.

My meeting with the experts was as I expected. They had a solution – re-sleeve the columns with stronger concrete and hope for the best. I had lost interest as I was going to argue that the true cause of the loss was a design fault (the chemical content of the water vs the chemical composition of the concrete should have been contemplated) and we didn't insure that – someone else did.

I had a morning flight with Richard to Jeddah so there was no prospect of another 'taxi incident'. The temperature and humidity in Jeddah were, if anything, more severe than in Al Khobar.

We were collected by one of Richard's colleagues, David, who was to drive us to the Taiwanese contractor's compound. On the journey, David teased me about my infamous 'taxi ride' (news travels fast I thought) and at that point, a Maserati sped past us doing something like 80 or 90 mph. The driver looked like a child. David said that it probably was a child, one of the dozens of Royal princes. He went on to explain that traffic law in Saudi was like no other. There was little logic, but I had noticed that all the cars were in good order, with no dents for example. I was told that in the event of any crash, the Police were called and you were given a piece of paper that meant you had to get the damage repaired within a certain number of days. No repair? No piece of paper or 'chit'? You were fined. If the Maserati had crashed into us, it was considered by the Police to be our fault, even if we were rear-ended by a 9-year-old doing 90mph in a 30mph zone or at traffic lights.

The reason was that as foreigners if we were not in their country, he would not have driven into us, so it was our fault. He went on to say that he was driving with his fiancé and she was in the front passenger seat and they were stopped by the Police and questioned. The Policemen had asked if the woman was his wife? He said no, my fiancé (she was English) to which the Policeman said she must be a prostitute as only prostitutes and married women sat in the front seat of the car, single women sat in the back. The policeman accepted no explanation from David so he paid a 'fine' on the spot (no receipt of course) and his fiancé went and sat in the back of the car for the rest of their journey. We had now come to a set of traffic lights and the moment the cars in the traffic came to a stop, they began honking their horns. Why do they do that? I asked. Whether the following is true or apocryphal I do not know, but David said that a rumour had spread that the traffic lights were controlled by sound and if you honked, they would change more quickly from red to green. All nonsense of course, but the locals must have believed it because they were pressing their horns day and night.

When we arrived at the compound the Taiwanese contractors, headed by Mr Chen, greeted us warmly. Their offices were heavily air-conditioned and the walls were adorned with wallpaper depicting jungle scenes. It was explained that nothing in Saudi is really 'green' everything is sandy and beige coloured and the staff missed simply seeing the colour green – hence the wallpaper. Nice touch I thought.

Looking at the 100s of claims for damage to utilities would take hours. By now Mr Chen said that they had paid all the default judgements and were out of pocket to the tune of millions of Riyals. My case was a simple one. We paid claims for accidents, not deliberate damage. They countered and said it was reasonable to expect that some of the utilities they encountered were not on local authority plans (not much in Saudi was) as the shifting sands of the desert meant that even if there were plans, the plotting of utilities could not be accurate. These were therefore 'accidents' and thus covered. I said that cables may move (though I doubted it), but not pipes. They accepted that but said that the depth of pipes was unknown as the sands could blow away the surface and a pipe that was thought to be 3 metres down may only be 50cm – again this was not their fault and so an accident.

I was not to be moved and said that there was all manner of utility detection equipment (they are called CAT-Scanners) available to them and they had not used any. A simple scanner could detect the electrical background 'noise' of an electricity or telephone cable and metal pipes were detected by magnetic means. By not using a scanner, that meant they were digging blindly and that, I said, was not just foolhardy but reckless, thus non-accidental. Furthermore, because they were behind in their program, facing heavy penalty charges, they had taken a commercial decision to do what they did, and insurers were not there to bail out their commercial problems.

Most of what I said needed to be translated to Taiwanese so the others around the table could understand and then answers translated back to English for my benefit, so it made the meeting longer than it needed to be and any subtleties of language were probably lost in both directions.

Eventually, we thrashed out a deal that was fair to everyone, though the adjusters always felt I had come to the meeting with a pre-determined deal in mind, which was quite perceptive of them.

Business over, the contractors asked if we would be their honoured guest at dinner that evening? David cried off but Richard and I accepted. A car was arranged to collect us from the hotel and freshly showered and changed we were driven back to the compound. We were taken to a large room where there was an enormous circular table, in the centre of which was a 'lazy Susan' (a table that turned) that would allow various dishes to be passed around to each guest. What immediately caught my eye was that the centrepiece - a huge orange lobster, intricately detailed with claws, legs, feelers and eyes on stalks... and all carved, so it appeared on closer inspection, from carrots! It was fabulous.

Once seated I noted that we each had a small 'shot glass' in front of our setting and the obligatory chopsticks. I was completely unskilled at that time with chopsticks and there was a worry that someone might get flicked with food or, of greater concern to me, I would go hungry.

I loved Chinese food and was starving! A waiter brought me a fork and so the meal began. With each course, another vegetable work of art was presented with it – a foot-high pagoda carved from swede, a massive koi carp (carrot again), a Buddha (swede again) and I think a dragon, made from what vegetable I cannot recall.

The waiter came around with a bottle of sake and filled up the shot glass. I was about to take a sip when I caught Richard's eye and he shook his head a little, so I replaced it on the table. At this point, one of our hosts looked at me, raised his glass and said 'Mr Cottington, gan bei!' Everyone else then raised their glass and said 'gan bei' (myself mumbling it a second or two late) and threw back their drink at which point all the glasses were refilled. [I later learned that 'gan bei' is the Chinese equivalent of 'cheers' though I believe it means 'dry cup' but it is considered bad manners to drink on your own, so a toast was required.]

A few minutes later another person was raising his glass and once again 'Mr Cottington, gan bei!' which was echoed and again the glasses were refilled. Courage stiffened by the rather lovely sake I thought I would give it a go and raising my glass I said 'Mr Chen, gan bei!' – more echoes and much laughter at my pronunciation. I was getting the hang of this so 'Mr Richard, gan bei!' and before long I had 'gan bei-ed' everyone round the table and was getting rather light-headed.

I turned to Mr Chen and asked about the vegetable carvings. I said that these were truly impressive – where did they come from? Mr Chen said that a man, Mr Ho, carved them in the kitchen for every meal and just doing the carvings was his job, he did nothing else. 'Wow,' I thought.

I then asked if Mr Ho was available, as I would like to thank him for his skill and artistry. Mr Chen looked a bit puzzled but said something to one of the waiters and a few minutes later a small elderly man came from the kitchen, walking with a stooped back and stood a few steps into the room, bowing slightly and rubbing his hands nervously. I asked Mr Chen to translate for me and said: 'You, Mr Ho, are a man of considerable skill and talent and you have brought me great joy and honour this evening with your wonderful carvings. Mr Ho, gam bei!' As the translation was made Mr Ho's face lit up with smiles and he briefly clapped his hands together, then nervously looked around as he had no glass, but someone handed him one, so he looked up at Mr Chen, who nodded and Mr Ho replied 'Gan bei', threw back the drink, turned on his heels and sped off back to the kitchen. Mr Chen turned to me and said that I had made Mr Ho a very happy man. I had meant it; Mr Ho was to my mind a genius.

The meal over I was driven back to the hotel. On checking out I asked the clerk to arrange for me a pre-paid taxi to the airport. I was then given my bill (in US Dollars and Riyal) and so figured this would be the way of using up my surplus cash and I handed the clerk the remaining bundle of Riyal notes from my wallet. The clerk thanked me, added them up and said that there was still a balance to pay so I put that on my credit card.

Whilst waiting for my pre-paid taxi I did a little mental maths as to how much my 'dodgy' taxi had cost. Around £200 apparently. I'd been ripped off big time... but I was alive, had a story to relate and besides, the company were paying!

Jeddah airport was not as impressive as the one in Riyadh, but splendid nonetheless and completely air-conditioned. Once on the aeroplane and we were in the air I asked a stewardess for a drink and was given a glass of water. That's being in 'economy' I thought. After another

20 minutes or so there was a 'ding dong' on the tannoy and the pilot announced that we were now out of Saudi airspace and suddenly there was an exodus of passengers toward the toilets. All were in Arab dress of one kind or another, dishdasha for men (the long white robe) or ladies in a burka. They returned to their seats in jeans and Western clothing and at that point, the real drinks trolley came round and all, now 'Westernised', were merrily getting stuck into the free alcoholic drinks.

In the office, there had been several adjusters leaving the liability team and we were asked if we wanted to undertake some of the routine, low value, employer's liability claims? I indicated a willingness and was given a few to investigate. My first one ended up with a little controversy, which for a simple 'slip and fall' was most unusual.

The accident circumstances in the letter of claim were simple and straightforward enough: In a confectionary factory a female employee, Mrs P, was in the ladies toilet block. She had slipped on a wet floor and in trying to save herself from falling, put her left hand through a 12 x 8" pane of glass and severed a finger badly which required many stitches and may need surgery to repair a tendon. Damages were claimed for a breach of duty in allowing the floor to become slippery. That all seemed simple enough, even for a novice like me.

The factory was in North London and I turned up on a sunny day around lunchtime and was met by a lady called Ruth, the head of personnel. I said I needed to see and, if possible, photograph the 'scene of the crime' as I cheekily put it. She said that the ladies' toilet block was also used as a canteen/rest room and as this was a food factory, I needed to wear a white lab coat, plastic bootees over my shoes, a hair net, a hat and a snood (a hairnet that goes over a beard). Once I was officially attired (and feeling a complete fool) off we went to the toilet block. Once I was through the door, there was jeering and ribald comments from the female staff sitting at a table having a rest break, about a 'pervert in a suit with a camera in the ladies' loo!' Ruth asked them to give us 5 minutes, so they left, still jeering at me on their way out. At the end of the room was an external wall of frosted 12 x 8" panes of glass and I figured that the cubicle closest to the windows must be the scene of the offending accident.

On entering the empty cubicle, I was rather surprised to see that one of the panes was now covered in cardboard... but it was about 5ft off the ground. All the other panes were intact. I was puzzled and asked if Mrs P was over 6ft tall? I went on to add that slipping and falling usually meant that when you stretched out your hands to save yourself, you'd naturally have your hands at, or below, chest height. Even if you throw your hands up, given the height of the broken window...well, it just didn't add up. Ruth explained that in point of fact, Mrs P was probably not even 5ft tall, she was extremely short as a lot of Asian women are. I pointed to the window and I could reach it, but I still could not understand how someone short like Mrs P had slipped and put her hand through a window that high up. Ruth looked at me for a few moments and then said: 'Mr Cottington, you obviously don't know how Asian ladies go to the loo.' I jokingly said that I had A-level biology and as far as I could recall, the mysteries of female internal plumbing were the same the world over. Ruth persisted, 'No, what I mean is, you don't know how they use the loo. You see, they stand on the ceramic bowl and squat, not sit on the seat like Westerners. In standing and squatting she must have rested her left hand on the window pane, slipped on the ceramic and losing her balance, pushed her hand through the glass window'. I was both flabbergasted and educated at the same time. I took my photos and scribbled a few notes on a pad.

Back at the office, I dictated my report and an hour or so later there was a deputation from the typing pool who came to see me. 'Is this true?' the head of the pool asked, 'about the standing on the bowl thing?' I confirmed it was. 'Incredible,' she said, and shaking her head went back to tell the other ladies in the pool the story. It seems a lot of us were educated that day, as was the claimant's solicitor whom I telephoned to explain why we would not be paying the claim. He was as dumbstruck as I was and he said that if what I was saying was true, we would hear no more about it. We didn't.

My personal life had moved on. I was now the proud owner of a 3 bedroomed flat in Selhurst (mortgaged to the hilt of course), right opposite a pub. My friend Malcolm was now a qualified Policeman on the beat in Brixton, and I was godfather to his two sons, but importantly, I now had a girlfriend. Her name was Jo and I'd met her whilst we were at a scout campsite. She was a guide leader and was camping with her guides on an adjacent pitch and we had got chatting and had exchanged phone numbers and promised to meet up, which we did.

I was busy redecorating my flat and despite the promises Malcolm had given me, he didn't help me one bit. His marriage was on the rocks and what with his shift work and frequent absences 'tup North to deal with the miner's strikes he was never around to lend me a hand.

Malcolm's confidence had significantly increased. His newfound confidence in public situations also translated to increased confidence with women. He'd already told me of some of his 'sexploits' in Sheffield where he'd been 'cracking a few strikers' heads' and now he had a girlfriend in Croydon too. My flat became for a while a second home to him, then he got a flat with his girlfriend. Both of his lives were miserable and he was unable to choose between them.

Jo lived in Reading and it became our practice to travel to meet up each weekend – Friday night to Sunday – either in Reading or Selhurst.

At work, I was keen to progress and was getting itchy feet. I had been at AIU for 6 years and although promoted a couple of times, it was plain that Tim was going nowhere and there was nowhere for me to go...at least in Croydon. Working for an International firm can have its benefits. I heard that there was a need for a construction claims manager in AIU's South Africa office. I had no ties in the UK of any consequence, so I contacted the new UK manager (John T) threw my hat in the ring as it were, and waited.

In bed one evening I began to notice that my right elbow was swelling alarmingly and was extremely painful. My GP diagnosed that a small insect bite on the tip of my elbow had become infected and I was now on antibiotics (a brand it turned out I had an allergy to as well) but my arm was so painful I could barely move it and I was wearing a sling. It was Jo's turn to come to my flat, which I was grateful for as cooking left-handed was difficult. I mentioned later about my possible move to South Africa and she burst into tears! I must have made more of an emotional impact there than I had thought. A few days later there was a diplomatic incident between the UK and South Africa and the company appointed an American to the South Africa position instead of me. As disappointed as I was, Jo seemed to be happy.

One day in the office Tim came over to my cubicle and said 'You've got a girlfriend in Reading, haven't you?' 'Yes,' I replied somewhat cautiously 'why do you ask?' 'Oh, nothing really, it's just I was at a meeting with Barry from INA and he mentioned that they were having a problem recruiting someone in their Reading office... thought you might be interested.'

I called Barry. 'Hi, Barry, Tim tells me you have a job vacancy in Reading – if that's true why haven't you offered it to me you swine?' (We were on good terms!) 'Would you be interested then?' 'Depends', I said, 'what's the job and the money?'

It was agreed we would meet up for a chat which happened a few days later. Barry asked me about my experience, he knew I did construction work, but the job was just UK-based (so I'd have to forgo any international travel) and there was a heavy emphasis not only on construction but employer liability (EL), public liability (PL) and product liability (prods) as well. I assured him my construction claims handling skills were a given. I had EL experience (yes, one lady slipping in a loo but didn't tell him that obviously) some PL and some prods. Barry thought I was skilled enough (or perhaps he was just desperate) and offered me the job. He explained that Reading was a small field office – there would be me, a claims adjuster and a secretary – but the money was £1000 more than I was currently on, plus a house move and a company car. It seemed a good deal and so without giving it much more thought, I accepted. I said that I would be able to start on 10th December 1984. This was six weeks away and as the annual pub crawl was on the 6th, I'd be able to go to that too!

Back in the office, I handed in my letter of resignation to Tim and he passed it to John T who called me into his office 'for a chat'. He said he didn't want to lose me but I said the offer INA had made was more than I was on + a house move and a car. He told me not to be rash and think about it, so I returned to my desk. An hour or so later he came into my cubicle put a folded scrap of paper on it and walked away. I opened the note and it gave a number £1500 more than my current salary or £500 more than Barry had offered. I was seething. If I was worth £1500 more today, why wasn't I worth that yesterday? I decided I'd move. Sod them.

Just coming across my desk at this time was a terrible landslide at a dam construction project in Columbia. The dam was in a remote area and the topography was mountainous.

The landslide had happened at the same time as a fortnightly change-over between crews. It was common that busloads of families would come to the massive project site to meet or drop off their husbands/brothers depending on whether they were being collected or delivered. On the fateful day, it was raining very heavily. A great deal of the sides of the gorge had been cleared of all vegetation which made the sides of the steep gorge very unstable, especially in the rain. The sudden landslip completely wiped out the bus park and carried the busses into the river submerging them in over 50ft of mud and debris. There were thought to be 147 or so fatalities. No one was ever sure as whole families had been lost in the tragedy. One USA foreman was driving a jeep when the landslide took him and his jeep from one side of the gorge to the other where he was found, unharmed, 50ft up a tree. Such is the power of nature.

It was by now getting close to my leaving date and Tim said to me that I was not permitted to attend the pub crawl on the basis that it was a company event, not my leaving 'do'. He was concerned that the attendees would be more interested in hearing about my new job rather than me promoting AIU. I thought that it was a bit unfair as that was not my style and did say that one of the pubs was opposite my own house and if I happened to be in there drinking at the time there was not a lot he could do about it was there? I was leaving the following day after all. But I didn't spoil the night and did not make an appearance.

My solicitors called. Bad news. The oil refinery crane collapse claim – the court had found that there was a clear intention that all contractors on the site were to be covered – our recovery action had failed. I never did find out what happened to my 'Swan Song', but the matter did make case law and became an exam question for a while.

I was selling my flat, packing up, and looking forward to my new job. Jo said I could share her rented house for a few weeks while I looked for a new property, so at least I had somewhere to live.

The following Monday I was off to Maidstone (for induction) – a new office, a new car and new people... I couldn't wait.

Chapter Nine

A NEW BEGINNING

Before I started with INA, I was of course familiar with the roads in Reading and knew where the office was located, but never knew my team. So, I thought it would be a good idea to meet up with my new assistant, Lin, and get to know her and any background issues before I landed in the office. We had met up at the Ramada Hotel, which to be honest was a bit too rich for my pocket. Lin arrived with her husband Steve and we sat and had a few drinks. I learned that my predecessor, Mike, was a bit disorganised and had a habit of keeping any files that might be considered on audit to be 'problematic' in the boot of his car. She went on to say that the office was friendly though, the branch manager was called Russ and was a nice guy and we had a secretary, Sue, who was also very good.

Lin had been Mike's secretary and had been promoted to a claim handler. Unfortunately, at that time she didn't drive so all the investigations had been farmed out to loss adjusters, and in consequence, there was a pile of backlogged post. She said she had no settlement authority and had to get other offices to come in from time to time to help out. 'Oh whoopy-do,' I thought. What have I let myself in for? I was rather nervous.

Barry had asked me to arrive at their Maidstone office at 10 a.m. where I would meet the team and be told the basic rules etc in an induction and pick up my company car. I was told I would be staying in a local hotel for two days and go to Manchester for three more days of training in a field office to learn how they did things 'in the field' before actually starting in Reading the following Monday.

As I mentioned, I lived in Selhurst and Maidstone is the County Town of Kent so I figured that the rail connection to the town would be simple and quick. I knew that I needed to go into London Victoria and then out to Maidstone. What I did not know is that Maidstone has three stations and not one is called Maidstone or Maidstone Central. No, there is Maidstone East, Maidstone West and Maidstone Barracks. Barry hadn't given me any directions and I figured that their offices are bound to be close to one of the stations, but which one? I had a suitcase to carry and so I decided to go from my station, Selhurst, to Victoria. What I had not allowed for was that East Croydon to Victoria is about 20 minutes but Selhurst to Victoria was 50 minutes as the train stopped at every station en route. I didn't get to Victoria until nearly 9 a.m. but I still figured I had enough time to get to Maidstone.

The ticket desk advised that Maidstone East was the 'main' station so I got a single ticket to there. The trains ran hourly and there was one around 9.15, so I was lucky... but the journey time was an hour too. I'd be late and there was no way of telling anyone.

At Maidstone East, I knew I had to get to Kent House, Lower Stone Street. But where was that? No map and the people I asked hadn't heard of it. I took a short walk into what looked like a shopping area and saw a road sign that said Stone Street which was sloping down a hill, so I guessed Lower Stone Street would be at the bottom. Indeed, it was... but there was no sign of Kent House. I asked a passing traffic warden where Kent House was and she pointed to an ugly 1960s concrete monstrosity opposite a multi-storey car park and said that the entrance was between some shops and through another car park. Clearly, they didn't get many visitors, because they didn't make it easy to find.

Arriving about 45 minutes late I climbed the steps to the reception area and Barry was summoned by phone. When he met me, he apologised for not giving me directions and said that the train journey was known to be a tedious one and he should have asked me to come at 11 a.m.! So, all was well.

We travelled up to an upper floor and I was quickly introduced to about twenty people all of whose names I instantly forgot. I was assigned to sit with Alan, a nice man I guessed about 40ish.

Alan was also an investigator who sat in a team that undertook investigations in their 'patch'. He explained how their files were kept and it was very similar to AIU in almost every respect. Even the files had a similar colour coding:

Red = Property
Buff = Construction
Yellow = Liability
Orange = Motor/Auto

Green = Accident and Health

Blue = Marine

Purple = Workers Compensation (a USA version of employer liability)

I then briefly met Diane from HR. I'd been sent an employee form to complete, but it only arrived the prior Wednesday and it looked 'odd'. The front page was from a company called AFIA (huh?) and it was A3 in size, folded in half. The front and back had boxes to complete, but the inside pages were blank. I explained that I'd no time to call and ask for another as it would never have arrived in time. Diane sighed and said that it was their fault and she got me another one to complete. I asked about the 'AFIA' form and she said that INA currently had a hiring freeze as the company was going through a renaming process. It was still 'hush-hush' and I'd hear more in a week or so, but there was no need to worry, it was just that my first week or so of employment would be with AFIA (a sister company apparently) and then I would be transferred to the new company name. It seemed a reasonable explanation so I signed on the dotted line and was now officially an employee of INA or AFIA or whatever we would be called.

I spent the rest of Monday and Tuesday morning sitting with Alan essentially just reading his yellow files and he then thought my time would be far better spent at a proper field office – the biggest one being Manchester. At that time there were 'field offices' in Birmingham, Bristol, Glasgow, Maidstone and Reading. Each office had its own 'territory' and these were essentially the counties within a reasonable area of the office. Reading sat in the centre of its territory, covering Dorset, Wiltshire, Hampshire, West Sussex, Surrey, Middlesex, Hertfordshire, Bucks and Bedfordshire, Oxfordshire and Berkshire as well as all of west London and Isle of Wight. Quite a patch to cover. I was also told that it was not considered the 'done thing' to stray over a border to another office's patch even though in some cases a lot of Wiltshire was closer to the Bristol office than the Reading office. I said I'd try not to stray.

Barry told me that my settlement authority on claims would be $500,000. Anything greater had to be reported to Maidstone for approval. My authority at AIU was $1m, so this was a step-down, but there was no international work and most claims were under $500,000 so I was not too bothered by that. Grabbing my bag, I said goodbye to the team and Barry took me to the car park to hand over the keys to my company car. He apologised for the state of it as it was Mike's old car (Mike being the previous claim superintendent in Reading who had left 6 months previously). The car was a dark blue Ford Sierra, a typical rep's car of the day. It had 75,000+ miles on it and sounded like a tractor. Barry assured me it had been valeted though I later found broken glass under the seats and it smelled of stale cigarette smoke, but it was my company car and way better than my own banana-coloured Mk1 Ford Escort. That reminded me, I'd probably need to sell it.

I was now off to Manchester! It must be remembered that at this time the M25 London orbital motorway was not completed. I had no maps and the sat nav had not been invented. I knew I needed to go North (that A-level in geography had to come into use at some point) so I decided to drive right through the centre of London to pick up the M1 at Staples Corner. I knew the way there at least. However, I needed to go back to my flat in Croydon on the way to pick up more clothes as I didn't know when I'd be able to get back there and was, of course, sharing a house with Jo. The drive to Manchester took five or six hours. A hotel had been booked for me and somehow or other I found it and prepared to meet up with my counterpart, called Brian, in the Manchester office in the morning.

I found the INA offices easily enough and took the lift to the appropriate floor where I asked the receptionist for Brian. A few minutes later a tall middle-aged man came to meet me. He shook my outstretched hand and took me to his office. There were files piled high around his desk, on the windowsills and the floor. He had a steely gaze and an abrupt manner. Two mugs of tea were brought in by a secretary and no sooner had I raised mine to my lips than he said in a broad Manc accent:

'Ow much are they paying you then?' I wasn't sure whether to answer or not, but Brian answered the question himself 'Too bloody much I bet. What experience do you have then?'

I explained that I'd had 7 years at AIU and had much construction and engineering experience, both domestic and international, as well as some liability and property losses. 'Much EL?' he questioned.

'Not a great deal' I answered somewhat truthfully.

'What about meeting claimant solicitors and court work?'

I answered 'Some'.

'Christ, you'll be bloody useless you will. I don't know why they hired you. You're too young, too inexperienced and over-bloody-paid. OK come and meet the team and we will see what you are made of.' That was quite an introduction! I later learned that this was 'typical Brian'. He was a very experienced claims investigator and negotiator. He was also the oldest of all the claims people in the field offices and consequently looked down on everyone, especially me, whom he always considered to be an upstart, and an overpaid Southerner.

I sat looking at files with Brian and his team for the rest of the day and the following morning. Brian thought, correctly, that I'd learn far more doing something constructive rather than reading files, so he figured I should leave Manchester that afternoon, go to Reading the following morning and actually do some 'proper' work. I agreed and called Lin and said I'd be there tomorrow, Friday, not Monday as we had previously arranged.

Chapter Ten

READING

I was not used to the traffic in Reading during the weekday rush hour, but I got to the office before 9 a.m. and parked in one of the parking spaces outside. Lin had told me which one to use – we had been allocated just one space, which was fine as she lived within walking distance anyway.

On entering the office, which was open plan, I saw Lin and she came over, directed me to the claims area and I was introduced to my/our secretary, Sue. She was young, blonde, and married, but had no children. She seemed (and was) very nice and I said that next week we would all go for lunch to get to know each other a little better.

Lin directed me to my desk which was in the shadow of a large grey open-doored steel filing cabinet. On sitting down behind the large desk, I could see that there were files piled high everywhere. Every surface was covered with files of all hues. Our one windowsill had files stacked on it, even the roof of the filing cabinet had files on it, as well as stacks on my desk and the floor around my desk. There was a tray on my desk full of letters still to be attached to files. It was chaos. Lin explained that as I wasn't expected that day, neither she nor Sue had time to 'tidy up' before my arrival. This would take a lot longer than a day to tidy up I thought.

I had decided that before I could deal with any of the files, I needed to get them in some sort of order and guessed, correctly, that the files on my desk were the supposed urgent ones and those elsewhere, well, less urgent. Of course, to answer anything, I needed to read the files first, and some of them were 2-6" thick. There was a great deal of reading to do. I made a start and rather like AIU dictation was undertaken on a machine that had mini-cassettes. I asked Sue about her preferences for dictation. I wanted to make things easier for her. She explained how she liked me to say things and that was fine. I asked her about the letters and noticed that each typed letter had the author's initials – so MH for Mike – followed a /then her three initials and then another/ and then a claim number like 972-4-1055449. I said as she was the secretary for the claims team... and there were only the two of us, why bother with her initials? It would save her 4 keystrokes and Lin and I knew who typed the letter. I also noted that every file was numbered 972-4 something. What did the 972-4 mean? Apparently, 972 meant the UK and 4 meant the Reading office. (I had noted in Maidstone letters were numbered 972-1 and Manchester 972-2 but hadn't figured out why). I reasoned that the identifying factor in all filing was the claim number – but if in this office they all began 972-4, putting that onto the file and typing it added nothing, so why not just use the last seven numbers? I said that I was saving her about ten key-stokes with every letter and that would save her time and overall make her turnaround of files a bit quicker. Lin was reluctant to make any changes but I said I really could not see what the problem was and would mention it to Barry on Monday.

Gathering up the remaining files on my desk around 5 p.m. I said I would take them home and work on them over the weekend.

On Monday I formally met the branch manager, Russ and his team of underwriters. I spent some time with them to learn about office structure, the lines of business they wrote and which brokers were supportive and which were not.

Barry gave me the OK to do what I thought necessary in the office regarding the typing but suggested that I make any changes gradually. I also received calls from my fellow field colleagues, Graham in Birmingham, Colin in Bristol and Sam from Glasgow all wishing me well and saying that if I had any problems go to them first, before Barry. Politics I guessed?

After a week of reading files and trying to get on top of the huge backlog, I thought it was time to go out and investigate my first few claims.

The very first one was in Millbrook, Southampton. I knew where Southampton was, but Millbrook? All I had as an address was the company name on their headed paper and the name of a road in Millbrook. How hard could that be to find? On Monday morning bright and early I set off to Southampton via Basingstoke. Just outside Basingstoke on the A3 was a Little Chef café and I thought... 'breakfast'. So, I stopped for a fry-up and a mug of tea which seemed to take longer than I expected and when I got back on the road the traffic was building up. I was due at the insured's factory at 9.30 a.m. I got to the outskirts of Southampton a little after 9 a.m. But could I find any sign for 'Millbrook'? No, I could not. I stopped at a petrol station and they pointed me in the direction of Millbrook but hadn't a clue about the address I was seeking. I got to Millbrook and drove around aimlessly trying to find the road. I stopped to ask an elderly lady walking a dog for directions and she gave me what still ranks as the weirdest set of directions I have ever been given.

'Well dearie, you drive up here until you get to where there used to be a bus stop. The council just moved it, which was a shame (where there was a bus stop? Huh? How do I find something that isn't there??), turn there (left or right?) until you get to a row of shops, ignore them, turn again (left or right??) near a big tree and you'd best ask someone there, 'cos I'm not terribly sure where that road is'.

So that was 5 minutes of explanation to surely get me lost again.

Curiously, I have found that women always give directions via shops and bus stops, whereas men seem to give landmarks like pubs and petrol stations. I finally found the factory. I was an hour late. The person I was due to meet was not best pleased. I said that the traffic was dreadful and apologised for the delay. I have never been late for anything – I get 'delayed'. That sounds so much better than being late, doesn't it?

The claim I was investigating was a back injury for Bob a 55-year-old man who had slipped a spinal disc moving a drum of wet ceramic waste dust. The company made electrical insulation components out of ceramic. The process was a mixture of hot from the kilns where the wet moulded ceramic clay was fired and wet from the grinding of the finished articles to make them smooth and shiny, and that produced sticky wet dust. It was Bob's job to sweep and shovel up the waste and put it into a metal dustbin which he would then carry to an external skip into which he tipped the waste. It was lifting the dustbin over his shoulder that put Bob's back out. The manager thought the claim had no merit. They had done nothing wrong and wanted the claim defended. (Hmmm...If I had a pound for every time, I heard that over my career, I'd be a rich man!). I was told that Bob was a hard worker who had been doing this job for years. He began at age 18 and was still doing the same job. The manager said that Bob had not needed any training, he'd been doing the same job for decades and nothing had changed. 'Bob has,' I said. 'What do you mean?' the manager shot back. I replied, 'Well, when Bob was 18 years old doubtless he was fit and strong, but he's now 55 and he's still being asked to lift the same bins of waste. He has changed. He's got older and less fit and strong and you haven't thought about that. All Bob needed,' I continued, 'was probably a trolley on which to pull the bins about. Oh, and maybe give him smaller bins.' The manager still thought that the claim was a 'try-on' and wanted the matter defended.

The next claim was in Bracknell on the way back to Reading. This time I found the factory as the person I had called had given me directions – Old Bracknell Road, next to the fire station, you can't miss it. Luckily, I didn't.

The factory was involved in woodworking and a man had hurt his hands on a 'vertical spindle moulder' (whatever that is). The injured man, Terry, was training someone new to use the machine when the accident happened. I was shown the offending machine. A vertical spindle moulder is a machine into which you feed long lengths of wood and special cutting dies spin at high revolutions and grind patterns onto the wood to form picture rails, architraves, skirting boards and the like. The problem comes when having fed the length of wood into the machine the last 9-12 inches or so need to be pushed through. This is done with a piece of waste wood called a 'push stick'.

It was explained that Terry was the foreman. He was teaching a new trainee, Janice, how to use the machine and had demonstrated the use of the push stick, then turned to the trainee and said, 'Oh, and whatever you do, don't ever do this,' and proceeded to push the last 6 inches or so of wood into the spinning dies when all of a sudden Janice was splattered with bits of bone, skin and blood as Terry stood there, stunned, holding up his hands now missing the top joints of index and middle fingers on both hands. Janice screamed at the top of her voice and had a panic attack. Terry remained rooted to the spot, standing his mouth open but not a sound came out. A claim had been lodged alleging that Terry had not been properly trained and the machine was improperly guarded. 'Who trains the trainer?' I pondered.

I dictated my reports and put them into the internal mail for Graham in Birmingham to cast his eyes over. He called me and said, unluckily, that for my first two investigations, I could not have chosen two more difficult cases. However, he agreed with my conclusions.

Bob (the back injury) needed to settle on best terms. Fingerless Terry was a more difficult case. The spindle moulder I had seen was very old and more modern ones were able to actually clamp onto the strips of wood and feed them through without a push stick. I thought the claim was completely defendable, bearing in mind that Terry was not only the trainer, but he'd even said 'Don't do this'. But, because of Legal Aid, it may cost more to defend than pay 'something' to resolve it. So, I settled it on the basis that Terry was 75% responsible for his injury.

By now it was coming up to Christmas and the company had indeed changed its name. We were no longer INA, or indeed AFIA, but having merged with another company called Connecticut General and taken over yet another company called Crusader, the initials were mashed together and we were now CIGNA Insurance Company of Europe. The only thing that affected us was that new policies were issued on CIGNA headed paper, but we had a long run-off of INA matters and that meant it kept Sue on her toes making sure the letters went out in the right

159

name.

For reasons that were never made clear, the company Christmas Party was always held in February and in 1985 that was to be in Maidstone. One year Maidstone, the next London. Most of the office decided that the coach trip from Reading was too long. Instead, we had a little gathering in the office with a few nibbles, wine and beer.

In early Spring 1985, I had found a house in Arborfield, to the south of Reading. I had sold my flat in Selhurst and Lin was learning to drive so she offered to buy my Ford Escort. I remember driving it to her house and parking outside when a water hose went and emptied the contents of the radiator onto the tarmac. I reasonably knocked £25 off the asking price for a new set of hoses.

I'd only been in my house for a week or so and got a call that shook me to the core. Malcolm was in a hospital. He'd drunk a bottle of whisky and then tried to hang himself. He'd been rescued by his girlfriend and was now in hospital, alive and semi-conscious. I drove back to Croydon the next day and saw him sitting in a chair by the side of a bed in the trauma ward. The chair had a table on it that had been locked in place to prevent Malcolm 'escaping'. My friend of years looked at me but hadn't a clue who I was. When he was reminded, he said 'Oh yes, Trevor, we used to work together in Croydon' but that was only repeating the words he'd just heard. He was quite unable to recognise anyone, the lack of oxygen to the brain had been severe, and although he could walk and talk he never recovered mentally. He was later confined to a psychiatric institution. I only saw him once again.

It had taken me six months or so, but I was now happy with the state of the office. The files were all in order and up to date. I had closed off a lot of 'dead-wood' and had ensured all reserves we had on the files were accurate, or as accurate as they could be. I then got a very strange phone call from a broker in Kingston called Mark.

'Is that you, Trevor? It's Mark here from Wrightson's in Kingston. I've got this letter from you and I'm not happy'.

'Oh? What letter is that?' I said, rather worried.

'It's a bloody reminder letter from you! Look, we send reminders to you, you don't send them to us!' (He was laughing at the time).

'Sorry Mark, under new management here – unlike my predecessor I keep on top of my files and so you are bound to get more, so smarten up eh?' Mark and I have been friends ever since.

(Some years later I found an internal memo dated November 1985 from the Reading branch manager, Russ, to my manager in which Mark had called me 'a hard bastard' but they knew where they stood. Not sure I'd agree with 'hard'...)

CIGNA was an American company at heart with HQ in Philadelphia but one of the things I soon learned was that they were frightfully keen on in-house conferences, particularly in their European HQ in Brussels, Belgium.

The first conference I recall was to be on the subjects of product liability claims and personal injury and how each would be handled around the region (Europe and South Africa).

Our hotel was in central Brussels close to the office. It was good to meet up with people from other countries. We rarely spoke on the phone, relying on internal postal memos. I'd had an issue with a claim in South Africa, the detail of which escapes me, but I knew a representative from SA was attending and I hoped to talk to him about it.

On the agenda was a session on 'Compare and Contrast' the different laws and how personal injury assessment of damages differed from country to country. All that seemed to be achieved was to confirm that each country is different. It seemed pointless to me to know that in Italy you would get a higher level of damages than in, say, Sweden. The legal systems were quite different, indeed in Italy a simple claim may take 5 years or more to get to a trial.

During the 'Compare and Contrast' session, the SA rep, Owen, said that he was completely unable to assess the damages for any of the claims for injury as there was insufficient information about the injured parties. The course leader asked him to explain and he said that any calculation was pointless until he knew whether the claimant was black or white-skinned, as it made a huge difference! We were, of course, as Europeans stunned by that.

In a breakout session, I asked Owen about my problem file. He asked who I was writing to? I said Thabo. He said 'Oh, that explains it. Your claim is with Xerxes. Although they sit at adjacent desks they come from different tribes. Thabo is Zulu and Xerxes is Xhosa. They don't talk to each other because of tribal differences, so your memo probably went into the bin'. Unbelievable, but true.

Our evenings were spent, perhaps typically, checking out the beer cellars of Brussels. The beer was cheap, and some of our numbers were suffering from jet lag. Owen and colleagues from Ireland and Glasgow looked as if they were going to be drinking all night, and I think they did. I wisely thought that as a 'new boy' I should not make a fool of myself and left them to it.

As I was checking out, I saw one of the Maidstone contingents trying to buy a postage stamp from the hotel reception. 'Who are you writing to?' I inquired. 'My wife' came the answer. 'But why? You'll be home this evening and that letter won't arrive until the middle of next week'. 'Oh,' he replied, 'I always write to my wife to let her know I arrived safe, tell her I love her and whatnot, and as it costs to make an international call (on expenses though I interjected) I write a letter.' I shook my head in disbelief, but there again... he had someone to write home to, I didn't.

I had by now moved into my house and started the task of decorating. I'd decided to put in a new bathroom and kitchen as well as decorate every room. It was going to take me ages. Strangely, Jo didn't offer to help with anything and once I moved out of her place and into my own, she moved house and never told me where she'd moved to. Even I could read the writing on the wall. I never saw her again.

Work began to completely absorb me. Once I had to travel to Luton to deal with an accident at the Vauxhall Car plant. When I turned up at the gatehouse in my Ford Sierra, they took one look at the car marque and directed me to the furthest car park from the plant. It took ages to walk back.

Then in March, I got great news that all company cars of over 3 years and/or had more than 75,000 miles on the clock were to be replaced. My car ticked both boxes so I was soon to get my first brand new company car. I chose a red Vauxhall Cavalier which was their latest design. It was delivered to the office and my Sierra was put onto a low loader for resale. I can still recall the registration number C429NMO and I was so happy that I took it for an immediate drive out. New car smell and I thought very fast, great! All I had to do now was get in 18000 business miles on the clock in a year. This was important because if you did under 18000 miles the personal tax allowance on the car doubled, and I didn't want that to happen.

I had mentioned that loss adjusters charged on a 'scale'. On the larger claims you paid more in fees and conversely on the small claims the fees were low. The adjusters worked based on 'swings and roundabouts' and provided they got a balance of high and low-value claims the fees spent averaged out. At least that was the theory. In practice, we were not supposed to give claims to loss adjusters under £10,000 (as we handled those ourselves) and as I put it, we only ever played on the swings. This came to a head when an adjuster I used frequently changed firms and I insisted that he take the files with him. The adjuster's branch manager called me in and I made my case about the need for continuity. The manager picked up each file and more or less weighed it in his hands and then said £500 on this one, £1250 on that, and so on. This seemed to me to be a highly unprofessional way of doing business. I, therefore, suggested to Barry that Reading should experiment with asking the adjusters to charge hourly rates in the same manner as solicitors. He agreed, suggesting a year experiment and asked that I keep a log of the expenses: scale vs hourly rate. I approached the firms I dealt with and said that all files needed time sheets and hourly rates applied.

After six months I had demonstrated fee savings of £100,000. The experiment was clearly successful, so the company wasted no time and adopted hourly rates for all loss adjusters. Over all offices, during the following year we made savings of well over £1m. Although some of the loss adjusters complained, I pointed out that if they chose the hourly rate, they could never lose. And did Trevor get a bonus or any thanks at all? Of course not.

It was my habit though of occasionally phoning an insured and asking about the service they got from the loss adjusters we appointed and that enabled me to cross-check the fees/hours we had been charged. One adjuster had charged me 2 hours to undertake a relatively routine claim. The person I spoke to at the insured was happy with the outcome, but I said that two hours to discuss it with you must have taken a chunk out of your day? The insured was surprised and said that the adjuster was there for 10, maybe 15 minutes at most. I returned the fee note for amendment and later fired the firm.

Sue, my secretary, had become concerned about my lack of female companionship. I had explained that I never went anywhere where I could meet women and had no time anyway. I was working all hours to get on top of the work and deal with all the new claims that came in not only from our local brokers but also from other field offices to investigate. Sue said if I didn't do something about it... she would. Eh?

I still rather missed the AIU annual December pub crawl and decided to do my own. I would however make a few changes. Firstly, there would be no 'crawl' around ten pubs. Instead, I found a nearby pub that served ten different real ales. Secondly, I would not restrict the guest list to just loss adjusters. I included my solicitors, accountants, my private investigator and, crucially, brokers. The first was a success and it duly became an annual event until I moved to London some years later.

Lin and I were sharing the business use of the car, so I was probably in the office just two or three days a week and spent most of that time dictating reports and getting on top of the postbag. The organisation was keen on writing insurance programs for big multinational companies. They are always very demanding as customers. Our files were to be audited annually so they needed to be in good order and we had to deal with all claims and claimants with care, compassion and politeness...even the 'nutters'. Oh yes, we had 'nutters'.

A customer had returned a jar of honey to a manufacturer because on opening it he saw 'to his horror and disbelief' a wasp (dead) in the top of the honey. He said he was so traumatised that he didn't think he could ever eat honey again and demanded compensation. He'd not eaten any honey. He'd not been poisoned by the honey; he'd not been stung by the wasp – no he'd just seen a dead wasp. His letters were long and rambling written on both sides of a spiral note pad and his handwriting was awful. I wrote as diplomatically as I could that he had no claim (apart from a replacement jar or cheque for the value of the honey – which he had already been sent by the manufacturer) as just seeing a wasp did not entitle him to compensation. That provoked another 12-page letter from him. I replied that my decision was final and that if he felt he'd been wronged then see a solicitor. I heard no more.

Lin had decided that she wanted to move on to do underwriting and it was becoming plain that she did not like my management style. One of the big global accounts we had written was for a Cola Company and we covered not only their EL/PL and product liability but their motor as well. Lin knew a motor claims handler at Royal

Insurance who she thought was good – Denise. I gave her a call and invited her for an interview.

A Cola driver had rear-ended another car that was being driven by an 18-year-old male who had a 17-year-old female passenger. The cars had dented bumpers and repair costs were nominal. Incredibly, the female passenger complained of whiplash. Now whiplash claims are difficult to disprove but they are not usually long lasting or expensive as the claimant usually recovers fully within a matter of weeks. This one didn't recover though. Over the next three years, she convinced herself that her left arm did not work and she had to move it with her right hand to, for example, hold down a loaf of bread as she cut it with her right hand. Her job was a typist and a one-handed typist was not much use, so she lost her job.

Doctors could not find any medical reason why she could not use the arm – it had full nerve function. But those years of not using her arm had caused her arm to wither until it was just skin and bone with no musculature at all. [At the time this was known as Sudeck's Atrophy. Today it is called 'Chronic Regional Pain Syndrome' or CPRS and results in very high awards]. I had the claimant seen by a top psychiatrist and neurologist. His recommendation to her was amputation as a prosthetic arm would probably have more function. This may have been the slap in the face that she needed... but it was two years too late.

Although she tried physiotherapy to regain muscle loss it was almost certainly too late. At the tender age of 21, she had ruined her life. The matter was in litigation and I had a meeting with her solicitors to try and seek a settlement. As liability for the minor accident was admitted, all we were arguing was that her injury was contrived. Maybe in her mind what probably started as a quick way of getting a small amount of compensation, had got out of hand and mind as she had mentally convinced herself that her arm didn't work. And now after three or so years, it truly didn't. We maintained that all we were liable for was minor whiplash. After much negotiation, we settled the matter for £50,000. This was low, even at the time, for what was effectively the loss of an arm.

I used to visit the Coca bottling plant in Sunbury-on-Thames probably every other month as their Insurance manager liked to have regular updates on all his claims. His name was Andreas and he always wanted to meet with both Lin and me. He was quite generous too, in many ways. On arrival at the depot, he would ask me to open the boot of the car and he'd put in it a case of 2-litre bottles of Cola, all with wonky labels that could not be sold. They would have been trashed so in reality he was giving nothing away. I got bottles of Cherry Cola before it was officially on the market.

I was interested to learn that those large 2 and 3-litre plastic bottles do not arrive at the factory that size. They arrive in hermetically sealed crates and are about the size of a test tube, or maybe about the size of an adult's middle finger. The plastic tubes are heated in a mould and are inflated with hot air to the mould size. This results in a huge transport cost saving. Only the caps are normal size.

Now Andreas was of Greek origin and wanted to take us to lunch on every visit. This became something that Lin dreaded and I have to say that this was something I was never keen on either, as Andreas had a habit of talking with his mouth full. He also seemed to have a permanent dew drop on the end of his extremely large nose and would sniff every few moments. We would just be enjoying a plate of food or having a drink and Andreas would begin an anecdote with a mouth full of Dover sole or salmon (he always ate fish, bones and all) which would be liberally sprayed over the table. Lin had taken to putting a beer mat over her drink 'to keep the flies out Andreas' she lied. Andreas would sometimes insist on coming to our offices as well for no other reason than to get up his business miles. Lin would always try to be out that day. But Andreas had absolutely no sense of direction. He refused to ask anyone either and would find a call box, call me and I had to drive out to find him and then he would follow me back to the office.

Lin had moved on to train as an Accident & Health underwriter. Sadly, she was all too soon off sick and later succumbed to breast cancer. It was a very moving funeral attended by the whole office, brokers and solicitors she had dealt with over the years.

Denise was a perfect fit for our small team as she had oodles of motor experience and I had very little. We had two large motor accounts to deal with and I was getting swamped. I offered her the job and she accepted.

A claim came in for a well-known manufacturer of disposable razors. The exchange went broadly as follows:

'My client used your razor product and he got a cut on the chin and we demand compensation.'

'Dear Sirs, razors are meant to be sharp. There is no defect in the product. Liability is denied.'

'But my client cut himself, compensation is appropriate in this case.'

'We believe that we have mentioned that razors are designed to be sharp. Are you suggesting that the manufacturer should advertise and market blunt razors? If so, we will pass that suggestion on, but we fear sales might plummet. Liability remains firmly denied.'

Sue was on my case again about a girlfriend. Denise was naturally backing her up. Computers were in their infancy at this time but the underground system in London was adorned with adverts for a computer dating site called Dateline. Sue had got the forms and began to fill them in for me. Seeing what she was doing, I grabbed them and filled them in myself. A week or so later a list arrived with 12 potentials or 'matches' in the Reading area – but just names, no other details. However, to get the full list a fee was needed and the completion of a much larger form. I paid up and filled in the form. Another week passed and a comprehensive list arrived. I noted that not one of the names was the same as the initial list. My second list was more successful as I met Karon in January 1986. We are still together 35+ years later.

Karon joined me at the next Christmas dinner, in February 1986. The event was in London but all I can remember about the evening was drunkenly berating Barry about my pay review, a paltry 7.5%. (Ah, those were the days).

A very peculiar property claim arrived, potentially a very big loss, exactly £5 million. We insured a firm of solicitors, let's call them Harrison Smith. It was common practice back in the 1980s for solicitors still to request payment for property transactions using a banker's draft. This is a check drawn on the bank itself and is essentially like a banknote, in this case, a £5 million banknote.

According to what I was told a bankers draft had been sent by courier to the offices of Harrison Smith and was in favour of Harrison Smith. The solicitor was waiting for the post room to deliver it, but it did not turn up. He waited for the afternoon post but again there was no delivery for him. He called the post room and they said that no envelope had been received and he'd best call the senders, just to make sure that they had sent it. He called the senders who indeed said that they hand-delivered the envelope to a young man in the Harrison Smith post room. Now panicking he again called the post room, but there was no answer as it had gone past 5.30 pm, the men there had gone home. The following morning the solicitor, now in a panic, went to the post room at 8 am. A member of post room staff was there, usually there would be two, but despite a thorough search the missing bank draft and the accompanying letter could not be found. In asking about his co-worker in the post room the man said that the lad

172

(called Jim) had come in yesterday, but complained of a migraine and had gone off sick about 9.15 am.

A call was made to the personnel dept and the solicitor managed to get Jim's phone number. No answer when he called. He got a taxi to where Jim lived and a flatmate answered the door. Of Jim, there was no sign and the flatmate said he saw Jim leave the property about 11 a.m. but had not seen him since.

Later enquiries revealed that Jim had bought a one-way ticket to Australia and had departed Heathrow on the first available flight.

It was at this point that a claim was made under a 'money' policy. I reported the matter to my management team and was surprised to get a call from Tony who was the chief exec. He was spitting tacks about the size of the claim and I did my best to calm him down. I pointed out that until Jim cashed the bank draft the only thing that was 'lost' was a bit of paper. The bank had not lost anything as no funds had left them either – they had just lost a bit of paper and, moreover, they had replaced it with another draft. Secondly, although there was an international 'watch' in the banking fraternity for the draft, it might be soon forgotten so it could, in theory, still be cashed. I went on to explain that strictly speaking the draft never would be out of date, but what could Jim do with it? He was apparently in Australia with a £5m bankers draft in the name of Harrison Smith. Is it likely that a young man would then go into a bank and try to open a new account in the name of Harrison Smith, without any proof of who he was, and his first deposit would be a £5m

173

banker's draft? I thought that might look a tad suspicious to any bank teller. Then for each passing day/week/month or year, any bank would have greater suspicions as to why it had taken so long to cash a £5m draft as the interest lost would be huge.

I suggested he forget the matter – I did not think anything would come of it. By now, Tony had calmed down somewhat but made me promise that if the draft was cashed, I was to call him immediately. I never needed to make the call.

A strange claim in Portsmouth at a swimming pool complex where a chap had nicked the skin on his ankle when sliding down a flume. The injury was tiny, but he was a deep-sea diver and apparently due to the pressure changes in diving any fresh cuts on the skin meant that he was unable to dive. This in turn resulted in him losing a three-month diving contract which he was due to begin two days after the accident. The injury was worth £500/750 but the wage loss was £12,000 after tax.

The flume was new and installed by a specialist firm. Our insured were the 'occupiers' and therefore first in line for a claim. I had asked how the flume was to be inspected as I could see that there were joints in the twisting, snake-like, flume. According to the manager one of the lifeguards 'walks' down the flume each morning before the water pump is switched on and feels each joint for any sharp edges. If they find none then the flume pump is turned on and the flume is considered safe for the public to use. The lifeguard then checks to see if the first few users of the flume do not emerge as if they have been sliding down a cheese grater. This all seemed a bit unscientific to me.

As the flume was only about four feet in diameter, I could not see how anyone could 'walk' down it and was told that the shortest lifeguard, a slim young lady, goes backwards down the flume on her knees, feeling the sides on the way, before dropping off the end into the pool for a dip. Although that seems reasonable, I pointed out that the flume was fibreglass and would naturally have a little 'flex' in it. Surely a heavier person would be more likely to make the flume joints flex than a waif-like young lady? Even though it was true, I was informed that a male lifeguard had attempted to perform the inspection. However, despite being dry, the flume still had smooth and slippery sides, and was steep. The lifeguard kept sliding down when they lost their footing, but this was the only way the inspection could be carried out.

I decided to draw in the manufacturers. The inspection method was daft and the flume was brand new. It shouldn't be a cheese grater. I wrote to their head office and got a reply, and I kid you not, from a chap called Dick Kiss. I mean if your first name was Richard and surname Kiss, you'd surely not abbreviate it, would you? I suppose it is unforgettable though. I've remembered it after 30-odd years after all. Anyway, their insurers were a firm that was to become notorious, Independent Insurance and they were represented by a firm called Davies-Lavery. I offered to split the claim with them 75/25, with them taking the larger share. They declined and suggested 50/50. The claimant had issued proceedings and my solicitors thought that my offer was reasonable, we had an impasse, and amazingly it went to trial. Damages had been pre-agreed; this was just a case between the parties on liability.

The judge listened to the evidence and apportioned the claim 50/50. This meant we were liable for a chunk of the co-defendant's costs. Now Dav-Lav (as they were known) were also used extensively by CIGNA in Maidstone. Their senior partner was having a beer with one of my colleagues in Maidstone and boasting how he had beaten me on the case. My colleague replied that his win of 25% had probably cost them a great deal more in any future instructions as I was highly unlikely to instruct them on anything, ever. For some years that was true. I came around eventually though. I only bear grudges for maybe five or ten years or so, I'm not obsessive.

We had written a new risk for a chain of DIY stores. At the time they operated out of converted cinemas and other old large stores. When they grew in size, they expanded into the 'tin sheds' in out-of-town retail parks that are so common now. However, back then the stores were generally shabby and customers were forever snagging their ankles on shelving or tripping over loose flooring. We received probably six claims a week. Few were serious, but I will come on to those.

Insurance companies make it a policy condition that all claim correspondence is sent to us 'unanswered' and no admission of liability can be made as this may prejudice our position. Whilst fine on paper, in practice it caused huge difficulties. The injured person would usually write to the store where they had their accident. The store would send that to the Head Office, who would send it to the brokers, who would send the claim to me. Weeks passed and by the time I wrote to the claimant about her stubbed toe, cut ankle or whatever, they were angry and had probably gone to see a solicitor. Not that having legal representation made the process any quicker, it doesn't, but it does make it more expensive for everyone, if not in money but in time. There had to be a better method.

I went to see the DIY insurance manager and I said that in reality all the injured person wanted was a prompt response, an apology and 'something'. What we agreed was that if a person had an accident at the store and reported it at the time the manager should say 'sorry' and give them a £10 pot-plant if the claimant was a woman or a £10 gift card if the claimant was a man. The reasoning behind this was, according to me, that the injured person was being treated as a human being, not a claimant. The £10 pot plant only cost the company £3, so they were giving nothing away really. The company worked on a 30% average mark-up on all goods and the average spend by a customer was around £30.

Consequently, the £10 gift card meant that if the person spent £30 the firm made no profit, but no real loss either. I said that this may not always work, particularly if the injury was serious, but if it reduced the number of claims it would mean less work for all of us and when it came to renewal, lower claims meant possibly lower premiums.

The 'pot-plant' scheme as it became known was introduced and the number of claims reported dropped dramatically.

I was also instrumental in another aspect of risk control for the DIY company. Not strictly my role, but this one seemed sensible, and it involved kitchen work-tops.

It seems to be human nature that when faced with a row of identical goods on shelves, a lot of people never take the one at the front, but always reach for one behind as if, somehow, that one will be superior. The same is true of packaging. Even though the contents may be undamaged, if the packaging is, the item is ignored in favour of undamaged packaging, which is thrown away anyway.

At the DIY stores kitchen counters were stacked (face-on) with the worktop facing the front, but leaning slightly backwards to a wall. However, the worktops were typically three or four metres long and being made of dense chipboard, were immensely heavy. Being stacked in the way they were, should have meant that the worktop facing the customer would have been the one they chose. But no, the customers tended to try and pick one further back in the stack and would move the stack to a vertical position to try and wriggle out another (probably identical) worktop. But manoeuvring the worktops meant that any change in equilibrium could result in the heavy worktops being held upright by the customer suddenly topping forwards onto the customer, or someone else passing by. It happened with grim regularity.

Following one nasty accident when a worktop being moved by a dad fell onto his 4-year-old daughter resulting in a brain injury, I questioned, with the number of accidents we have seen, why wasn't the stacking method changed? How, they asked? For one thing, I suggested, they could be stacked flat on the ground in the aisles. If there was insufficient room for that, then stack them 'edge-on', that is vertically, but only the edge showing. Given the number that gets damaged, I said that all it needed was a sample to be cut – maybe a foot or so – to allow the customer to see the surface design of the worktop. There was still the problem of customers pulling a four-metre worktop out of a stack, so chain them up and put up a sign asking the customer to get help. And that is what they did.

The DIY store was opening a new branch and had organised a grand opening that involved an advertising 'blimp' launched over the store, but tethered to the ground. On the day the blimp arrived the manager and staff set about inflating it with a large bottle of helium. The blimp began to inflate and slowly rise, but no one had remembered to fix the guy line to the special peg that had been driven into the ground. It was a windy day and as the blimp rose higher and higher the manager held onto the guy rope for all he was worth as he yelled at his colleague to get the other end of the rope tied to the peg. The blimp was now thirty or forty feet in the air and with the manager now dangling underneath about ten feet off the ground, he could grip no longer and let go. Luckily by now, his crew had secured the blimp to the peg. Unluckily, the manager broke his ankle.

Although a claim was not made (it was thought that the manager was too embarrassed to bring one) I did receive a report of the accident. I sent it back to the brokers as the injured party, although an employee, was, at the time of the accident, a pilot... and we did not cover aviation risks! The brokers and insured were initially incredulous, but I was right. Blimps are covered by aviation insurance, in the same way are hovercraft.

It was alleged that a contractor laying cables in a road using saws to cut through the tarmac had created sufficient airborne dust to cause fish to die in an ornamental pond. I thought this was ludicrous and went to see the claimant and take a look at the pond. The pond was massive and partially drained to allow me to see the 'damage' caused by the dust. I could not see anything at all and the claimant said that his koi carp had all died after being poisoned by the dust. I said that to get to the pond the dust would have to come from about 20ft away and then over a 6ft fence. I thought it was impossible and he had no evidence of any fish dying, photos or anything. I suggested he prove his case.

Two days later the office was evacuated due to the pervading smell of rotting fish. The idiot had sent us dead fish in paper envelopes through the post... and the Post Office had delivered the stinking mess. There is nowt so queer as folk, eh? I sent him £100 and told him that if that was not accepted, we would counterclaim for fumigating the office.

Talking of dust. I became suspicious of a series of aggressive letters from a small firm of solicitors in Slough. It was alleged that the claimant had suffered repeated asthma attacks from the dust generated from our insured's building site during demolition works. The claim included a month's loss of wages, general damages and the cost of air travel for a month's holiday to allow the claimant and her whole family to escape the dust to get cleaner air. The claim was quite sizable.

The odd thing was that they had travelled from Slough to Delhi for 'fresh air' and coincidentally the claimant just happened to work for the same firm of solicitors who authored the letter of claim. My road map of Slough demonstrated that the route to the solicitor's office from the claimant's home did not pass the building site and she did not even live close to the dusty site either. Furthermore, in declining the claim I pointed out that Delhi has worse air pollution than anywhere else in the world. If you want clean air you go to Canada, not India.

I then received a strange call from the solicitor's office. The person I spoke to said they did not know the claim I referring to! After discussion, it seemed that the claimant was actually a secretary/typist at the firm and she was obviously sending out the letters on the firm's headed paper and as she opened the post in the mornings, she was able to intercept my responses without anyone knowing. However, she was off ill today and my letter of denial had been passed to a partner, who did not recognise the case; hence the call. The solicitor said that his firm was not representing the typist, who was shortly to become an ex-typist...

The latest in vogue claim was RSI or Repetitive Strain Injury, a fancy name for something that had been around for years, such as 'housemaid's knee', golfer's or tennis elbow, writer's cramp and nowadays I suppose, PlayStation thumb. A lot of manual work involves manual dexterity of a repetitive nature and wrist and hand injury can result. The constant use of vibrating tools can result in nerve damage causing the fingers to turn white and a loss of sensation. Years later I even suffered a RSI of my own due to the constant movement of a computer mouse, though my bad posture was also a cause. Preventing such a problem means rotating tasks, and taking regular breaks is recommended.

One of the first RSI claims I was sent involved a company that had a lot of machinery and the claimant was an engineer who was tasked with repairing delicate machines that had a large number of screws and small nuts to manipulate. It was said in the letter of claim that the non-rotation of tasks and the constant twisting and turning of his wrist had caused tenosynovitis and that he may need surgery to relieve the tendon sheaths and may never return to his previous work. It looked like a very expensive claim.

I travelled down to the insured who were near Portsmouth and there met a very gruff and irritated managing director. I had gone through the claimant's work history and noted all the tasks the claimant had to do and said casually that RSI claims were very difficult to defend as the courts always seemed to side with the claimant and that the employers needed to do more to prevent injury, such as job rotation etcetera.

'RSI?' he said, 'what's that then?'

'Er, repetitive strain injuries, like writer's cramp or tennis elbow. It's frightfully popular at the moment as a claim and difficult to defend, unfortunately.'

The MD harrumphed in response and added 'The only bloody thing he (the claimant) did repetitively was to fail to turn up for work! He was off sick for weeks at a time and these doctors' notes just say "wrist inflammation".'

'Well, there you are then. That's what I was saying. He has a wrist problem, and comes back to work and that inflames the problem. It's a really difficult cycle to break I'm afraid.'

The MD then dropped a bombshell.

'You do know he's a championship darts player, don't you? He's in the local paper having won a competition only last week, when he was off bloody sick with his alleged wrist injury. Look, here's the photo!" and with that he handed over the local rag.

'I don't believe it!' I exclaimed and took a photocopy of the article. I thanked the MD for his time and duly sent the photocopy of the newspaper article to the claimant's solicitor hinting that the claim was probably fraudulent.

I later heard that the claim was withdrawn and the engineer had resigned his position.

The company had taken over another insurer and their book of business was being placed in run-off. The outstanding claims were distributed to us and we were instructed to settle them as rapidly as possible to get the claims off the books. I had to travel to Weymouth to see a claimant solicitor who had brought a claim for a 12-year-old child who had been knocked over by one of our policyholders, a member of the Swanage and District Vintage Motor Cycle Club. From the papers there was a dispute on liability, the child had gone backward and forwards when crossing the road. In discussion, the solicitor asked if this club was a normal policyholder for us? I demurred and said that the book was in run-off and the policy would not be renewed. 'You do know', he added, 'that the Swanage & District Vintage Motor Cycle Club is the local chapter of the Hells Angels and your man was doing wheelies up and down the high street on a very powerful motorcycle, just as my client was trying to cross the road. She didn't know which way to go!'

The 'Hells Angels'!! I had a feeling that this was not a case to take to trial. We settled amicably.

Chapter Eleven

ARSON AND SO FORTH

A new piece of technology had arrived at our offices. A telex machine! Telex was the typed version of what we now call texting. Similar to text a telex machine uses a telephone line. An operator sits in front of a small screen and types the message. The message is then 'printed' as a string of holes on a ribbon of paper that could be, depending on the length of the message, three or four feet long. The operator then dials the number of the recipient and on receiving an electronic beep that confirms a connection, feeds in the ribbon of paper and that sends the message as code to the receiver. At the receiver's end, the message gets printed out on a roll of paper for someone to actually read.

It was our practice that any large claim over a certain value had to be reported to Maidstone, Brussels and Philadelphia using a form called a Large Claim Summary, or LCS as we called it. Before telex, the LCS needed to be typed on a manual typewriter, photocopied and sent in the mail to the offices. Now with telex the LCS narrative could be sent to the offices in a matter of moments and similarly, we could get replies or queries in return just as rapidly. However, it was necessary to keep the message as brief as possible because making an error in the message meant retyping the message with a new paper ribbon.

Not all claims involved blood and gore. Sometimes we received plain property losses – such as thefts and fires.

I reported a new claim. A pub we insured in Dorset, said to be the oldest pub in England (there must be a dozen or more with that boast!) and seemingly built using timber washed up on the beaches from wrecked ships from the Spanish Armada, had burned down. Nothing was left and the claim was thought to be more than £1m for property damage and business profit loss (called business interruption). I dutifully sent the telex message: "New Loss Advice. Property loss: 'World's End' public house. Sparks from chimney ignited thatch resulting in total loss by fire. Estimate £1m for PD/BI. More details to follow. Cottington, Reading office, UK."

Within an hour of sending the message, I got a phone call from a manager in Philadelphia.

'Got your telex. You say 'Sparks from chimney ignited thatch'. What the hell is 'thatch'?'

I explained that thatch was an old-fashioned roofing material made of reeds and it looked sort of like straw.

'Jesus Christ!' he exclaimed, 'You Brits build houses out of fucking straw?! Who lived there? The Three Little Pigs?' and with that, he hung up. I hadn't the heart to tell him that the walls of the pub were made of 'wattle and daub' – clay/mud and animal dung mixed and spread on supporting interwoven sticks, as he would have thought we were truly primitive!

The property team had written a risk that on the face of it looked new and innovative. A company had been set up to open small boutique shops at maternity wards in hospitals where visitors could buy cards, clothing and teddy bears to give to the new mums and the babies. It was called New Arrivals. We were insuring the stock at the shops and the warehouse.

I got a call from the brokers to say that the New Arrivals warehouse was on fire and it looked as if there was going to be a huge stock loss. We were not covering the building but from the outset, it looked like we needed a loss adjuster and possibly a forensic accountant to deal with any claim for loss of profits.

The adjuster gave me a call and said that the fire had started in the warehouse where an old packaging machine was supposed to have ignited and the stock of 100,000 videocassette boxes and some teddy bears were totally lost. The machine was burned so badly that the cause was not known. Maybe electrical in origin? The machine was used for putting plastic film on the outside of the video cassette boxes. Huh? I naturally queried the VC boxes as I could not understand what that had to do with items to be sold at shops intended for babies and new mums. The broker explained that the New Arrivals business was not taking off as the owner had hoped and to keep the staff employed, he was temporarily branching out into making VC boxes for a business friend.

As far as I could tell the change in risk was, as we call it, 'a material fact' and should have been declared. The packaging/shrink wrap machine had been declared, but underwriters had taken the description to be for packaging

187

teddy bears and clothing in plastic bags, not for VC boxes. The claim, advanced by a firm of Loss Assessors, was for over £500,000. (Loss adjusters work for insurance companies. Loss Assessors on the other hand work for policyholders and take a hefty percentage of the insurance pay-out as their fee. It was therefore in their interests to make the claim as large as possible. Assessors were (and still are) generally regarded by insurance claims handlers as unprofessional, bottom-feeding, scum-sucking bastards...at least when being polite.)

There was external CCTV footage of the warehouse that showed the New Arrivals director, Vick, running out of a fire exit door with his staff and later haranguing the fire brigade to put the fire out quickly. It looked very plausible.

Whilst the debate over coverage went on, we were being threatened by the assessors with legal proceedings and were on the brink of paying, when we received an anonymous phone call. The caller had asked why were we possibly paying the claim when the cause was arson? We asked for a private meeting with the caller which I attended at a rather seedy looking pub in North London with the adjuster.

The caller was Tony, who said he was the bookkeeper of New Arrivals. He explained to us that if we paid the claim, he'd still be in a job, but if we declined, he'd be unemployed probably for a year, and therefore if he was going to give us evidence to deny the claim, he'd need paying. This was irregular but not unheard of. We said that if we were to consider his request, we'd need to know that he would be prepared to give evidence in court, stick to his story and that his 'fee' would be no more than one year's salary, about £20,000 at that time, but paid in two tranches. The first of £5,000 when he signed a sworn statement and the second of £15,000 if the claim was withdrawn or the case went to trial. He accepted our offer.

I stated that our forensic team had inspected the warehouse, but did not find any incendiary devices. They determined that the wrapping machine was likely the origin of the fire, but its damage was so severe that they couldn't be certain. If the cause was electrical then we probably had to pay. Tony asked what an 'incendiary device' was? I said typically a device used to start a fire by delay – like a filling can of petrol that had matches stuffed in the neck with a taper sticking out. A candle is lit underneath the taper, and it burns down gradually, allowing time for the arsonist to get out of the building... but then the taper ignites the matches and 'whoosh' major fire. Tony nodded and said that there was nothing like that here. He said that Vick had 'rolled up a newspaper and stuffed it under the corner of a pallet of video cassette boxes, got out his cigarette lighter and ignited the paper. Then once the fire took hold, he pressed the fire alarm button and we all got out'. I asked, 'How do you know this?' Tony said, 'Because I watched him do it! I was standing close by. Vick didn't see me until he had lit the newspaper, then he saw me, put his finger to his lips as if to say nothing...then he pressed the fire alarm.'

It seemed good evidence to me and we got solicitors to draw up an agreement with Tony. He signed it and I sent him £5,000. We then declined the claim. The assessors threatened all manner of dire retribution, but we heard nothing. New Arrivals went into Liquidation and their Liquidators did not press the matter any further. Six months later I sent Tony his £15,000 with our thanks.

We insured a lot of hotels and they were always suffering from loss of guests' luggage, particularly tourists. A would-be thief would notice a coach outside a hotel and see that luggage was being loaded. By pretending to be with the coach or a member of hotel staff, he would assist in the loading of the hold and then saying there was not enough room on this side of the coach, would take a couple of suitcases round to the far side of the coach... and be away on his toes.

I was investigating one such theft, this time of golf clubs, and the manager of the hotel was surprised that the thief only took this particular set of clubs when there were others around the lobby, all of higher value. I asked what was unusual about the lost clubs and was told that they were really small clubs as the owner was a dwarf! The clubs had to be specifically made for the owner, doubling the price of a normal set of clubs.

I was dealing with a tricky claim for a contractor who had flooded an optician's shop and the matter was in litigation. A settlement meeting was arranged and I attended with the broker (Ann), the insured (Dennis), the loss adjusters and the solicitor. I'd known Ann for a while and she was a very prim and proper lady, but unlike most brokers, she knew each file and contract in detail. Her knowledge was encyclopaedic. She travelled to work on the same train every day, sitting in the same seat, for forty years and had never taken more than a week as a holiday as, in her words, 'she didn't like things to back up'. Ann introduced me to the insured's insurance manager, Dennis, with the comment:

'Dennis, this is Trevor. You'll get on with him as he is a 'contractors' man' – a plain speaker, he calls a spade a shovel if you know what I mean.' To which Dennis replied:

'If he doesn't know the bloody difference between a spade and a shovel, he doesn't know a bloody thing about construction!'

Protesting my encyclopaedic knowledge of spades and shovels, the meeting progressed. Liability was not an issue, but quantum was. The parties argued back and forwards with only the claimant and myself being silent. The discussion was tedious and got nowhere. I saw the claimant whisper something to his solicitor and stand, presumably to get a breath of air. I followed and went to the toilets and standing at the next urinal was the claimant. I said to him:

'This meeting is getting tedious. It doesn't have to be like this you know.'

'What do you mean?' he answered, clearly intrigued.

'Well, this is all about money, isn't it? I'm standing here, metaphorically, with a cheque book but I can't write a cheque out until we get a sensible number from you. You know that parts of your claim are heavily inflated. Come on, what's your absolute bottom line?'

'£70,000.'

'OK, done.'

We cheerily washed our hands and went back into the meeting where the solicitors were still arguing. I called the meeting to a halt and said that we had agreed on a figure and all that remained was for the solicitors to draft a settlement release, known as a Tomlin Order. There were several legal jaws on the table, but the matter was settled. I'd not wanted to go much over £60,000, but there was a real risk of going down at trial for £80,000 or even £90,000, plus all of the legal and counsel fees.

Maybe I'd paid too much, maybe he'd accepted too little, but those are the ingredients of a fair settlement. Dennis was happy too as he did not want his people tied up for days at trial.

Based on this success, Ann had requested that I take over the handling of all the claims for Dennis.

The policy had many coinsurers, but due to a couple pulling out of the market the schedule changed year after year and it seemed that the Maidstone team kept getting the maths incorrect. Ann had requested that just one person handle the claims and that I review all the outstanding past years' claims to ensure all were correct. Few were as I later found out. It was quite a task and it took me months to gather the files as some were at field offices in Bristol and Birmingham. All had been processed incorrectly with the coinsurers, although the settlements were correct.

The trouble with the arrangement I had with Ann was that I now had to undertake investigations slightly out of my patch. One such claim was for a child accident in Coventry. Child accidents are always tricky. Building sites act as an 'allurement' in law and children trespassing can still result in a claim and in the worst cases, a fine from the authorities.

The contractors were undertaking the refurbishment of a school. A child, presumably intent on vandalism, had climbed onto a roof and had fallen through a skylight and landed face down, fracturing her jaw. When I arrived on site there was also a man from the HSE (Heath and Safety Executive – the UK safety inspectorate) investigating the same accident. We gathered all the facts at a joint interview with the site agent, but the HSE chap said that he wasn't taking the matter any further even though there was a potential breach of regulations as a fence and scaffold had not been 'secured' and could, and was, accessible by miscreants.

'Why's that?' I cautiously asked.

'Oh, before I came here,' he said, 'I went to see the family. The mother answered the door and when I explained who I was and that I needed to hear from the child what had happened, the mother told me to 'fuck off my doorstep – my daughter has suffered enough' and with that slammed the door in my face. So, without the child's testimony we can't get a case together, so just secure your fence and scaffolding in future, OK?'

We had a new field manager. Barry's job had been split and he was now in charge of just Maidstone and a new man, Kerin (an American) was moved from the USA to the UK to take charge of field operations. I cannot say I got on with him, he never understood our geography, practice and procedure. Whenever he heard about a serious injury claim his first question was always 'How much are the medical costs' and we had to keep pointing out the NHS was free. I don't think he ever learned.

October 1987 was memorable due to the 'hurricane' (actually a storm with gale-force winds) that ripped through Southern England. Every loss adjuster was overloaded with work and that included me. We had so many claims submitted that we ran out of red file jackets to put them in. I sent Sue to Rymans to buy some more and got berated by 'facilities management' for not going through the proper procurement process!

Sue soon left us to become a mum and was replaced by Tracey. If I recall correctly, she was straight from secretarial college, or maybe even school, as she was very young, but settled in well with the team.

Sometimes it pays to keep your mouth shut. I was never paid enough to do that though.

We had a field meeting as the company had written a new global account of many diverse manufacturers from jet engines and helicopters to passenger lifts. Somebody quipped that 'doubtless we would now be looking at claims for people plummeting to their doom in lift accidents?' 'Actually,' I said, 'I think that when a lift car fails you are more likely to up than down. If all lift cables failed then you'd probably just stay where you were as one of the cables holds back bolts that shoot out to the side of the lift shaft and into a ratchet, stopping the lift car from moving. So you could be winched up manually to the next floor, but not down.' There was a moment of silence, then 'Oh, so you know about lifts? – you can handle all the lift claims then!' And that is how I came to deal with numerous lift accidents. A little knowledge is a dangerous thing. I should have kept my mouth shut!

A few of the lift accidents I dealt with were funny, indeed one was tragic, but all were caused by the stupidity of people and none were actually the fault of the lift.

Six or eight drunken students at a major university were in the new passenger lift in the student block. They thought it would be fun to start jumping up and down as the lift was ascending. The lift was not designed for such abuse and so it stopped. Someone pressed the emergency button and they were told via the intercom that the Fire Brigade had been summoned and they would be there shortly to rescue them. However, maybe it was due to impatience, a weak or full bladder, but one student decided to open the lift doors and seeing that he was about five feet above the floor below decided to jump down. The only way the doors can be opened from the inside of the lift car is to use a special key. The key here was triangular-shaped and was not the sort of key anyone would ever have. But opening the car door in this way also opened the doors on the floor below. The student jumped out of the car, landed on the floor below, lost his balance and fell backward down the lift shaft to his death.

The matter proceeded to a Coroner's Inquest and the deceased was found to have the special key still in his pocket, although how he had come about it no one knew, and so it was concluded that there was nothing wrong with the lift itself, which operated as it was designed to, and the verdict was 'Misadventure'.

Generally, the older the lift the greater the likelihood of a breakdown. We have all seen the signs inside a lift car saying something like 'maximum of twelve people or 1200kg' and you start to wonder how twelve people could even get in a lift that small and given that most of us measure our weight in stones and pounds, few of us could convert that plus the weights of our fellow passengers into kilos, before the lift has begun to move. But in a lift designed for six persons, somehow nine rather bulky gentlemen at a Masonic Lodge did indeed squeeze themselves into a lift. The lift was on the second (top) floor and they managed to get the old-fashioned lattice doors closed behind them. Someone must have pressed the Ground floor button and the lift slowly began to move and then the motors began to make a loud noise and the lift gradually built up speed until it crashed with a bump onto the buffers at the bottom of the lift shaft.

Although people may think the opposite, lift cars go up because the motor lowers the counterweight as the counterweight is always heavier than the car plus the weight of the passengers plus an allowance of 50% or so. Conversely, the car goes down because the counterweight is lifted by the motor.

So, in the case of the "fat men in a lift claim" (as it became known), the counterweight was now slightly lighter than the lift car plus the nine men, and the motor was attempting to lift the counterweight at the same time as the weight of the men and car was forcing the lift car down. This caused the motor to overrun and burn out allowing the car to freefall onto the bumper at the foot of the shaft (the lift only had one floor to travel). The claims were not serious – bruises only, but the whole matter raised an important issue about contributory negligence. Arguably the first six men into the lift were not breaking any rules, but the last three were. Also, did the person who pressed the 'G' button on the control panel have a duty to not press the button or demand that three exit the lift? As the person who pressed the G button was one of the first in the lift too, was he more negligent than anyone else? It was tricky. I could not figure out the right answer so I deducted 20% off each of their claims!

At an old hotel, there was a goods lift only used by hotel staff and the occasional delivery driver, even though delivery people were not supposed to use it. The lift, installed in 1920, only went from the ground floor to the basement where the kitchens and store rooms were located. A delivery lorry arrived and saw that the lift was about to descend with a full load. The driver shouted down from the lattice gates to 'send the lift back when you're done' and got a 'Righto' in answer. A few minutes later the lift began its ascent along with a scream from the basement and when the lift arrived the driver saw a

197

mangled and very bloody thumb dangling from the lattice gate!

What had happened was that the man in the basement closed the two sets of lattice gates, but the only way to get the lift to go up was to press the 'up' button on the far side of the car. He put his whole arm through the two lattice gates and pressed the 'up' button and immediately the lift began to rise. The man managed to pull his arm back quickly but his thumb was caught in the diamond shapes of the lattice gate grid and traumatically amputated his thumb. Although the thumb was surgically reattached, he never regained full function. Once again, no fault with the lift, the only fault lay in the fallibility of humans.

Sometimes accidents are so bizarre that they defy belief or suggest that people do not understand what a product is for or how to use it for what it was intended.

We insured a manufacturer of condoms. One might think that a condom only has one usage? Not so apparently.

A claim was submitted for a lady who had suffered internal injury after placing a domestic hamster into the condom, tying the end and then inserting the poor imprisoned animal into an orifice in her lower anatomy where it was believed that its wriggling would bring about a sexual thrill. The hamster was clearly not enjoying the experience however and chewed its way out of the condom and inflicted numerous bites on the female anatomy as it made its escape. And a claim was made on the basis that the product didn't say you could not use a condom in this way! The claim was, as you may expect, denied.

A more normal claim for condom use (or misuse) came invariably from women who claimed that the product had split during normal usage. 'I used your product and it got me pregnant' was a typical letter making a claim. Pointing out that a condom cannot possibly cause pregnancy, if there was however a fault, then send the condom in for analysis and we will consider the matter. Very few people ever keep used condoms (unsurprisingly I suppose), so in the absence of any product to inspect the claims could go no further, but some did send them in (which gave the post room some concern). It was usually found that the condom had teeth marks on it which had damaged the thin latex and as the packaging says 'do not use your teeth when applying the condom'. Those claims never got very far either.

Some years had passed and both Denise had left to have children, and Tracey had moved departments to work with the marine claims chap (who she ended up marrying) so I was on the lookout for replacements.

The secretary I chose was Alison, but in the office, the lady at an adjacent desk was also Alison so it was confusing. 'My' Alison was a lovely girl and pointing out the difficulty it was causing me (and others) in having two Alison's sitting side by side, could I give her a nickname instead? I suggested 'Charlie' as it was sort of cheeky for a lady, but also the name of a very popular perfume at the time, and she was OK with that, so Charlie she became.

Indeed, over the next three or so years everyone called her Charlie and she even answered the phone with it, even long after Alison number 1 had left. Years later I bumped into her in the Reading shopping precinct and I couldn't remember her real name. She will always be Charlie to me.

The replacement for Denise was more problematic. I saw dozens of CVs and no one had the right level of experience or they wanted too much money. I was bemoaning this to Karon and said to her – 'look the damn agency has sent me the CV of someone with no experience at all, the woman hasn't even worked before, she can't drive and all she has is a bunch of A-levels and a degree in German! What use is she to me?' Karon said, 'Well, at least it proves she can learn.' So, I interviewed Helen. She impressed me greatly and I offered her the position on the understanding that she passed a driving test within six months or so. She did pass, the first time of course.

But for sheer weirdness and bizarre these next two claims remain stuck in my mind... for various reasons.

I had to investigate an accident for a builder who had fallen from a roof. Falls of greater than 6'6" meant that there was almost certainly a breach of regulations – the lack of a safety rail or safety harness for example. In this case the man was said to have fallen just 32", at least that is what it said on the claim report form.

The building site was north of Oxford and by now Karon and I had bought our first home together in South

Oxfordshire, just north of Reading in the village of Woodcote. I found the building site easily enough and learned from the site agent that the injured man had been stripping a roof of slates and had fallen forward and landed astride a rafter (so 32 inches then – his inside leg measurement), turned 180° and fell to the ground below. He was doubled-up in pain and had to be removed from the site in a wheelbarrow as he was unable to stand. He was then taken to hospital with his head on the dashboard as he was unable to sit upright. The witnesses on the site were also doubled over, only in their cases with laughter, not pain.

The Letter of Claim came in and so I went to see the claimant's solicitor. We thrashed out a deal on liability and turned to the injuries. One of the allegations was that as a result of the injury it took the claimant longer to reach orgasm than it had before the accident and there was a belief that he may be unable to father children in consequence.

Our conversation went something like this:

'How many children does your client have?'

'Well, none at the moment, he's not married.'

'So how do you know he could father children then? I mean, if 50% of all men are below normal fertility, statistically your client could be in that half. He has no 'track record' as it were about being able to father children, so it is pure speculation that he could. Accordingly, I want a discount for that. As to the second part... 'it takes him longer to reach orgasm than it did before'... how subjective is that? I mean, he may have been 'Minute-Man' before...

of course, his girlfriend may think that's a positive benefit...'

The solicitor was incandescent. 'Mr Cottington if you think for one moment that by dropping my client onto the most sensitive part of his anatomy you have done him some kind of perverse favour; I shall have to ask you to leave my office immediately!' I tried to calm him down.

'Look, all I am saying is that the allegation is unprovable, but we'll get him seen by Dr McDonald in Harley Street for a sperm count and see what that says. She's very good, a leading specialist...' The solicitor interrupted my flow.

'Are you suggesting that my client is seen by a lady doctor?'

'Yes, what's the problem with that? I believe that most gynaecologists are men... maybe she's getting her own back for womenkind eh?' He seemed unimpressed by my comment.

'How do they do these...' er, tests then?'

'Not too sure really, I think the chap is given a specialist 'gentleman's magazine' and a sample pot and told to go into a room to, you know... produce a sample.'

He looked horrified, 'Oh, I don't think I can allow him to see a lady doctor. We'll get our own report.'

It transpired later that the chap had a 'normal' count so the allegation was dropped, but his true injury was a fractured coccyx, not exactly 'funny' and quite debilitating and there is nothing the medical profession can really do for it, but let nature take its time.

On to another investigation, this time at a plastic injection moulding factory where a large machine made the coloured plastic windows for vehicle brake and indicator lights.

The huge machine involved had a large hopper on the top into which plastic granules were automatically tipped at the touch of a button. There was a Perspex window on the side of the hopper through which the level of granules within could be seen and when the level became low were topped up. At least, that was the idea. However, after years of use, the widow had become scratched by the abrasive plastic granules and had become useless as a window. According to the manager the injured supervisor, who was only 21 years old, should not have been climbing onto the machine as the practice was dangerous and so forbidden. If he had wanted to see the level of granules in the hopper, he ought to have used a step ladder. But of course, getting a ladder was troublesome and a fit, athletic young man could climb the machine in a matter of moments. On inspecting the machine, the footprints and wear marks on the paint rather proved that climbing onto the machine to look over the top of the hopper was something happening as a matter of routine.

On the day in question, a cleaner, Rose, was sweeping the floors of spilt granules when she stopped for a chat with a friend. She propped her broom up against the moulding machine and carried on her conversation, unaware that the supervisor had just climbed the machine to look at the granule levels in the hopper when he

203

launched himself backwards off the machine and impaled himself on the broom handle.

Upon landing on the ground, screaming at the top of his voice, the young man was embarrassed beyond imagination. The workforce hooted with laughter as the chap waddled to the 'gents' apparently giving credence to the saying 'if you stick a broom up my arse, I'll sweep the floor as well.' A more perceptive staff member noticed the trail of blood and followed it to the 'gents' where he found the young man in a great deal of distress. By now the man had pulled out the broom and the ceramic floor tiles were awash with blood. An ambulance was called and on reaching the hospital the heavily sedated man underwent emergency surgery. I later learned that it was revealed that the broom handle had penetrated him deeply. Another half inch or so and it would have penetrated the man's diaphragm. Had it done so, when removing the broom, he probably would have died. As it was his intestines were ruptured and approximately four feet of his gut had to be removed. He also had a colostomy, which was later successfully reversed. Unsurprisingly he never returned to work at the factory.

There was patently an unsafe system of work. This was going to be a difficult case to defend and I told the director that but for a replacement piece of Perspex costing no more than £5 a young man's life was probably ruined. The wear marks on the paint were indicative that an unsafe practice had built up and he was lucky that the Health and Safety Executive hadn't prosecuted the firm. I was just leaving when the director asked me 'Haven't you forgotten something?' I mentally checked my equipment – tape measure, camera, file and note pad 'No,' I replied, shaking my head, 'I don't think so, I've got everything thanks.' 'Oh, no,' he said, 'I mean this' and he was offering me the broom! The handle was wrapped in a plastic bag, but all the same... it was THE broom! 'It says on the report form', he continued 'that we had to preserve all the evidence. So here it is, you know, the broom.'

'That's OK, please keep it,' I said and made a hasty exit.

In all my years of investigating claims I don't think any policyholder, with the exception perhaps of the occasional bottle of wonky labelled Cola, had ever given me anything by way of a 'gift'. (No one has ever tried to bribe me either, and I'm not sure whether I am upset or thankful about that!)

One factory very close to our office in Reading was a firm that printed paperbacks. Every time I went there the latest novel was coming off the presses. The odd misprint, or defect, such as where the cover was glued slightly askew, was lobbed into a bin. Not once was I ever offered one and I must have been going there three or four times a year. I mentioned this to Helen who was now investigating claims herself – don't expect any freebies and don't ask either. She came back from the printers with about a dozen or so of the latest print runs and not one was a 'defect'. 'Oh, they just handed them to me on the way out. I didn't ask for anything, honestly.' She came back with packets of bacon too from a pork packaging factory. It made me wonder if I ought to wear a short skirt too...

Helen and I shared the matters that needed investigating between ourselves. I tended to do the longer journeys as I could make an early start from home. Helen lived just a few hundred yards from the office and was habitually late in the mornings. I was pretty flexible about working hours as Helen always made up any lost time so I was not bothered. Apparently, according to her logic, if I were running late, I could hurry and get to work on time. But if she was late and hurried, she'd already be at the office!

But if there was one area of my patch I didn't like going to, it was Surrey. Whatever time I made an appointment for, the traffic or roadworks got me delayed and we didn't have many investigations in that area anyway, so they tended not to get to the top of the pile very often. After weeks of gathering dust in a tray, an investigation in Weybridge finally reached the top of the pile once more. I re-read the report form. An operative had "lacerations to four fingers" – it didn't seem serious. I called the insured and spoke to the director. Sometimes the British can be masters of understatement.

'I'm surprised it has taken you this long to call me Mr Cottington.'

'Why's that? It's just a laceration to four fingers...'

'Yes, but they were lacerated off.'

'What?' I was aghast, 'four fingers have been traumatically amputated?'

'Oh yes, two off each hand.'

'But, but on the form' I stammered, 'you have put 'lacerations', which are 'cuts'.'

'Yes... well they were cut - cut off – two on each hand.'

'Were they able to be re-attached?'

'Oh no, they were pretty mangled.'

Good grief. I went down there that day. A straightforward lack of guarding on the machine, so another one to settle on 'best terms possible'.

Talking of guarding...

At a secure factory where chequebooks were printed for banks, a claim came in for a man who had trapped his hand underneath a guard on a machine and crushed a few fingers.

The machine in question was a paper guillotine that was used to cut and trim stacks of paper chequebooks. This guillotine was capable of cutting through a stack of paper two feet high with ease. To operate the machine, the paper would be aligned and the operator would use both arms to press two buttons on the machine. This action would lower a guard and a massive clamp that secured the paper stack in place. By keeping the operator's hands out of harm's way, the design was intended to prevent any possibility of finger or hand injuries. Then, the operator would press a foot pedal, and as the hands were kept clear of the clamp, a razor-sharp metal guillotine blade would descend and slice through the paper effortlessly. I observed a demonstration of the machine in operation, and it appeared to be a very safe system. 'What went wrong then?' I asked.

'Adrian found a way of bypassing the clamp buttons. He fashioned a bamboo cane with two short pieces of bamboo tied at right angles with a rubber foot on the ends. In this way he could press the two clamp buttons using just one hand and the wally got his right hand under the clamp.'

'What would have happened if he'd pressed the foot pedal? He'd have lost a hand surely?'

'Oh no,' said the supervisor, 'this machine has a 'magic eye' that can detect if something is soft and it won't operate.'

'Really?' I said, intrigued. 'Go on then, show me. Stick your hand under and I'll press the buttons.'

'Fuck off! This is a machine, and machines go wrong mate, I'm not testing it!'

So much for faith I thought.

Chapter Twelve

NEW FACES

During the preceding 4 or 5 years the CIGNA branch underwriting network had grown. We now had four additional offices in my patch – Southampton, Watford, London West End and Redhill. All were generating new local business and with business came claims.

Helen and I were becoming overloaded with work and I secured a budget to recruit another adjuster. Eventually, I recruited Colin, who was a broker with whom I'd had dealings. He was very good at talking to policyholders, other brokers and insurers and had been in the industry for quite a while. I thought he'd be a good fit.

Charlie the secretary had left and so had her replacement, Judith. The next arrival was Sarah. A sweet young lady for whom nothing was too much trouble. She took on the task of arranging all our appointments and was very good at 'bullying' (in the nicest possible way) people to make sure they would be around on a certain day. She was great at getting accurate directions too. Sarah also had this charming attribute that if anyone complained of a headache, stomach upset or whatever – she'd have a pill for it in her huge handbag. If someone had requested a defibrillator, she'd probably have one tucked away. She was a real asset and an excellent typist too, even though she wasn't too hot on the occasional Latin word. She typed 'excreta claim' instead of 'ex gratia'... well, it probably was a shit claim!

Before a mobile phone (about the size of a house brick) was fitted to the car, we would have to buy pre-paid phone cards, find public phone boxes that took the cards and then call our appointments to say we might be late, sorry, delayed. I also made a habit of calling the office in the morning or afternoon in case anyone had cancelled. It was such a waste of time to get to one of the furthest reaches of the patch, such as Weymouth, only to find that the person with whom you'd had an appointment had called in sick. That could be a whole day wasted, especially in the summer when you could get stuck behind a caravan for miles on the narrow roads.

Colin was a hard-working man but somewhat vain. I was concerned that his vision was not good, but he refused to have an eye exam, even though the company paid for them. One day he returned from his calls and apologised for 'dinking' my car. Apparently, he tried to queue jump at some roadworks and had been side-swiped by an articulated HGV. The truck had caused rubber wheel marks all down the passenger side of the car, ripping off all the trim, and the wing mirror and damaging the front and rear bumpers. The car was six weeks old.

He did much the same again a little later and so I insisted he go for an eye exam. He returned with spectacles and seemed amazed at how much more he could see... like the traffic in front I wondered?

Without any fanfare, Kerin our manager had gone back to the States and Jerry was our new field manager. Now Jerry was a 'marine man' and had been in a past life a master mariner and was thus entitled to use the term 'Captain'. We called him 'Popeye'.

We were all invited to a conference and the chairman was a broker. Jerry was giving the main talk (about what I cannot recall) and was introduced by the broker with a shortish background and then said:

'Actually, Jerry is known to all his colleagues as 'Digger' ... his initials being JCB...ha ha.' What? 'Digger'?? The chairman could only have known about that if Jerry had told him. What kind of self-centred person gives themselves their own nickname?

At an internal meeting, Jerry was trying his best to get us enthused by some changes and then said:

'Look, you are the guys with the ideas. You are the ones with the knowledge!' I found this unbelievable from 'senior' management and replied, 'Jerry, I have no ideas and no knowledge... can I be a manager then?'

Digger didn't last.

Two new items of technology arrived in the office. We were given a new-fangled computer terminal that allowed us to set up our claims and make our payments. This was just a financial tool (called Meridian); it was not a computer as we know them today. However, at the time it was innovative and it meant we no longer had to fill in forms and send them to Maidstone for processing. It meant that any errors were ours, but we had ownership of the financials and I was pleased about that. We were given a list of all outstanding files on Meridian, and cross-checked them against the physical files. We found several errors and closed them down saving many thousands of pounds in reserves.

The other piece of kit was a fax machine. The messages and letters arrived on 'hot' paper that came on a big reel. The downside of the paper was that the print faded within months and as we needed to maintain paper records, the faxes then had to be photocopied. We only became aware of the fading issue after a few months and then had to frantically photocopy all the old faxes, just in case they were ever needed.

We had only had the fax machine in the office for a few days when the manager of Redhill, Steve, wound me up about something or other. He was a really nice guy, larger than life and we got on well, but I decided to prank him. One evening after the rest of the office had left, I got out three pieces of blank A4 paper and sellotaped them together to form one long piece of paper. I wrote Steve a big handwritten message along the lines of:

"VERY URGENT
Steve...
it's Gerry
call me urgently
fantastic new business opportunity
call me on my new number on..."

I fed the daft message into the machine, typed in the Redhill office number and pressed the 'send' button. When the top of the message was fed out of the machine I sellotaped the top and bottom together, so the message was now in a complete loop... and the 'urgent, message was duly sent...and sent...and sent...all night long.

The following day Steve called me and in fits of laughter he said that about a mile of fax paper was on the floor of the office and they had to send out for another £50 reel of paper! ...I wondered what the phone bill might have been too? Mea Culpa – I fully accept it was childish of me.

Gosh, a fax machine and a computer! The future had arrived.

I'd been invited by a firm of loss adjusters to attend the Welsh Rugby Union final at Cardiff Arms Park, I think in 1991. Travel was by train and I joined the London crowd at Reading around 10 a.m. and was given a beer as a 'loosener'. A few more looseners passed my lips before the train pulled into Cardiff and we were picked up by coach to travel to a hotel where we enjoyed lunch and yet more beers. Another coach to the Park, and another beer or two before finding our seats. I was unsure who was playing (Llanelli and Pontypool apparently) and we found ourselves sitting down at the 'Pool' end, so I guessed it was best to support them.

The spectator sitting next to me was a small chap of some advanced years and was not with our group, but judging from his vocalisation he knew more about the rules of the game than the referee and more about tactics than the manager - and told (yelled) them both advice as to what they were doing wrong. I was enjoying myself in the sunshine when after 40 minutes the half-time whistle blew. It could not have come a moment too soon as I was, in the vernacular, starting to cry yellow tears. I needed the loo big time. I stood up and turned to the small chap who was donned in Pontypool regalia and expected him to either stand or at least let me squeeze by. 'Sit down boy,' he said rather sternly, 'this is a MAN's game!' And with that, I sat down. I was worried for the chap in front of me because I was sure he was going to get a wet neck before the game was over. He didn't, although I suspect he would now, some 30+ years on – prostates being prostates. Llanelli won, not that I really cared, as by the time of the final whistle I had only one thing on my mind - I dashed to the loo as fast as I could.

Kerin had been replaced by Graham from Birmingham and Barry had retired to be replaced by Jack, another American. It is fair to say we did not get on...at all. The field claims superintendents had all been summoned to a meeting in London. It was Jack's plan that we should all be in 'teams' and he had already divided the Maidstone operation into self-governing teams. Eight or so adjusters would choose a team leader and each team would have a four-letter acronym to differentiate them. There was the Speedy Efficient Claims Team (SECT) and the Property and Casualty Team (PACT) and Jack asked if we could come up with a name? I suggested that as we were in the

Field and responded quickly to claims, maybe we could be the Fast Action Response Team? Jack thought for a moment, smiled and then as the acronym registered, he grimaced and said to me, 'You're not taking this very seriously, are you?' I suppose that was probably true. [I later learned that another insurer had a similar idea and called one team 'Claims Unit Non-Technical'. What were they thinking?]

The only thing that I give Jack credit for was he reorganised the filing system. He implemented a system called 'terminal digit filing' and it's great, I wholly recommend it... but it's far too boring to describe here.

Jack had lured Helen away to Maidstone to become a team leader and I knew she would be a good one. That left Colin, Sarah and me.

Colin and I had been invited to a 'Sportsman's Dinner' as guests of a firm of solicitors in Cheltenham. We were to be staying overnight and the Dinner was a 'black tie' event. I told Colin it would be a good idea to arrive early and he said that he would do a call on the way and be there in good time. He wasn't.

I was standing in the reception with our hosts, all togged up in our DJs when there was a crunch on the gravel outside, a slamming of car doors and Colin came rushing in, bag in hand wearing a brown suit. He took one look at us and said:

'Er, why are you wearing dinner suits?'

'It's a 'black-tie' event Colin, it said so on the invitation,' I replied.

'But I'm wearing a black tie!' he blustered, waving his black tie for us to see. We all burst out laughing.

'Don't worry Colin,' said one of our hosts 'I came in a black suit, you can borrow that.' So, Colin did.

It was a fun evening and we had a good time.

The following morning Colin left early, with our host's suit in his bag, leaving our host to go to his office in his dinner suit! That must have been quite a sight.

Sometime later I received a strange call from Chris, the property manager in Maidstone, asking for a 'private word' one evening at home. I was intrigued. Chris called me that evening at home and said that there were corporate changes in the offing and he was setting up a team in the London Office concentrating on construction, engineering, energy and boiler & machinery, but on a global basis. He wanted me to be his #2. There were going to be ten in the team altogether but only two had any liability claims experience. If I wished to take the position as Executive Loss Adjuster there would be a pay rise plus extra to cover the travel expense. It seemed a good opportunity.

I had by now been in the Reading office for 10 years, so it was probably time for a change and so after discussing it with Karon, I accepted the position which was to start in a month or so.

Meantime I was required to advise Jack I was moving departments, but would still be around for 4-6 weeks and would take with me all the construction cases to London, so Colin and Sarah ought to be able to cope once I had moved. Jack was less than pleased and rather churlishly immediately cut me off from all internal correspondence. Colin was happy as not only did it mean he was likely to be promoted, but he would get his own company car. That was fine with me, he'd dinked mine about four times!

I suppose we all learn in different ways and I am more of a hands-on type. Certain tasks, like learning to drive cannot be done by reading a manual and then taking a test. I know of people who learned how to work computer programs by reading the manual, and then putting it into practice, but that is not for me. I recall being on a training course set in the bowels of our London office and we were in teams and given identical boxes of Lego. The task was to build a tower as quickly as possible, and the end of the task was done by a team shouting 'Stop', the other teams then had two minutes to finish their construction and see if they could get their tower higher. Seems simple enough eh?

As the other teams began building a tower by putting bricks on bricks, I suggested to my team that as a self-confessed Lego 'expert' (I was a very keen modeller in my youth, but 'expert' was stretching it a bit) we should do things differently. My suggestion was to use the flat biscuit-shaped plates and simply lay them end to end and using another 'biscuit', join them together making a very long, thin, train track, whilst others in the team built simply a large block. At a given signal, the block would be attached to the long track, and then the whole lot turned through 90 degrees.

The block would now be the base on which the 'tower' would be supported. Having constructed a long horizontal 'tower' and a chunky block we put the operation into action and lo and behold the tower was raised in seconds and was so tall that it touched the ceiling of the office. We shouted 'Stop' and the other teams simply looked on aghast at what we had done. The tallest of the other team's towers was about three feet and there was no way anyone was going to get a taller tower in the extra two minutes. We had won by a considerable margin. The course leader said that he had been doing this challenge pretty much every week for three years and had never seen anyone do the task like we did. I said that doing things in a traditional way was not always the best way and sometimes you need to think 'outside the box' as it were.

To this day, when confronted with an unusual claim, I still endeavor to approach problems from a different perspective in order to find unique solutions. This came into focus some years later when dealing with an expensive nasty injury claim but one where there was an agreed level of contributory negligence, in this case, 50%. The claim was pitched at £4m or so and its true 100% value was probably closer to £2/2.5m, so after contributory negligence, about £1/1.25m.

The normal way of dealing with these huge schedules of loss is to tackle each head individually and then you get a 100% figure and then divide by two and you should have a number that is acceptable to the claimant. The issue is that the claimant only sees that his claim has been reduced by half, and then I'm perceived as the 'bad guy'. I suggested that I meet with the claimant's team and asked them to humour me, by putting the schedule of loss into a 'Christmas wish list', by putting the schedule in order based on the claimant's priorities, with the most important on top and the least important at the bottom.

The claimants did as I suggested and it surprised me that some of the things that the claimant thought important, I did not. For example, the person needed wheelchairs for life, but these were lower down the list than having adapted transport. A care allowance (always one of the largest heads of claim) was similarly much lower down.

When I saw the list, I was able to say that as far as the items at the top of the list were concerned, we would pay for them all, but the somewhat fanciful heads, such as the cost of holidays and a hydrotherapy pool which were at the bottom, we would not pay for... but all of the important items he would be getting in full, such as his transport costs, his adapted housing and his wheelchairs. All of this came to about £1.2m and I said that what he was now going to do was, in theory, going to court to get half of the cost of the things that were least important to him, which seemed a bit silly.

When put like that he reconsidered the matter and took the very sensible offer of £1.2m.

Chapter Thirteen

LONDON CALLING

Before actually going to the London office, Chris called me and said that there was to be an Energy conference in Euston. 'What in North London?' 'No,' he said, 'Houston, Texas. It will last a week.'

When I received the itinerary, it seemed a very full week, beginning on the Sunday when we were flying out from Heathrow. The flight to Houston was 8 hours of boredom and we were picked up at the airport by a limousine to take us to the hotel. We were due to have dinner with some of the other attendees so I went to my room to freshen up. I do not know what my problem is with American plumbing, but although I managed to turn both the taps on, I could not turn them off again. It didn't seem to matter which way I turned the damn taps I could not get the water flow to stop... I had to call the maintenance team! They must have thought I was a complete idiot. A chap arrived in a boiler suit, looked at all the flowing water, turned the taps, one way or another, I still had no clue... and looking at me as if I was indeed a complete idiot, turned and left. After that, I only used one tap for the rest of my stay... just in case of repetition.

The conference itself was run by a firm of consulting engineers and there was a lot to learn. Each evening we were treated to dinner at a different restaurant. I clearly remember a Mexican evening. The food was buffet-style and was great. Whilst we were chatting, I picked up from the table a 'shrimp' although it was the size of a baby lobster. The shrimp had been stuffed into a jalapeno pepper and deep-fried in batter. It was lovely. One of the hosts asked me if I liked the shrimp? I said I did and he suggested I try another. I did, then another. 'Didn't you find that, er... kinda hot?' he asked. 'Nope,' I said and started chomping on another one. The Americans seemed to think that all the Mexican food was too hot for them. I didn't. They nicknamed me 'Rubber Lips'.

By Wednesday the jet lag was kicking in and by mid-afternoon, I was nodding off and had to have a nap before the next assault on my digestive system. It was a steak restaurant and I am sorry to say that my steak was so big that I could not finish it, I was obviously letting England down.

Thursday saw us off to the Humble Oil Refinery. This was the first oil refinery in the world and we were treated to a guided tour of the facility. I happened to mention when we were in one of the computer rooms that the oil industry was not just unique, it was distinctly odd. 'How so?' someone asked. I said that I had been to a lot of factories and in each, you see a raw product coming in, such as milk and you see cheese going out, or trees coming in and paper going out. But here, at a refinery, you see nothing, just a maze of pipes and dials that show that 'something' is going through the pipes. One of the supervisors laughed and said in a Texan drawl, 'Man, if you do see any of the product here... run like fuck because you got 'bout 30 seconds before you are going to be incinerated!' Sound advice indeed.

I did cause some controversy though. We had all learned about how crude oil was 'cracked' into components, such as lighter oils (gasoline, kerosene and diesel), gases (butane and propane) and the heavy ends (lubricant oils and tars) and all involve the same basic chemistry, the breaking down of the benzene rings and chains. One of the by-products was used to make plastic. I said that when one looked at all the products that Humble made, nothing was re-cyclable, in effect, all they made was, well, pollution. The room went silent. I carried on with my theme and said that if they could find a way to turn plastics back into something useful, rather than create a landfill, they might be doing something progressive and different. This was way back in 1997 and I have to think I was ahead of the times with my views. Back in 1997, it seemed like nothing was recycled and as far as the technicians at the refinery were concerned, the sooner the Limey idiot was out of their refinery the better.

Friday morning was a wrap-up session followed by a 'BB' game in the evening. This turned out to be a Basketball game, the Houston Rockets vs Dallas Mavericks (I think). We were all given the T-Shirt as a souvenir and of course, wore them to the game. One thing about Houston that surprised me, apart from the humidity, was that all the women I saw were truly 'Southern Belles'. All were made up to the 'nines' and very well dressed. If I happened to speak to any of them, they were all taken in by my accent and frequently said, 'Oh honey, say something, anything at all, but say it again in that British accent! Hey, Delores!! Come on over here and hear this guy speak! It's awesome.'

The game seemed to go on forever and luckily Houston won, something like 110 to 108. Just one basket in it. Apparently, it was thrilling. I thought it tedious.

The flight home was on Saturday and I didn't have time to get over the jet lag before my new start in London on Monday.

I had my commute to the office worked out to a fine detail. Drive to Goring, train to Paddington, a walk to Lancaster Gate, Central line to Bank, then a walk to Lime Street. The problem was the time it took and the cost. However, I thought I would give it a go for six months.

The office had been refurbished and we were on the 6th floor. I met the new team as apart from Chris, all the others were from Maidstone. The team consisted of Chris, Peter, Paul, David, Karl, Mark, Mike, Gerry, me and our secretary, Justine. Mike and Gerry were seconded to our team although they only looked at multi-million-dollar claims and were globetrotting adjusters. I was the only one in the team who was new and aside from Gerry, Mike and Chris, the others were reporting to me.

I needed to try and build some team cohesion especially with David and Karl as they struck me as two lazy individuals who did nothing more than the bare essentials. At the bottom of one of their filing cabinets was a stack of post. 'What's that?' I asked. 'Dunno,' one of them said, 'It's been there for months.' 'And you didn't think to look at it?' 'Not my problem,' came the answer. I did look at the post. There were many payment requests and new claims, all now months old. I was unimpressed by these two. But I digress.

The National Lottery had just begun and at the time the cost of a 'line' was £1. If you got three numbers up you won £10. There were 10 of us, so I figured that if we each put in £1 and won £10, it would be free next week. In the unlikely event that we won something more, it would be split 10 ways ... this was a cheap and easy way of building team spirit, or so I thought. Eight of us were in the syndicate, but David and Karl declined to join in, probably because I had thought of it. In a small office behind ours sat two people in 'Facilities' and they made up the required numbers to 10.

During the first eleven weeks, we had nine £10 wins. I then went on a two-week holiday to France with the family. When I came back to work there was a rail strike so I drove to Hangar Lane on the A40, parked and tried to get a tube train to the city, but the tube drivers were striking too. It was tipping with rain and after a long wait I got a bus going to Embankment and there, without an umbrella, I walked along the Thames Embankment to the office. By the time I arrived, very late, I was soaked to the skin, miserable and in a foul mood.

Peter came up to me smiling, 'Have a good holiday?' he asked.

'Yes, it was fine thanks. Didn't know about this bloody strike though. I'm soaked. Anything happen of interest whilst I was away?'

'Oh, not much. We won the Lottery though.'

'Another tenner?'

'No, eighty-seven grand.'

I glared at him, 'Peter, if you're taking the piss, you are fired, 'cos I'm in no mood!'

'No, truly,' he said and showed me a cheque from the National Lottery. It was indeed true. He continued, 'We won on the first Saturday you were away. We tried to call you on your mobile phone but you must have been in France by then and there was no signal. Wanted to tell you to have a good time. Last week we didn't win anything though. Had we got the five and bonus we would have got £123,000, but £87,000 wasn't so bad. Anyway, here's your share.' And he handed me a cheque for £8,700. Not a bad return for a £2 investment.

I was of course thrilled. I called Karon and gave her the good news and said that the loan we had just taken out for the kitchen refurbishment could be paid off and with the surplus I went and bought a suit.

Karl and David weren't speaking to anyone... and didn't for weeks after.

You can't keep an enthusiastic claims investigator down and I was itching to undertake some investigations but realised that I could only do the more serious ones.

A broker called and said that there had been a fatality on a building site in Milton Keynes. She said that there were nominated adjusters on the account. I knew that this broker was, quite literally, in bed with this particular adjuster who was a property adjuster, not a liability adjuster. Moreover, he was based in Leeds. I said I would deal with it myself. The broker insisted on coming too 'to protect the client's interests' she said. I thought that's what I was doing, but did not object.

The accident was rather typical. A sub-contract roofer, not wearing a safety harness, had stepped onto unsecured roofing sheets, which slipped and he fell 50ft or so onto a concrete base and was killed instantly. He was 21 years old. Tragic.

Back into the site office with the main contractor, I explained that based on what we learned I could not see that there was any liability on the main contractor. The accident was all down to a lack of training and provision of safety apparel by the sub-contractor. I said there would be an Inquest and an investigation by the HSE, but I did not think they had anything to worry about. The site agent then asked me the question I get asked at every accident.

'So, what's a case like that worth then?'

'Well, from what we know, he was 21, lived at home with his parents, and had no dependents so this will be a basic fatal damages case plus funeral expenses. I'm afraid that Prince to a pauper we are all worth the same on a mortuary slab as a piece of meat... about £10,000, so with funeral expenses and solicitor fees, £15000 would cover it. Not much is it? So sad, such a young chap too.'

I left the site and Justine typed up my report a few days later.

I then got summoned to Chris's office.

'There's been a complaint about you,' he said.

'Really? Who from?' I was rather dumbfounded.

'You know that fatal accident you investigated?'

'Yes.'

'Well, you said something that apparently caused offence.'

'Really?' I was puzzled. 'What did I say and who's offended?'

'Apparently, you referred to the deceased as 'a piece of meat'. Is that true?'

I relayed the words I did say, pointing out that I could not believe the site agent was offended.

'Not the agent. The broker.'

'Oh, good grief Chris, she was pissed off because I wouldn't let her appoint her pet adjuster on the investigation. This was just spite.'

'OK, just watch what you say in future.' I would.

How accurate do loss estimates have to be? Sometimes you can get it spectacularly wrong.

I do not know what it is about Hull, but we had written another major project. The EU had told the good burghers of Kingston-Upon-Hull that they should stop tipping their sewage into the Humber and build a new sewage treatment plant, plus all the ancillary sewer pipes, instead. The project involved using a tunnel boring machine (TBM) digging/boring the main sewer line, behind which came a train and conveyor belts taking away the spoil and laying segments of concrete wall to form rings.

The TBM was called Maureen, after Maureen Lipman the actor who hailed from Hull. If there is an issue with TBMs it is that they cannot reverse as the concrete rings that are now behind the cutting face make the diameter smaller. So, they have to go in a straight line and can only be removed by digging a vertical shaft and then they are removed by crane. The Channel Tunnel was dug in the same way, but as two TBMs were coming in opposite directions, one from France and one from England, they would have met head-on. However, just before meeting up, the French one was driven sideways so that the final breakthrough came from the English one. The English machine was dismantled and removed. The French one remains at the bottom of the English Channel.

Back in Hull, it was mid-December and Maureen was proceeding rapidly as the ground was found to be unusually soft. At the end of a shift, the cutting crew were returning on the small train that ran inside the tunnel and saw that there was a trickle of soil coming from the roof between some ring segments. This was not good. They hurried to the main shaft, alerted a supervisor and a huge flange plate was installed and the tunnel deliberately flooded to prevent collapse. What to do now?

The loss adjusters called me.

'Trevor, it's bad news. There is a tunnel collapse in Hull, well, sort of, the tunnel is flooded and the contractor is unsure what the fix is, but it's going to be expensive. My current estimate is £2.5m.'

We went through the numbers and thought that £1.75m might cover it. It was year-end and putting on such a large figure was never received well by senior management.

By early New Year, the adjusters said that the loss might be £3.5m. The cause was said to be 'unforeseen ground conditions'. This was good news, as I noted that the contract between the insured and the Water Authority was on 'I.C.E. Conditions of Contract'. I knew that under the terms of the Institute of Civil Engineering contract the risk of unforeseen ground conditions was at the risk of the Employer, Anglian Water and not the contractor.

I called the brokers and told them the 'good news' that under the I.C.E conditions, the insured could put the claim to the Employers. The brokers asked me to repeat what I'd said.

'Under the I.C.E conditions of contract, the risk of unforeseen ground conditions is at the risk of the Employer. So, good news, eh?'

'I'd agree,' replied the broker, 'if this were the Institute of Civil Engineers contract, but this is the Institute of *Chemical* Engineers contract and under that, the risk of ground conditions is still with the contractors.'

I could not believe my ears or what was there in black and white on the 'slip' that the underwriter had signed, so I went to see him. On the slip it stated 'I.C.E conditions' and

I asked him if he took that to mean Civil Engineers or Chemical Engineers? He asked what was the difference? I said about £3.5m. The underwriter said that the premium was greater than £3.5m so maybe I ought not to make such a fuss? Realising that in a legal fight I'd still be up against the contra proferentem rule (see p91) and if there were ambiguity over Chemical or Civil, the underwriter should have asked for clarity and as he didn't, we would lose. To this day I still do not believe for one moment he had even heard of the 'Chemical' terms. Nevertheless, we accepted the claim.

By mid-January, the loss estimate had risen to £5m and I decided I needed to take a look for myself to gain a fuller understanding of the problem and suggested solutions.

Maureen was stuck under a car park. The area where the flexing of the sewer line was located and where the sewer was surely going to collapse, was under a tributary of the Humber. The tributary was small, but a river nonetheless.

The proposal was simple in practice but complicated in engineering terms and expensive. Firstly, it was considered impossible to abandon Maureen and dig a parallel sewer as that would require obtaining hundreds of easements from the people who owned the land above. That would take years. Secondly, it was also impossible to put another TBM down the original shaft and bore towards Maureen as the TBM would be boring through a good half mile of 'good' but flooded tunnel. If the water pressure were removed the tunnel would collapse along with, perhaps buildings above.

The only solution that seemed to have merit was to dig another shaft in the car park around 50 metres from Maureen and lower a new TBM (called 'John' after John Prescott the local MP) and bore towards Maureen. But as the ground around Maureen was soft it was suggested that ground freezing would be needed. This involved drilling pipes into the ground and pumping down liquid nitrogen. The pipes needed to be two bores – a middle pipe down which the liquid nitrogen was pumped and the outer pipe for the release of the gas, bringing it back to the surface. When the ground was frozen, 'John' would be lowered down the shaft and drilled towards Maureen. When the two met, as John could not reverse, his cutting head would be dismantled, allowing Maureen to be dismantled from her frozen condition and removed back up John's shaft. John would then have his cutting head replaced and drill through all the frozen water and concrete segments until after the area of weakness. There he would be dismantled, taken back to his shaft, re-assembled on the surface and lowered back again this time in the opposite direction and allowed to carry on boring fresh sewer.

That all seemed simple enough (it wasn't) but how much would it cost and how long would it take? The sewer had to be finished by an agreed time, otherwise huge penalties were likely from the EU.

The whole program was adjusted to allow the building of the treatment plants to be accelerated whilst the crew at the 'car park' carried out the remedial work. As to how much? The estimate of £5m had so many variables I felt the costs would inevitably escalate. I raised the number to £7.5m.

The ground freezing required huge quantities of liquid nitrogen, which were sourced from British Oxygen Co. The contract with BOC was initially for three months for all the liquid nitrogen they could make. This was then extended to six months all at an agreed fixed price per litre. The contract ended up lasting nearly two and a half years.

By the middle of summer, my estimate of £7.5m was raised to £10m, then to £12.5m.

I went back to the site to see how things were progressing. When I arrived at the 'car park' that had been leased by the contractors to carry out the repairs, the first thing I noticed was the noise. There was a constant whistling, rather like old-fashioned kettles on a gas stove. I was shown the liquid nitrogen pipes and all the pumping equipment which looked like a mass of tangled spaghetti. The pipes stuck out of the ground vertically, but the tops were covered in ice, even though it was a hot day. It was explained that the venting nitrogen gas was still very cold and this caused the tops of the pipes to become frosted, then icy and as the ice built up the venting hole became smaller and smaller causing the 'whistling' noises. There were dozens of pipes and all were whistling at a very high pitch. I was concerned that the neighbours would be complaining and was told that every couple of hours someone would go around and knock off the ice with a hammer.

I was then taken to see the progress, such as it was, down the shaft. That involved me standing in a 'man cradle' and then hoisted by a crane and swung out over the shaft and lowered. I was just a few feet from the top when there was a 'jolt' on the cradle as if the brake had been momentarily applied and released. It had. The operator of the crane liked to give 'the suits' a bit of a shock as a 'joke'. I suppose it passed the time.

At the bottom of the shaft, I was released from the cradle and began to walk toward the tunnel face. It was freezing cold and I could see my breath in the air. There were men on scaffolding with pneumatic hammers drilling against the face of the tunnel which should have been soft silt, but with the liquid nitrogen, the silt had frozen and was like concrete. Every few moments the hammer might hit a flinty stone and there was a spark and pieces of frozen silt would fly in all directions. I was wearing a hard hat and safety goggles when a piece of the rock hit me on the cheek like a bee sting. I thought I had seen enough.

Back at the compound, we readdressed the timeframe and cost model. There was seemingly no prospect of getting the project finished by the EU deadline, but the delay costs did not concern me as they were uninsured. The construction costs were now not thought to be £12.5m, but closer to £20m!

Two years later I settled the claim for just over £43m. That one section of sewer repair of a few hundred metres cost more than the whole project of 2.5 miles. I never got to ask the underwriter whether he might have rethought the 'I.C.E.' point because he had left. To this day I maintain he was conned by the brokers.

Chapter Fourteen

THE VIKINGS

Our man in Stockholm had left to go to a firm of loss adjusters and I was asked whether I would take on the additional role of being 'our man in Scandinavia', but from London. It would mean the occasional trip to the region and I would need to meet with loss adjusters and lawyers in all three countries (we did not write enough business in Finland to qualify as needing a visit). It seemed to me to be a tough job, but, sighing, I suppose if push came to shove...I'd do it. Free trips to Scandinavia? What's not to like?

Over the next eight years or so I travelled to the region probably twice a year and sometimes for special claims.

One thing I have learned over the years is that although international travel sounds glamorous, it rarely is. A lot of time is spent at airports and travelling and there is no time for sightseeing, not that there are many 'sights' in Saudi Arabia, but I had hoped for some free time in Scandinavia. I soon learned to allow at least half a day in each country to go to a museum or art gallery.

Denmark, or rather Copenhagen, was probably the only place I went to just twice. Most of the claims were very small in value and involved people breaking their teeth on stones in salads (can you believe it - stones?) and were all outsourced for handling by a firm of solicitors.

We insured a global catering company and they serviced a lot of staff canteens and airports with catering facilities. The salad meals all had olives as part of the salad and the 'stones' were olive pits, not the gravel that I had supposed.

The solicitors bought a lovely dinner though. This was something I was especially grateful for as my 'hotel' was in fact above a sex shop and had no restaurant facilities. My room was so tiny that I could sit on the toilet seat and place the palm of my hand on my bed. The shower was above and a little to the side of the toilet, the drain in the middle of the floor. With my arms outstretched I could touch all four walls in the bedroom. This is what happens when you allow corporate booking to get you a hotel in the 'business district' of Copenhagen. Judging by the noises coming from the other rooms I think the bedrooms were probably rented by the hour.

On one trip I was accompanied by a loss adjuster from Sweden. The countries share similar judicial codes and their languages are understood in both...or so I was told. I was walking down a busy street chatting away with the loss adjuster when he bumped into a lady coming in the opposite direction. As in the UK, the automatic response is for both parties to say 'sorry' and walk on. He and she said something and we carried on. A few paces onward, he suddenly stopped and burst out laughing.

'What's so funny?' I asked.

'She just told me she was a virgin!' he guffawed. I asked him to explain and he replied she had said in Danish something like 'I'm innocent or my fault' which in Swedish sounded like 'I'm a virgin'. I got him to say the two phrases time and again, but to my English ear, I could not hear any difference.

The one thing I did learn in Copenhagen when crossing the road is to always wait for the traffic lights to change or use a zebra crossing and follow other people, never going first. The number of cars and cycles that jumped the lights or ignored pedestrian crossings was immeasurable... and they all drove like maniacs too.

Apart from seeing the Little Mermaid on the Copenhagen waterfront, I didn't see any of the touristy sights. The Little Mermaid is tiny too, so very appropriately named.

Stockholm is a lovely city, set in an archipelago. Each island is connected to others by a series of bridges and a lot of the time I could not work out whether I was on an island or mainland. I have always found Stockholm a difficult place to navigate as there was not, for me at least, any visual point of reference.

My first meetings were with the chap I had effectively taken over from and we went through all the files, 80% of which seemed to be motor claims.

I soon learned that in Sweden the insured party is the car, not the driver, so even if you crash your car into a lamp post, you can make a claim for your own injury. That seemed very peculiar to me. Indeed, one sad case involved a lad who 'borrowed' his father's company car and tried to commit suicide by driving it at high speed into a tree. He failed to kill himself, but to my amazement was still able to claim for his injury.

There was a huge 'however' though and that was concerning damages. It seems you could only claim for the time you were actually in hospital as an in-patient and then only for so much per day, so the awards were never particularly high.

I was looking at another matter where a driver had knocked over an elderly lady in a supermarket car park and had broken her arm. I considered that the claim would be a serious one and was surprised at how low the loss estimate was. I was told that the lady 'got better' so the claim was miniscule.

One afternoon I was walking with my loss adjuster colleague (probably on the way to a bar if I am honest) along a waterfront and I commented on how nice all the houses along the waterfront looked. There was no graffiti and all the houses were well decorated in a variety of pastel shades. It looked charming.

'Oh, yes Trevor. The houses here have to look nice. It makes for a pleasant outlook for everyone. Actually, it is a requirement that everyone has to paint the outsides of their houses every four years.'

'And if they don't?'

'Oh, the council come and do it anyway and send the owner a bill. As the council charges more, people do it themselves.'

How very enlightened I thought. If only the UK could do the same.

During one trip I had, out of necessity of course, to pay a visit to the Icebar. The bar was set to the side of the IceHotel and I think was sponsored by Absolut, the Swedish vodka distiller. The bar itself is at a permanent - 7C and you need to wear a thermal coat, which supplied by the staff. The only drinks available were vodka-based cocktails, sweet or sour, and were themselves served in a 'glass' made of clear ice. No washing up – when you finish your drink the 'glass' is thrown away. The bar itself was carved from blocks of river ice and I could see traces of river weeds entombed within. Around the sides were ice sculptures too.

It is so cold inside that you have to wear gloves otherwise your skin sticks to the 'glass' and it is not thought to be a good idea to have more than two drinks (which you pay for in advance) as staying any longer than half an hour could result in hypothermia. Of course, I had three drinks. Even the bar staff are only able to work in 20- or 30-minute shifts at a time. Yes, it's a tourist trap and certainly not cheap... nothing in Scandinavia is, but it was an experience.

I had a very difficult claim in southern Sweden for a company that recycles refuse. Rather than use landfills as a way of getting rid of rubbish, this company burned the rubbish in a massive rotary kiln with the heat generated being used to run turbines and in turn, generate electricity. Hot water was also a by-product and went as free heating to the community. The kiln was, by necessity huge and unusually also burned liquids. Waste liquids, such as paint, oils and even contaminated water were sprayed into the kiln and burned at high temperatures. The resultant ash was also sometimes able to be used, I think as 'clinker' for road surfaces.

The problem was that there was only one kiln and it broke down. We covered the machinery breakdown and business interruption losses.

The business of waste recycling is fascinating, in that it must be the only industry that gets paid for destroying things. Demolition I suppose comes close, but even then, the resultant rubble needs to be disposed of.

In Sweden, there was only one factory that could dispose of hazardous waste and it was this one we insured. The factory financial model runs on the basis that customers turn up with a lorry full of certain waste. The type of waste has to be listed on a manifest and the lorry is weighed. The waste load is then tipped at designated points and the lorry re-weighed on exit, the differential in weight being the weight of the load. The customer is then charged based on the type of load multiplied by the cost of destruction for that type. Waste wood for example is easier to burn than contaminated water. The point of all this was that the customer paid for the destruction of the goods in advance of the destruction even happening.

When it came to the claim the cost of the breakdown was simple, we paid for the repairs even though the repairs took months to complete. The problem was the business interruption. The insured said that they operated the facility in effect 24/7/365 with only a two-week shutdown in August for maintenance. Their argument ran that because of a 12-week shutdown they could never catch up. I thought the argument was flawed.

I said that whilst I understood the logic that they worked currently 24/7 it only would take one customer to go bust or go elsewhere and suddenly capacity would be gained. Meantime I accepted that there would be an increase in storage and movement costs (known as increased cost of working) and that was covered, but the loss of profits – no.

The insured wished the claim settled there and then, but I said according to the policy we could wait until the end of the policy period to calculate the loss, which was another six months' time... but if they wished to compromise...? They did.

That example could be an exam question as it highlighted a potential flaw in the policy – the insured had paid for business interruption cover, but as they saw it, they could never make a claim. That was not entirely true, but close. The construction of a new bridge linking southern Sweden to Denmark meant that customers in southern Sweden did indeed move their custom to another waste facility, so my point was entirely valid.

A strange call came to me on 23rd December from the same global waste management company. The conversation went something like this:

'Trevor, it's Chas in Houston. Got a fatal accident to report to you and we need it investigated today.' There was a very heavy emphasis on 'today'.

'OK, Chas. Where is the accident location?'

'Just outside Helsinki in Finland.'

'And you want this investigated today? What happened?'

'Our guys were unloading a refuse truck of waste paper and this body tumbled out. He was pretty mashed up. The guys think that he was sleeping in one of those big green wheelie bins full of waste paper and the guys never noticed him and he was tipped into the truck and got crushed.'

'So let me get this straight Chas. You are in Houston; you are eight hours behind me and here it's coming up to four in the afternoon. In Helsinki, it's got to be six p.m. And you want this investigated today? Impossible.'

'Tomorrow then Trevor, we want you to investigate this tomorrow, OK?'

'Chas, you are asking me to go to Finland on Christmas Eve, I repeat, on Christmas Eve. A four-hour flight. Even assuming I could get a flight, which I probably can't, what is there to investigate? You know the circumstances, what you don't know is who the deceased is, or, sadly was. If he was sleeping in a wheelie bin, the chances are he was a homeless tramp. It's -10C in Helsinki and tramps frequently use wheelie bins as temporary shelters. But think about it Chas, who's going to make a claim and for what? He's hardly likely to be a breadwinner is he and have dependents? Even if there is a liability, which is unlikely, any claim is going to be small. Any fatal accident is going to be the subject of a Police investigation and everything will be impounded. I don't think for a moment the Police are going to bust a gut on Christmas Eve to do much or any, investigation until the New Year.'

'OK... you may have a point, but I want you to get hold of that Police report and get me a copy without delay.'

'Will do Chas. Oh, by the way, how's your Finnish?'

'What?'

'Well, the Police report will be from the Helsinki Police and the report will be in Finnish, not English. Finnish is a difficult language and there will be a chunky translation fee. My advice is to wait and see if there is a claim and then as we will need local lawyers, which we have, they can do the translation for free. How's that sound?'

'Yeah...OK we'll wait then.'

'Great. Have a happy holiday.' And the call ended.

Of course, no claim was ever advanced. Why is it that Americans think that the world speaks English? OK in Finland a lot do, but as for going to Finland on Christmas Eve? No thanks... I'd miss Santa!

What surprised me about Sweden was that the Swedes don't like their Norwegian neighbours, whom they regard as a waste of 'good air'... and the feeling seems to be mutual. I learned that the animosity stretches back to the time that Norway gained its independence from Sweden, as recently as 1905. WWII didn't help matters when Sweden threw in their 'neutrality' card and Norway was invaded, leaving the Norwegian Royal Family to seek sanctuary in England. This is why the Norwegian Government still sends a Christmas tree to London to be erected in Trafalgar Square every year as a 'thank you'. After the war ended there was then a further bond with the UK when schoolchildren were no longer taught German as a second language, but English instead. Accordingly, asking a Norwegian if they speak English, is like asking a maths professor if he can count up to three.

However, the main area of contention was oil: Norway had it and Sweden had none. Sweden had the rain and that generated electricity, but oil brought in massive wealth to a small nation of 9 million or so. University education was free and so almost everyone I met had a degree or a doctorate. A surprising number had law degrees too, but few practiced. The high taxation and oil wealth meant that the State looked after the elderly. The basic and lowest level of old age pension was around £50,000 p.a. about 10 times that of the UK (at that time). Thus, no one was considered poor and I saw no evidence of homelessness.

On my first visit to Oslo, the airport was at Arlanda and involved a bus ride into the city centre. A new airport was being built and on the day of the changeover everything worked, I mean everything...the computer systems, the escalators and lifts, the check-in procedures and the new train that takes you directly to the city centre. The train was smooth with video screens showing touristy films of Norway as well as the news. It made the journey time, about 20 minutes or so as I recall, pass quickly. Incredibly efficient and reasonably priced. When I asked a colleague whether there were any 'teething problems' he replied, with a chuckle, 'No, why would there be? This was built in Norway, not England.' Yes, quite so.

My hotel was a short walk from the station and I was soon to learn that Oslo is a tiny city. It is possible to walk from one end of the city to the other in about 45 minutes, although in the winter no one walks anywhere. Being a small city and on the edge of a fjord I was soon able to have my points of reference – if the mountains were behind me, I knew the fjord and docks were in front. The docks also contained a shopping precinct called Arthur Brikke which I strolled around, jaw wide open at the prices. A humble pair of gent's shoes was the equivalent of £300. Everything was expensive and heavily taxed. The basic rate of income tax was around 45% but wages were comparably much higher.

Due to high wages many jobs, such as waiters and bar staff, were habitually filled by Swedes which caused yet more resentment.

My first meeting was with our loss adjusters and the head of the firm was a lady called Charlotte.

We met in my hotel bar and began chatting about business and so forth. After twenty minutes or so I asked her 'What part of western Canada are you from?' Charlotte looked horrified, I thought I'd made some kind of faux pas.

'Sorry, I mean to say, either you come from Western Canada or were perhaps taught English by a Canadian, as I can detect an accent.'

She replied, eyes wide open with incredulity 'I was born in Vancouver and came to Norway aged nine with my parents. How do you know this?'

'Oh, it's just the way you structure sentences, the pauses and sometimes ending a sentence with 'eh' which is very Canadian. I pick up on accents and have family in Alberta and you sounded sort of Canadian, that's all.' I'm not entirely sure she believed me, but it was true.

I had a meeting with her team who were in a business park, way outside the city centre so a taxi was needed. Taxis are frequently used in Norway, partly because the cost of cars is so high and journeys fairly short, but also because there is zero tolerance for drunk driving. The UK limit is I think 35mg of alcohol in samples, in Norway it is 1mg. This might mean that a wine gum or sherry trifle can put you over the limit. The penalty for drunk driving is also a fine and a mandatory prison sentence of a minimum of one month.

However, this being Norway, even the prison sentence is 'when it suits you'. Drivers are not taken from court to jail, no, they take time off at work and say they will do their jail time in a couple of months. Very civilised.

As it turned out, the offices of the adjusters were adjacent to one of the low-security prisons, which from the outside looked rather like a Butlins holiday camp.

The adjusters' offices were on the top floor of a five-storey building. One of the adjusters I met was in a wheelchair. Nothing too unusual about that, except I saw on the side of a window a large emergency contraption. On enquiry, I was told that in the event of a fire the lift could not be used and the disabled chap was considered too big to carry, down ten flights of stairs anyway, so a safety chute had to be installed. It was an elephant trunk of canvas and in an emergency the chute was released and the disabled guy was picked up and 'posted' down the chute. I asked what broke his fall and was told that the trunk narrows at the bottom and he shouldn't hit the ground 'too hard'. Then they said the classic – 'well, he's paralysed anyway from the waist down, he won't feel anything!'

I went through the files they had and got myself up to speed with the outstanding matters. There were a few tricky ones (the aforementioned rotary kiln being one) and Charlotte gave me a lift back to Arthur Brikke where we enjoyed a few beers. I was introduced to a couple of solicitors, Eivind and Trond, who worked at a firm with whom we did business. Over the coming years, we became rather firm friends (see later).

We had written an account that I felt was going to be a sink for money. The risk was a scheme for people selling houses. Under Norwegian law, the seller of a house is liable to pay for any hidden defects for up to three years after the sale. The defects could be things like uneven floors, leaky pipes or defective drains and the like. Initially, our market was to be the sale of commercial premises, but the take-up was not good, so the brokers persuaded our underwriters to extend the scheme to house sales. Historically, no company had made money with the scheme, but somehow, we would, even by selling the policies cheaper than the competition. Our underwriter, who was based in Stockholm, was called Per. He was a short, overweight chap who had a phobia about lifts, so would walk up the stairs to meet people in their offices. The law firm we had retained to look over our wording and deal with any litigation that may result was situated on the 10th floor of a tower block in the heart of Oslo. We had several meetings there and at each one I would go to the offices by lift and Per would turn up 15 minutes later, dishevelled, sweating profusely and out of breath. It would take him a further 15 minutes to calm down along with copious amounts of water.

In consequence, the meetings would take quite some time, especially as technical matters were discussed in Norwegian and Swedish, and then translated to me in English. The lawyer was a young man who had an eidetic (photographic) memory and was able to quote word-for-word great chunks of Norwegian law. He got the highest test result in the Norwegian bar exams, having undertaken no revision. Amazing.

The premiums were coming in thick and fast and this made Per a very happy man. He had exceeded his premium income budget very early and this enabled him to buy the brokers some of the most expensive dinners I have ever been invited to. Then the claims came in...

The first few claims were difficult and required a legal view before we could consider a settlement. That took time and additional money. Before long, instead of the dozens of claims per year I was told to expect, we were getting dozens a month, then weekly. I arranged with the brokers a 'handling fee' and they employed two or three people just to process the claims. My job was to audit the files. To say the files were boring was an understatement. Nearly all involved leaky shower trays and the discovery of mould and mildew.

I saw so many mildew photos that I teased the brokers that Black Mould was the national flower of Norway.

There was even a claim for the smell of cat pee that required a house to be sanitised. I questioned how it was that the buyer didn't notice that when they were looking at the house? Didn't they have a nose? The point was that the seller did not declare the smell on the seller's pack, so there was a breach of sale and this is what the policy picked up as the defect (the smell) was 'hidden'. The seller retained a liability as a policy excess of NOK500 (around £50) but because the amount was so small, it rather paid the seller to have a selective memory and 'forget' to mention defects as the insurance would pay for any repairs. The whole scheme was open to fraud and I am sure it was.

One file I audited had the claimant as Eivind! He had bought a new house, but the floors were uneven, so he made a claim. He told me that most houses have wooden floors and scatter rugs rather than fitted carpets. When viewing a house to purchase, the buyer carries a few glass marbles in their pocket. They put the marbles on the floor and if they don't move, the floor is flat, but if they scoot away, the floor is uneven. He knew the floors were uneven due to his marble test, but the seller didn't say they were uneven...so it was a claim.

We ran with the scheme for about two years with a three-year run-off, so I had to go back to Oslo many times. I am not sure what the loss ratio was but I think it ran into the 1000's%. Per was, I believe, 'requested to seek alternative career opportunities'... Shame, I liked him, but he could not admit the scheme was inherently flawed and should have dropped it after a year.

On one visit to Oslo during the summer months, I was invited by a colleague of Charlotte, called Camilla, to pay a visit to the Vigeland Sculpture Park. The Park was designed by an artist, who sadly died before completion, but the park was certainly worth a visit and I have been back a couple of times.

The sculptures in the park all represent the human condition from birth to death and every emotion in between. All the sculptures are of people and all are naked. The most famous one is of a small boy standing on one leg throwing a tantrum. It's considered good luck to rub his foot, so I did. A short stroll away was 'Strength' where three burly naked men were carrying a massive girder over their shoulders. I'm sorry, but one cannot help but look at a certain nether region and I jokingly said to Camilla, 'Are all Norwegian men like this? Or was this carved on a cold day? Ha ha!'

'Oh no', she replied sadly with a sigh 'all Norwegian men are like this...' Camilla later married an English guy!

At the centre of the park is a massive column of people, each holding another up in the air as they entwine the column. As I say, impressive.

We had many outstanding claims for divers who were injured on oil rigs, well, actually diving deep under the rigs. It was curious (at least to me) that all of them seemed to have suffered an inner ear problem at roughly the same age, about their mid-forties. The cause was put down to excessive diving and all were bringing workers compensation claims. The significant difference between workers comp and employer's liability is that to bring a WC claim it is unnecessary to prove negligence, simply that you are injured at work. Our Chicago office had written the policy believing that WC was the same the world over. It isn't. Significantly, in Norway a WC claim is rarely closed. The claim is assessed and paid and you'd think that would be that, but no. If the claimant's condition deteriorates then he can come back and have the claim reopened, and that is what all the divers were doing.

The only solution was simply to overpay them in return for a binding release. It took ages to wrap up and it is fair to say our Chicago office was not happy with the outcome.

Much more fun, at least for me, was a claim involving welding rods. A company we insured had supplied welding rods to a company manufacturing oil rigs.

Unfortunately, a huge number of rods had been mislabelled and did not contain the right amount of chrome and that meant that the welds in which they were used were considered 'suspect'. I think it is fair to say that sending out a multi-million-dollar rig with dodgy welds would not be considered a 'good thing'. The only solution was to grind out all the suspect welds and re-do them and the cost was considerable.

I went with my lawyer, Artur, to see the claimants at their factory at Sandefjord, which was a short drive from Oslo. The managing director met me and introduced his team of lawyers and we sat down to go through the claim. Of course, the lawyers were all trying to score procedural points off each other and I thought this was tiresome as we were not getting close to settling anything.

Exasperated, I said to the MD: 'may I suggest that you and I fire our legal teams and send them into another room to discuss international tort reform or how to resolve the Arab/Israeli conflict, or 'something' and leave you and I to talk about what matters – money. If you and I cannot resolve this between us then we can ask the reptiles to come back and they can play their legal games. What do you say?'

'Mr Cottington, that sounds like a very good idea' and with that, both legal teams went off to pull the wings off flies or whatever they do for fun.

The MD had a spreadsheet of proposed figures for the repairs and some actual invoices for the repairs carried out. I looked at the huge numbers and I could see that there was some scope for savings here and there. I also said that if we were to settle the matter now, rather than in a year or two with conventional litigation, I would be paying up-front, so wanted a further discount. The MD smiled and said I drove a hard bargain, but he could see I was being fair, so we concluded the matter and shook hands. When the legal teams returned, they were somewhat dismayed that the case had settled, presumably they were looking to bill the case for a couple more years!

Chapter Fifteen

BILLY

Not long after I joined CIGNA in 1986, I was sent a worker's comp (WC) claim for Billy.

Billy is, and was, one of the saddest cases I have ever dealt with. Billy worked in Saudi Arabia for an oil company and was driving back one evening to his compound and did not see that ahead of him on the road another car had crashed into a massive lamppost and it had fallen horizontally, but not to the ground. The lamppost was now lying across the carriageway but at windscreen height and Billy never saw it and he drove straight into the post at around 60 mph in his pick-up truck. The concrete post came through the windscreen and smashed into his face.

Billy was married to Linda and they lived on the Isle of Wight. I was asked to visit Linda to arrange the care package for Billy.

I drove to the IoW, crossing over by ferry, and eventually found Linda's house. She was a very nice lady and had a very young daughter aged about 4 years. In speaking to Linda, she told me she was a nurse and knew precisely not only the extent of Billy's injuries but the gloomy prognosis. It looked very bleak indeed. Billy had a compressed brain injury; he was unable to speak much and when he did it was a mixture of English and Arabic. He was blind in one eye and had lost a lot of teeth and had fractures to his skull and arms.

Fractures heal, but the lack of cognisance meant that

Billy could not do any meaningful physiotherapy and that resulted in his wrists and hands becoming like claws. He had (and has) no appreciable comprehension of his surroundings, but was able to recognise Linda.

The WC package that had been procured for Billy only paid for his medical care, but as I said to Linda, it was for life. His wage losses would be paid by his company, but I guessed for only so long. Things were going to get tough for Linda and her daughter. However, I said that my duty was to do what was medically best for Billy and until his condition stabilised, that meant a long stay in hospital on the 'mainland' as the folk on IoW call it.

Over the next year or two I got Billy transferred to a specialist unit in Cheshire until it became apparent that they could not do any more for him.

Linda had naturally wanted him back home, but I told her that Billy needed 24/7 care with specialist nurses and doing that at your own home was an invasion of her privacy and might not be the best for Billy. Via Social Services on IoW, we managed to source the rental of a three-bedroom bungalow. One bedroom could be used for Billy, another for his night shift with the third used for storage and physiotherapy. By now Billy was incontinent too, suffered fits and could barely walk.

I dealt with Billy for the next 9 years until my move to London, during which time Linda and I had a very good professional relationship. She frequently phoned me with a shopping list of appliances and aids for Billy's care and I would go over to see the team annually and make sure everything was running smoothly. Sometimes it wasn't. When mobile phones became commonplace, I got to see the bills and could see that one of the carers had a lot of calls to 'non-Billy' numbers. The carer was told that she would have to pay the extra charges for which she became resentful and then violent towards Billy. I knew he was difficult sometimes; he had a brain injury and could be very uncooperative, but violence to a patient was unacceptable in any circumstance. We got her fired.

Whilst I can deal with people with physical injuries, I have always found it hard to deal with brain injuries. In the early days, Billy used to recognise me – mainly because I had a beard and Billy hates people with beards – he pointed and said loudly 'Beard!' which was usually my cue to go and sit out of his vision as he could get upset with any change in routine. Even if his lunchtime sandwich is cut in a different way it can cause a tantrum. I have the utmost admiration for those who can care for patients such as Billy, but it is beyond my abilities.

By the early 2000s, I was back in Maidstone and a colleague had the Billy file, which as a paper file was about two feet thick. I knew the file and had invested a lot of time in the early days into the handling, so I offered to take it back. It was returned with a rather alarming amount of speed. I dealt with it for another eight or nine years until I was able to transfer it to Glasgow as by now the payments on the file were pretty routine and that mundane task was something I could easily delegate.

Over the years we arranged a lot of outings for Billy to try to give him some enjoyment in his life. He used to go horse riding at a special school and trips just to get an ice cream at a café, but sadly he cannot walk any longer and rarely leaves the bungalow. His carers have been with him for many years too.

The company that deals with the nursing staff, by purest chance, operate out of offices in my village. If I hopped over the back garden fence, I could practically be in their car park, so I still undertake annual audits of the invoices and troubleshoot for Linda from time to time.

I suppose I have been dealing with Billy and Linda on and off now for something like 35 years. Our children have grown and Linda remains married and devoted to Billy, though I believe she does have a new man in her life.

Billy is very disabled now, wheelchair-bound and arthritic. He watches TV all day but no one is entirely sure whether he has any comprehension of what he is watching, but turn it off and he shouts! However, Billy only needs to sneeze or cough twice and a doctor is summoned. He has better healthcare than any pensioner I know.

I fully realise that this story is not in the least humorous... sometimes certain claims can leave an indelible mark on one's conscience and soul. Billy's case certainly left an impression on me.

Linda and I still exchange Christmas cards.

Chapter Sixteen

THINGS GET A BIT HOT

One summer I had been asked to audit a reinsurers portfolio of claims in Austria. Smashing! I had never been to Austria and arranged my flights so I would have at least half a day to do a small bit of sightseeing in Vienna, where the audit was to take place. I was learning how to manage a bit of 'me time'!

I'm not keen on audits, especially the way we had to do them. To my mind if the right result is obtained and everyone is happy, does it matter at all that a letter was answered after eleven days, instead of ten? Criticising a fellow professional, internal or external, for that misdemeanour seems utterly pointless to me, but that is what we are supposed to do, only I won't. When the auditor comes to be audited (which we do) I always come out as the most lenient scorer. That is not to say I won't give a bad score for inaccuracies, poor file management and making wrong decisions, but a day or two late in answering a letter? Oh, come on.

The files were of course in German and sometimes French, but numbers are numbers and I can read those. I had an independent loss adjuster with me who could read the languages and after a day and a half, we decided to have an early finish and beetle off to a museum. The museum we chose happened to have an exhibition of Austrian gold and the Royal Family, the Habsburgs. The exhibition was interesting and there seemed to be an awful lot of picnic sets. Judging by the wear on the cutlery I guess they picnicked a great deal, but to sit on a lawn with gold cutlery, massive gold candlesticks and other fripperies seemed to take opulence and wealth to a ridiculous extreme. We had been at the exhibition for about an hour when I got a phone call.

'Trevor, it's Chris. Are you still in Austria?'

'Oh yes, hard at it, just leaving the office now and we have another half day to go.'

'Well, forget that, let the adjuster wrap up, you are off to the Czech Republic as an oil refinery is on fire. If you get a move on you can get an evening flight to Prague. The brokers will meet you at the airport and drive you to Litvinov where the refinery is on fire. I want you to report back with the loss estimates as soon as possible. OK?'

So, explaining all to my colleague, I hurried back to the hotel, checked out and got a taxi to the airport. I had about an hour to get a ticket and as I only had hand luggage check-in was easy. I made the flight with about 10 minutes to spare before take-off. Looking out of the window of the fairly small aeroplane I saw the wings had propellors. Yes, propellors! I'd not been on a light aircraft like that since a trip to Rotterdam in my AIU days. There was, to my astonishment, a stewardess and I am convinced that every time she walked up and down the aisle with a tray of snacks and drinks the plane tipped up or down. It was still relatively light in the evening and I had a good view of the Alps as we flew over them.

At Prague airport, I was met by the broker and he drove us to a hotel in Litvinov, where I was greeted by another broker and another claims guy like me from the 'lead' carrier of the risk and a loss adjuster. We were told that the refinery was still on fire (yikes) so a site visit would not be possible until at least tomorrow.

We had a few beers and wondered what the following day would bring. As it turned out, not a lot. The refinery burned all of the following day but CCTV footage was available for us to watch on videotape.

The brokers put in the video and we began to watch. The fire was well underway and every so often there was an explosion and a massive plume of fire and black smoke billowed into the air.

'Oops, there goes another five million dollars!' said the broker, rather too cheerily for my liking.

'Nah, I doubt it' I replied. 'Those are storage tanks of fuel. If the refinery machinery were damaged, the cat cracker etc, that would be more expensive... but what we can see there is fuel going up.' No sooner had I said that, than another 'boom' and fireball.

I was puzzled though. I asked the broker, 'Where was the bund?'

(All storage tanks of chemicals and fuel, are surrounded by an impenetrable wall, called a bund, so that in the event of a leak, the liquid is retained within the bund. The volume capacity of any bund is supposed to be the volume of the contents of the tank, plus at least 25% to allow for the extinguishment water.)

We replayed the video and freeze-framed the image. I could not see the bund at all. Then as the video played, we could just see the top of the tank blow like a champagne cork, but there was no sideways spread of fire.

The adjuster was looking at the file and the history of the risk. 'Got it' he said, 'the refinery was built by the Germans in 1943 or so and the storage tanks have bunds that go to the full height of the tank, with only a small gap between the metal tank and the concrete bund. They were built like that to withstand Allied bombing. Only a direct hit from on top would cause much damage. Quite ingenious really. I've certainly never seen anything like it.' Neither had any of us.

The brokers were convinced that the claim would be north of $50m. I said I would be surprised if it went over $10m but I added that the market needed a big loss as premium rates were lowering and no one was making money.

The strange thing about insurance companies is that the general public seems to dislike the fact that insurers make money at all. If an insurance company is making money, it means they can afford to pay claims. But some people seem to regard insurance as a Christmas saving club. 'I've paid my premiums for years and now you tell me the claim is not covered!' is a familiar cry. Yes, well, Mr Policyholder if the claim you are making is excluded by the policy which is a contract, then it is no surprise the claim is denied. We are not a charity. I have had many arguments over the years with policyholders who buy a 'plain vanilla' policy and then exclaim we are thieves and charlatans when the claim they make falls within an exclusion. When that happens, I often ask what car they drive?

'A Bentley if you must know.'

'You do know that you can buy a much cheaper car? A Ford Escort for example. Oh, it doesn't come with a drink cabinet and electric windows or heated seats. But it will still get you from A to B and probably just as quickly and with cheaper tax and fuel cost. It's strange isn't it, that you are prepared to put your backside into an expensive car whose sole function is to get you from A to B, but when it comes to your business, something that matters, you shop around for the cheapest policy you can find and buy one without the car equivalent of heated leather seats and a self-adjusting fog lamps... and then you complain your backside is cold.' That usually shuts them up.

The fire continued to rage the whole of the day and the news was that the extinguishment foam (which is toxic by the way) was three metres deep in places so it may take days before a proper schedule of damage could be prepared. I had decided that there was nothing more we could do, in fact, we hadn't done anything at all apart from drinking beer and watching CCTV videos, but I was satisfied that the damage was confined to pipework, tanks and lost fuel. There was no apparent damage to any process equipment so I thought the loss potential would be $10m or so. A proper assessment of the physical damage would have to wait for a week until access was permitted. Meantime, as the policyholder did not have business interruption cover, I need not concern myself with how long the repairs would eventually take. I decided to return home and reported to the underwriters that I was suggesting a loss of $10m. 'Not enough,' they said, 'we need a big one to move the market.' They seemed genuinely disappointed that the policyholder had not bought business interruption cover as that would certainly have added millions to the loss. The claim was settled a few months later for around $7m...and rates didn't increase.

Off to Riyadh again, this time no taxi 'issues'! A large glass works had a fire and there was a big claim in the offing. The insured predominantly made glass perfume bottles as well as ashtrays and vases. A fire had gone out of control on one of their furnaces and a lot of machinery had been destroyed, or so they said.

In desert regions water is of course scarce, so the fire services (often a division of the army) tend to control the fire by bulldozing down the burning property, often along with the neighbouring, but unaffected buildings, to prevent any spread.

The list of machinery that the policyholder said had been bulldozed into the desert was lengthy. I could tell that the sheer size of a furnace and other equipment 'lost' meant a huge pile of debris. The bricks for a glass furnace alone weigh about 200 tons.

My loss adjuster and I sat in a boardroom with all the claim papers, cross-checking with the 'invoices' or 'orders' most of which were in Arabic. I told the insured that I could not read all the Arabic script but what I would like to do is go and see all the debris in the desert, photograph it and cross-check it against the orders they had placed. I was told that this was 'not possible'. 'Why not?' I asked. I was told that the debris was bulldozed a long way into the desert and the scrap would probably have been taken away by thieves. I persisted and said that some of these items were so big only a crane could lift them, but I'd like to take a look anyway. Once more I was told it would not be possible to see the debris.

After an hour or more of gentle negotiations, I said that we would consider the claim if the insured sent us the photos of the damaged equipment together with the replacement invoices, not orders.

Before I left the MD of the company who was referred to as 'Doctor Doctor' (on the basis that he had two doctorates, though in what subjects, no one was brave enough to ask) offered us both a leaving gift - a selection box of the perfumes and colognes that the company made. I thanked him profusely for the kind gifts and assured the good Doctor(s) that we would not delay in dealing with his claim.

Back in the car to the hotel, I was wondering out loud how I would get the perfumes home as there were a lot of them and would doubtlessly have to be declared at Customs. The loss adjuster told me not to bother and toss them in a bin as the scents were not to the Western taste and would probably burn my skin anyway. Hmm, but free is free and Karon may like them. Brownie points could be earned. Back in my room I looked at all the bottles and had a brainwave. I put each into a plastic bag and labelled them 'INSURANCE CLAIM: fire damaged stock/contaminated – for analysis only' and hoped that would be good enough if I got stopped at customs.

I wasn't stopped at Customs and got all the bottles back home safely. The names on the bottles meant nothing to me as they were in Arabic and I could not tell whether they were for men or women. Karon came to see what I was doing, took a sniff of each bottle, declared them 'rank' and tossed each into a waste bin. No Brownie points there then!

Eventually, the amended claim came in from the glass factory together with an apology. Apparently, the fire was much smaller than they had told me and the orders I was looking at were for a new extension to the factory and they had inadvertently become mixed up with the claim papers. I raised an eyebrow...of course they did.

Chapter Seventeen

FREYA

One January, Eivind from Oslo phoned me with an invitation. He and Trond had set up their law firm and were anxious to improve their English language skills so they had booked a week-long course in London; would I like to meet up for dinner? Of course I would.

A few days later there was a change of plan. Both Eivind's and Trond's wives had said that it was too dangerous to travel to London 'because of the war'. I was slightly puzzled as I did not think Norway was at war with anyone, possibly the Swedes or Finns at a pinch, but the BBC News said all was quiet on the Nordic front.

Eivind went on to explain that as the UK was at war in Iraq their wives didn't feel it safe to come to the UK, so instead would I like to go to Norway for a week and teach them English and a bit of English law? So, if I understood that right, it was safe for me to go to Norway but not for them to come to our war zone? The rate of exchange is one Englishman equals two Norwegians. All my expenses would be paid and they would pay for my time. They reasoned that provided my time and travel costs were below what it would have cost the two of them to come to London, they were ahead of the game. I said I would go, but I could not be paid as that was against company rules and I'd be taxed on it anyway. It was agreed I would go over for a week in February so I booked a week's leave.

I flew to Oslo on a Sunday and was picked up at the

train station by Eivind and taken to his house. I had taken gifts for his three children. Whatever I had chosen for his girls turned out to be far too young for them, but the gift of Lego for his boy was accepted with glee. Peder and I then set about assembling the spaceship on the floor (I commented, with a knowing wink, on how 'flat' it was). I spoke no Norwegian and Peder no English but the universal language of Lego ensured we both had fun.

After dinner the children were retiring to bed and the girls were whispering to their parents about 'something'. I commented that whispering was pointless as I couldn't understand them if they'd been shouting. The girls were learning English at school and gave me a lovely rendition of 'London Bridge is Falling Down'.

The next day Trond came by and we drove out of Oslo up into the mountains to a place called Skien. We stopped by the massive ski jump and I could immediately see how brave/foolish ski jumpers are. Just looking up to the top gave me vertigo. I was told that the jump at Lillehammer, where the Winter Olympics had been held a few years before, was even higher.

The snow was quite deep and after a drive of an hour or two, we pulled up outside an enormous house. This was Eivind's 'winter house'. He had a 'summer house' too down on the Oslo fjord. There was a great number of boxes of food and holdalls to take out of the 4x4 to the house and the snow was waist high. It was tough going just to reach the front door. Front doors in a lot of countries open outwards, for fire safety I believe, and this meant digging out about 5-6ft of compacted snow before we could get in. We took turns shovelling and eventually, we had cleared enough for Eivind to get his key into the lock. He pulled back the door and we stepped in to be met by a gust of heat. I said, 'Did you leave the heating on??'

'Oh, yes' came the response, 'otherwise it would be very cold!'

All the houses leave the heating permanently on over the winter and Eivind used this house for about 6 weeks in every 6 months. Global warming? Blame the Vikings.

Inside the house was fully equipped, cosy and huge. I was convinced it was bigger than my own house.

So, there we were, three men in a snow-bound cabin, miles from anywhere. I'm sure I'd heard of 'specialist' films where that was the premise.

I had brought gifts too for them, books on English language, grammar, a thesaurus, a dictionary, a book on crosswords and a book of poetry. I was not sure what the structure of the 'teaching' would be, but they said that just spending a week talking would be good.

We spent the days chatting and trying to go for a walk in the snow, but it was too deep, so instead we concentrated on drinking aquavit, beer and wine. We each took turns to cook and I think I could hold my own in the cooking stakes.

I was returning on Friday, so in effect, we were only there mid-week, and as the days progressed, we did discuss the origin of English, accents and a whole range of other things.

When it came to my discussion on the English legal system, combined with how insurance is placed I hoped I had not bored them too much. In Norway legal fees are usually the responsibility of each party, although you can claim court fees and expert fees against the losing party, but only a small amount of your legal costs, known in England as party/party costs. I explained that in England the losing party ends up paying up to 80% of the winning party's costs and that can be considerable, sometimes even greater than the claim itself. My audience looked surprised at this, so I said that when you did receive the other side's bill of costs it was normal practice to phone them and say:

'Got your bill. You are having a laugh? Yes?'

'You phone them and say 'You are having a laughs?' This does not seem very professional to me.'

'Well,' I answered casually, 'it might seem so, but what you are doing is telling the other side the bill is outrageous and that there must be a mistake. Yes, we all do it – you are having a laugh mate.'

'OK, we will practise this: it is a laugh you are having?'

'Not quite: you are having a laugh. You are having a laugh.'

'OK, you are having a laugh. Got it.'

Not sure I was doing an awful lot for Anglo/Nordic business relations, but I was having a laugh.

Later that afternoon Trond came back from his bedroom pulling a wheeled black suitcase, one which I had dragged a few days before through the snow – it was fairly heavy – and offered me the handle. He said it was a small take-home gift for the family and inside were four Norwegian pullovers of traditional designs. They were really splendid and very warm. What a lovely thought. I still wear mine to this day.

On the final evening, we were discussing something meaningful, women probably, when Eivind repeated that he must pay me for my time. Once again, I refused pointing out I had already been given the pullovers, but they were persistent and suggested a gift instead. I said that the family were soon to get a dog, a female black Labrador, and if they wished they could put something towards the cost, but I made a strict condition – they had to name the dog. The name should be Norwegian, and something the family and I could easily pronounce. In the cabin, there were several books and Eivind and Trond began flicking through them to find something suitable. They came up with some names, but I said they were too difficult for the English tongue.

In the back of the crossword book, there were many lists of the gods and goddesses of various countries. I then noticed that the Norse goddess of love was called Freyja. The guys said that this would be a fine name for a female dog and so when I did get the dog, Freya she was. I dropped the 'j' though as the dog couldn't spell too well.

On the flight home, the non-veggie food option was (as always) meat or fish. I chose meat. My little tray arrived and peeling back the foil top there sat an ominous-looking chunk of brown meat. 'And this is?' I asked the attractive stewardess. 'Oh, elk, sir. I believe you also call it reindeer'. Sitting on top of the meat was a little cherry tomato. It soon dawned on me; I was eating Rudolph! I think the Norwegians were definitely having a laugh.

I gave them regular updates on 'their' dog and Freya lived to just short of 17 years.

Chapter Eighteen

STANDING ON MY OWN TWO FEET

Our Marketing department had decided that the company needed to be more visible in the insurance market with an emphasis on construction and suggested a 'roadshow' featuring several departments. The underwriters had said that whilst they were happy to do a couple of slots, it would be better if the event lasted a whole day, finishing perhaps around 3 or 4 pm.

A team was assembled and I was chosen to be the voice of claims. I roped in a firm of solicitors to help with two of the presentations. It was thought that the roadshow would be put on at hotels in key regions and brokers and policyholders would be invited. Over two weeks, we would do the talks in Southampton, Watford, Swindon, Birmingham, Manchester and Hitchin. Eventually, a plan was put together and the running order would be:

History and Overview of the company
Our appetite for construction and underwriting
Risk surveys
Health & Safety update
Lunch
Claims stories
Legal Update
Question time

As can be seen, I had been consigned the slot after lunch, the one that nobody likes to do, though I didn't mind. I planned to tell a few 'war stories' such as the chap who fell from the roof, together with how we are there to help get matters resolved. 'Safety is no accident' would be one of my messages, because whilst there may be an injured person at the end, the time taken by all parties in reporting and investigating on building sites should not be overlooked. For every hour that parties are dealing with paperwork and the HSE is an hour lost building something and that can cause delays and hidden costs. Specifically aimed at contractors I included a piece about the familiar road sign 'DANGER – MUD ON ROAD' and asked the audience what they thought it meant. I got the typical answers, namely that there was mud on the road and that motorists needed to take care. I explained that the sign meant different things to different people – it all depended on what hat you were wearing.

I said that if a similar sign were in a supermarket where someone had spilled a bottle of ketchup, would you expect the spill to be cleared up, or the sign left there for days or weeks? After all, what is the worst that can happen if someone slips over on ketchup? I then played a Police video of a road traffic accident involving three cars all badly smashed up. Roofs taken off, that sort of thing. In one car the hand of a young girl can be briefly seen, the rest of her body is covered by a blanket. I said that the car accident was the third on that stretch of road in two weeks and the contractor had done nothing to sweep up the mud. The site agent could be prosecuted for manslaughter. I had asked a stooge in the audience to assist me with the next part. I stood in my black three-piece suit and putting on a barrister's wig and gown, I pointed to my 'stooge' and asked him to stand. He did so, wearing a construction hard hat. I then began in my sternest tone:

'You and you alone are responsible for the death of a 17-year-old girl' I boomed. 'Her life was cut short because you Sir, did nothing about the dangerous and very obvious hazard of mud on the public highway. You knew that mud is a hazard because you put up a sign, but that is all you did. You could have sent a couple of chaps out with brooms to sweep it up, but no, you thought a sign was all that was needed and motorists were to look out for themselves. Ladies and gentlemen of the jury, I ask you to find this man guilty of all charges and that the court make an example of him by imposing a lengthy prison sentence to the maximum allowed by law.'

I paused for a moment and then added:

'OK, I know I am mixing up criminal and civil matters here, just for effect, but you take my point? You need to do something. A sign like that does not absolve you of responsibility – don't think of it as a 'get-out-of-jail-free' card. Indeed, you could end up inside jail, nervous in case you drop the soap in the showers.'

You could have heard a pin drop.

The first talk did not go so well, the history of the company was boring and frankly, no one was in the least interested. We had feedback forms and using the data from those it was decided to drop the 'history' slot altogether. My talk seemed to be well received.

As I grew in confidence my talk began to flow more

easily and wherever I could I would refer to solicitors as 'scaly reptiles' which usually got a small laugh.

By the third talk, the chap who preceded me was a solicitor called Ron. Now Ron was an experienced orator and was a natural speaker. He knew his talk by heart and so delivered it with slides all without notes – the swine. But Ron started to steal my gags: 'After lunch, you will hear from Trevor who refers to solicitors as 'scaly reptiles'. We are not like that; we prefer to be thought of as rhinoceroses, you know, thick-skinned, hard-nosed and always ready to charge!' Which of course got a great laugh.

I needed to think fast. Over the sandwich lunch, I changed part of my talk.

'I know you have just heard Ron compare solicitors to rhinoceroses. Complete nonsense. Rhinos are much cuddlier for a start. Yes, I have referred to solicitors in the past as reptiles, but now that I come to think about it, they are more like wasps. Most of us have no idea what they do, they seem to be completely useless, you see them everywhere, they all look the same, they are irritating and occasionally you get stung by one, but it is not usually fatal!' Which got a greater laugh. I didn't know it, but a gauntlet had been metaphorically thrown down.

During the presentation in Birmingham, I was midway through my talk and had finished the story about the chap falling off the roof onto his delicate parts, when a man stood up at the back of the room and yelled:

'Telling that story is highly inappropriate! That man was my brother and I object in the strongest possible terms about it being used in this way.'

I was visibly flustered and said that I had not used any names and the story was largely untrue anyway (it wasn't, but I needed a get-out-of-jail-free card) but the man continued:

'Yeah, well it wasn't funny... that's what Ron told me to say!' and there was huge laughter and applause.

Ron and I agreed to keep our jokes in but I needed just one final little dig and the lady solicitor who followed me, Claire, was unfortunately the brunt end.

Claire was not needed in the morning slot so she tended to arrive after lunch, to get in more billable hours, I suspected. I had known Claire for many years, indeed when I first met her, she was a trainee and now she was in charge of a department (she later became the Senior Partner/CEO). Crucially she had not heard the banter between Ron and me and on this day, she arrived mid-way through my talk. As I was concluding, I said:

'In a moment you will hear from Claire. As wasps go, she's a nice one. But what Claire may have missed from the lunchtime news is that from April 1st, there is to be a new Government regulator to standardise solicitors' fees. (At this point I could see Claire furiously scribbling notes). Water is regulated with Ofwat, gas and electric with Ofgen and solicitors will be regulated with... Ofrip!' (Big laughs from the audience). Throwing her pen down, Claire gave me a steely look and a grim smile.

Many years later it was decided that we ought to do a similar 'roadshow' but this time all the speakers were to be in-house and the audience was just brokers. We had a marketing department and they were organising the venues and sending out the invitations. The proposal was to start the talks start at 8 a.m. and finish by 10 a.m. Breakfast was to be supplied and the early finish was timed to enable people to attend and not have much taken out of their working day.

The speakers all attended for a run-through and to offer critiques of their colleagues. This allowed us to tweak what we were to say and make for a smooth and professional talk. It was agreed that there needed to be a chairman and he would introduce each speaker. We each had twenty minutes and my talk was on 'Exporting to the USA, the Perils and the Pitfalls'.

In the running order, I was last on. This enabled me to take some of the references from earlier speakers and enmesh them into my presentation. During the rehearsal, I gave my talk and at the end, I waited for the critique.

'It's not bad Trevor, but there seem to be an awful lot of pauses.'

'Yes, the pauses are when I play the music.'

'Music? Music? What music? You are playing music?'

'Oh, yes. Whenever I refer to American juries I play some music, not much, just a few seconds.'

'What music?'

'Oh, the banjo bit from the film 'Deliverance'. I will also develop a bit of an eye twitch too.'

'Oh my God' he exclaimed, 'This will either work well... or you will crash and burn.'

Marketing had told me to be at the venue by 7.30 a.m. for a sound check. But I said I was last on at 9.30 and my train did not get into London until 8.00 a.m. so it was not possible, besides, I said, I'm the headline act. The speakers before me will have sorted out any sound problems! She gave me a withering glare.

The venue was packed. Give brokers a free breakfast and they will come. The talk before mine was one which I had said ought to have been cut. It was all about statistics and loss ratios, actuarial figures and such like. It was tediously dull to me and I don't think the audience thought it was interesting either. That talk over, I was introduced and I took to the lectern.

'Well, thanks Stan for that absolutely riveting talk, the audience is as high as a kite...I've no idea how I'm to follow that, but I suppose I'll give it a go'. And I launched into my talk. My opening was a gag:

'How do you stop an American attorney from becoming so depressed they are on the verge of suicide? No one knows? Oh, good!'

As soon as I came to one of the 'pauses' I flicked a button on a CD player and the familiar banjo music began to play and I twitched an eye. Someone at the back of the room said 'That's Deliverance' and there was some general laughter. My talk was not all laughs, there were some serious points made, but I think I delivered it with a certain style. When I finished, I had on the screen a picture of the banjo player from the film with the title 'a typical juror' and as the last banjo notes faded away, I sat down. There was huge applause and from some, I even got a standing ovation, although I accept that they may have been trying to be first out the door.

I was warmly congratulated by my colleagues and it was agreed that we ought to do it again. The lady from

277

marketing said nothing to me, in fact completely blanked me.

In the audience, that day was Andrew, a broker from a major broking house and he asked me if I would do my talk at Lloyds? I said I would and when it happened it was one of my proudest achievements. The Lloyd's library was fairly packed and there were a lot of friendly faces there too. I knew that there were many solicitors, and international lawyers attending as well as USA attorneys... so I kept my risqué opening gag in! There were quite a few laughs as well as stifled gasps of horror.

I think the talk was well received.

And then there was the story of the Two Trevors. I was one and Trevor D was the other. One was younger, one was richer, I will leave you to work out which is which.

I had just won a major action in the High Court and then the Court of Appeal (CoA) on a technical point that was pretty boring, but saved the company around £60m and of that I saw not a penny. TD on the other hand was the lead lawyer on the case and his firm trousered more than a few bob. The background to the claim, a construction project, was interesting. Answer this: how do you build over land on existing land? This is not a trick question, but at its simplest, how can you build something on top of something else and create new land? One answer is to build over an existing railway cutting. By covering the cutting with concrete arches, you create a tunnel underneath so the trains can pass, and by covering the top of the concrete arches with backfill/soil etc you create land on which to build something, like a supermarket for example. That was the plan but due to incorrect backfilling, the whole bloody lot collapsed causing masses of damage and other losses. Part of the claim was covered by our policy and some was not. The bit that was not covered resulted in the insured suing, but the High Court and then the CoA said Cottington was right... so I made case law (again).

The upshot of that was that the two Trevors were able to turn that case into a presentation, which we did successfully at a couple of major brokers. With blood rushing to the head and sensing stardom it was suggested that we then promote the difficulties faced with certain product liability claims.

At this point, I have to declare that in certain instances 'the law is an ass' and makes a mockery of product liability cover. The details of this are complex and pretty boring, to be honest, but I will try and pep it up a bit.

Imagine you are a factory making a bottled chocolate milkshake drink. It needs two ingredients – milk and chocolate which are mixed and bottled then packaged for distribution and sale. Got it so far?

OK, now imagine that within the chocolate you have brought in is something nasty...like, say arsenic.

You mix milk and chocolate to make a milkshake and on quality control testing someone says 'Hang on a cotton-picking minute, this chocolate milkshake has arsenic in it and cannot be sold or someone might drink it and die.'

The question then: is the milkshake *damaged*? I think most people would say yes, but curiously the CoA said no it isn't damaged because chocolate milkshake was never made. Arsenic is not an ingredient in chocolate milkshake and therefore chocolate milkshake never actually existed. (Yeah, I know, this needs thinking about – wrap a few wet towels around your head...I had to).

As it happened in the court case(s), we insured both the chocolate supplier and the milkshake manufacturer, so we were bound to get stung whichever way the court(s) decided, but as happens with grim regularity, we had to be seen to be doing what was right for both policyholders, so the case was taken all the way. I still think it is bad law though and I am quoted in an insurance magazine that the decision was/is 'weird'. However, it remains the law and using this and a few other cases we decided it would be a good thing to allow both uninformed insurance people and manufacturers to hear our talk. Shamefully, Trevor D would not allow me to use any music. My suggestion of using 'Ten Green Bottles' was dismissed without a moment's consideration, even though it was apt.

We had three gigs lined up, not quite the worldwide tour we had hoped for, but the final one was to be the showstopper, for it was at AIRMIC (the Association of Insurance and Risk Managers in Industry and Commerce) who were the people the talk was aimed at. We turned up on the morning in question and our host said that not quite as many people had shown up as had expressed an interest in the talk via email. 'How many?' I enquired.

'Just one I'm afraid,' came the sorrowful answer 'and to be honest he would turn up for the opening of an envelope, he comes to everything we advertise.'

'Which manufacturer does he work for?' I asked.

'Oh, the Catholic Church. Thinking about it, your talk is not really relevant to them, is it?'

'No, it isn't... and besides we will look pretty daft with two of us doing the presentation for 45 minutes to an audience of just one. I think we will have to cancel, OK?'

So AIRMIC remains ignorant of the nuances of milkshakes and other beverage manufacturing concerning product liability cover. Had they heard that there was to be a rendition of 'Ten Green Bottles' I have little doubt it would have been standing room only.

Chapter Nineteen

ODDS AND SODS

There are times when dealing with claims that you see a pattern of events and this causes you to 'raise an eyebrow'. A typical example is theft. Of course, people can be unlucky and homes or premises broken into numerous times, but more often than not it is simply that people do not learn from their mistakes.

A contractor on the south coast also had a small plant-hire business and one of the items that was forever being stolen were scaffold tubes. In this case rather than just the tubes, this particular type was of interlocking tubes, the sort that snap together to form a framework. After the fourth such theft from a 'secure' compound, I decided when the fifth claim came in, to take a look. I had agreed to a time to meet with the policyholder and as it happened, I was early.

The yard was surrounded by a chain link fence, and hedges and the main gate was a four-foot high, aluminium tubular gate, typical of the sort you find on farms. The gate was padlocked with a hefty chain. I walked around the perimeter of the compound and found that although there was a high metal fence, in places the fence posts (which slot into concrete blocks) were easily lifted out and it was possible to squeeze in as the sections of the fence were missing their interlocking braces. I didn't even get my suit dirty. I wandered about the compound, taking photographs, noting that there was a considerable quantity of scaffolding there, but it must have been there a long while as plants and weeds were growing between the stacks. I was wandering around inside the compound for twenty minutes or so when I heard a chap shouting 'Hello, hello'. I walked back to the main gate and there, leaning on it with his elbows was, as I soon learned, the policyholder, a man I thought to be in his late 50s/early 60s.

'I got here a bit earlier than I expected,' I said, 'thought I'd have a bit of a look around while I waited.'

'Oh, no problem,' the policyholder said and added 'nice and secure isn't it?' I don't think he saw the irony of that, what with me being in his 'secure' compound at the time.

'Not sure it really is secure actually,' I replied, 'what with me getting in here without any bother at all.'

'Hang on a moment, I can't really hear what you are saying,' and with that, he vaulted (yes vaulted) the gate and took a few steps to get closer to me. I repeated myself and added about him being able to get in without even opening the gate which, if nothing else, demonstrated how ill-secured the place was. I said that his compound was certainly not secure, he'd had five thefts in as many months and each one had cost him £1000 as a policy excess. With £1000 he could easily have made the fencing stronger and fixed properly. As for the loose scaffolding, I agreed that it would be difficult to secure, but all he needed to do was buy a few cans of fluorescent pink spray paint and mark them. The black and rusty examples we could see were pretty generic and impossible to trace... but pink scaffolding? It would stand out on any building site. The policyholder thought for a moment and then said that he thought that the scaffold was being sold as scrap. I said I could see why, the tubes I could see looked too rusty to be considered safe. I said that whatever the value of the stolen scaffolding was on a replacement basis, the policy only provided for written-down value. Given that thieves would have stolen the best stuff first, which we had paid for by the way, what was left were the dregs and said that his latest claim would not be entertained. Although he threatened to sue us, he didn't.

Talking of fences...

We insured a 'theme park' and I was asked to investigate a claim for a 14-year-old girl who had cut her finger on a fence. Theme parks have a lot of fences, not just around the perimeter, but around the roller coasters too and other attractions. There was no explanation in the letter of claim as to where in the park the accident had happened, but according to the letter, the accident was put into the accident book so I guessed that they would know the location. I was attending the park during opening hours and I felt rather smug by-passing the queue to gain entry, even though I was dressed in a suit and carrying a briefcase. From the reception area, I was taken to the security guard's office (actually a small portacabin) and introduced to a guard. I explained I needed to see the accident location and the guard said that it was he who found the girl in a distressed state out by the perimeter fence close to a roller coaster.

We walked to the spot with the guard smoking roll-ups all the way, complaining about how busy it was and how hot the weather was. The fencing in question was typical chain-link fencing about twelve or more feet high. The fence looked in good order and as I rubbed my hand over it, I said I could not see anything sharp where anyone could hurt themselves.

'No, not here' said the guard, 'up there' pointing to the top of the fence.

'But the top is covered in razor wire!' I exclaimed.

'Yeah, it does what it says on the tin' he replied with a crooked smile on his face. 'Little thieving cow was trying to climb in through the razor wire and must have got her hand in the loops of the razor wire. She had a nasty cut on her hand and had obviously just dropped the twelve feet or so to here, inside the fence. There was blood everywhere so I took her to the first-aid station and they patched her up, but I think they called an ambulance to take her to hospital.'

'And you are sure it was here, this spot, where it happened?'

'Oh yes, quite sure. I came back later and found her finger on the ground.'

'You found her finger?' I said, rather stunned.

'Yeah, picked it on from the grass and put in an old baccy tin. Still got it in the office if you want it? Looks like a little finger to me.'

I decided that perhaps I didn't need the finger after all (yuk) and when I called the claimant's solicitor, I gave him a metaphorical two-finger response to his spurious claim.

It was about 9.15 am and I was standing outside of Preston Coroner's Court, about to go in to hear a very difficult case, when I got a phone call. A broker was advising of a new claim for a fairly well-known contractor. I said to the broker that we didn't insure that company. He said we did, well, as of midnight last night we did and they had a serious accident at 8 am this morning. Nasty one too. Two guys had fallen from a window cleaning cradle at Canary Wharf and fell about 4-7 storeys. One dangled from a safety line, and the other landed on the concrete ground but was alive. Could I go and investigate? I explained that geography precluded any investigation by me for a few days, but I would get someone else to do it. We had been at risk for eight hours and already the annual premium had been blown!

As I was standing on the steps of the Coroner's court, I asked the Policeman at the door why the streets were closed and why there were so many Police about? He said that the Crown Court was next door and the 'Harold Shipman' murder trial was on... and at that moment a large prison van turned the corner flanked by four Police motorcyclists. Shipman was eventually convicted of 15 murders.

Coroner's Inquests are not for the faint-hearted and although open to the public they are not the place to go for a day out. I have attended more Inquests than I care to recall, all of them grim, but attending them is important as this is usually the first time all of the accident evidence is heard. We learn about the deceased, their family circumstances (married, children etc) as well as hearing an autopsy report, which can provide evidence about any underlying diseases which may have affected life expectancy.

The Coroner's Court is possibly the oldest in the world, established under Richard I in 1194. The Coroner has many rights and responsibilities, but for my purposes, the most important one is that a jury (by law all fatalities at work have to be heard before a Coroner's jury) has to hear sworn evidence from witnesses and come to a verdict. In reality, the jury has limited powers as they are only there to confirm who the deceased was, where and when they met their death and the cause of death. For the majority of the cases I dealt with these were 'accidental death/misadventure', 'death by neglect', or 'corporate manslaughter'. 'The one thing the Court/jury cannot do is find or apportion blame. As Inquests almost always precede HSE criminal prosecutions witnesses are at liberty not to answer questions if they feel they may incriminate themselves at a later prosecution, but if they do answer and later say something different, they can be found guilty of perjury.

I was attending an Inquest in Swindon about a sad case of a fork-lift truck engineer who was tinkering with the mechanism in between the fork mast and the body of the truck. The fork mast could be tipped forwards and backwards on this model of truck. For reasons only known to the deceased, he was in between the mast and body of the truck and reached up to move a lever and instead of pushing the mast away from the truck body, he must have been disorientated and pulled the lever in the wrong direction, and the mast squeezed him tight, crushing all the air out of his lungs. Unable to inhale, he could not yell for assistance and died of asphyxia in about two minutes. He lay there for about 45 minutes before anyone thought that something was wrong. As I say, grim.

However, the evidence in the case was not going quickly and the Coroner told the parties that the matter would be heard today and ordered the court policeman to lock the doors to prevent anyone coming in or out. The matter was over by 6.30 pm, two and a half hours later than normal... and in consequence, I got my first (and last) parking ticket. Annoyingly, I was not permitted to put it on expenses either.

A well-known confectionary manufacturer had a redundant building that was to be sold off. The company used to print their sweet wrappers and so had all the necessary machinery and paper and ink stores. As time progressed it was found to be cheaper to purchase printed wrappers from other printers rather than manufacture their own, so the printing factory was to be sold along with all the machinery and contents. Once the building was empty a schedule of dilapidations was needed and this was outsourced to a firm of chartered surveyors. The surveyor who came to the site was not just any rank-and-file surveyor, but the senior partner of the firm, a man of considerable experience and arrogance to match.

According to the young property manager (witness of the insured), the surveyor turned up on time and was asked if he needed a tour of the factory first, to get the layout. The offer was perfunctorily dismissed with a wave of the hand and a comment that he had undertaken hundreds of schedules in his time and did not need a 'youth' to accompany him. Being reminded that the factory was redundant, it had no electricity and so no lighting, would he like a torch? Again, the offer was refused as the surveyor said he had one in his briefcase, so the manager left him to it.

The survey was expected to last about an hour, but after two hours the property manager thought that maybe the surveyor was being a little too thorough, or he'd got lost, so he went to find him. On opening a door to the old main print room, by torchlight he could see that there was the surveyor spreadeagled on the floor, clearly in pain. He said he'd got into the main part of the factory, the light was dingy, but sufficient and then opened a huge door, stepped in and found that there was no floor on the other side and had fallen to the ground. His briefcase still containing his torch had skittered across the floor and in near total darkness had had to crawl across the floor trying to find an exit, with what turned out to be a broken ankle.

A claim was naturally made alleging that 'the building was unsafe to enter given that it had no electrical or natural lighting and was, therefore, a hazard'. The door through which the surveyor had come was defective too, given that there was no floor on the other side allowing a fall of 5-6 feet. My investigation concluded that had the surveyor looked at his plans first he would have seen that the building, constructed in the 1920s, had been designed so that barrels of ink could be rolled into the print room, leaving their taps over the edge of a platform (it wasn't a 'floor' as such) so that the printers could draw off the ink from below. The platform was about desk height and clearly to step off the edge in the dark was likely to cause someone to fall and injure themselves. The surveyor had not turned on his torch before entering the building, let alone entering the room, so this was a stupid act on his behalf, not my policyholder. Additionally, he was the senior partner of the firm who'd undertaken hundreds of surveys (so hardly a 'babe in arms' as we like to call the inexperienced) and more pointedly, had refused any offer of an accompanied tour. I decided the case was defendable.

As to the injuries it was also alleged, that in addition to the ankle fracture, he had suffered an ingrowing toe-nail because of the pressure of the ankle and foot plaster cast.

I had made a nuisance offer of settlement, but the claimant refused it and so the matter went to trial.

The judge found for the claimant in every respect. He thought it entirely reasonable not to turn on a torch until after entering a room (thus ignoring the fact that the torch was still in the surveyor's briefcase and what if the door had led to a lift shaft? Would that have been reasonable?). He said that our property manager was mistaken in that he'd offered to assist the surveyor, and that had such an offer been made, the surveyor would have accepted. Then he dismissed my surgeon's evidence (who had set hundreds of ankles in his 50-year career and had never seen an in-growing toe-nail from a plaster cast) in favour of the junior doctor of three years who had seen a few toe-nail problems in his short time in A&E.

I crashed and burned. You win some, you lose some I suppose.

Incredibly, a stolen car we had paid out on had been recovered by the Police. They were undertaking a numberplate check of a vehicle and found that the plates were false and did not match the etched numbers on the windows. The poor chap who had bought the car via an advert in a car magazine had been duped and had paid £3000 in cash for what he thought was a bargain price for a good used car. I now had to appear at Kingston Magistrate's Court to claim, on behalf of the company, the ownership of the vehicle.

Before my case came on, I met the chap (let's call him Adam) who had purchased the car. He was claiming that he had put on new tyres and wheels and was counterclaiming the value of the 'additions' he'd made. He had invoices to prove it, so that wasn't really in question. I did say, however, that I had no argument with his wheels and tyres and would give him the credit or he could buy the car from us legitimately. He said he'd take the cash as the car was, in his mind, 'tainted'.

The Court was busy. This was just after Ascot racing week and the court was packed with drunk drivers who were awaiting their turn at the gallows. Adam and I started to bet how much of a fine and sentence each driver would get. We soon found a major inequity. One guy, over the limit admittedly, was caught on a routine breath test and was about 20mg over the limit. He said he lived in Norfolk, was the manager of a hotel and lived 25 miles from his place of work and asked for some leniency. He got fined £750, six points on his licence and an 18-month ban. The next chap was stopped by a Police motorcycle patrol as he had two (female) passengers in the front seat of his

Porsche convertible and was found to be 35mg over the limit. His solicitor said he was a Harley St consultant and the loss of his licence would cause grave difficulties for him in undertaking his charity work and getting to his NHS Hospital where he worked for free. A letter saying something was handed to the Magistrates in support. He got a £500 fine, six points and a 12-month ban. The bare minimum. Adam and I agreed that there was no justice there.

This was, and remains, the only time in my life I have ever given evidence in court. My solicitor decided it might be fun if I read out for the benefit of the court the VIN (Vehicle Identification Number) of the car from the Vehicle Registration Certificate (called a V5) to compare it to that on the Police record. I do not know if you have ever looked at a VIN, but they are long, very long and a mixture of numbers and letters. I took the oath and when asked for my name and job title etc... I had to ask for a drink of water. My mind had gone blank. I knew I had a name, I'm sure I did when I came into court that morning. I blinked a few times and gave the right answer. Then after a few questions about my role and where I worked, I was then asked to read out the VIN from the V5. I did so. Then I was asked to read out the number on the Police record, in order 'to verify that they were the same'. I started to read it out for the second time and happened to catch the eye of the lead magistrate who started to smile, presumably at the verbal torture that I was undergoing. I gave the value of the amount we had paid on the stolen car and that we accepted that Adam had purchased the car in good faith, but the title remained with the insurance company and we were prepared to refund Adam the cost of the wheels and tyres once we sold the salvage. The court accepted this and agreed we could have the car returned to us for re-sale. The salvage was sold at auction and I sent Adam his money for the agreed amount for the wheels and tyres.

It had been a time of unusually high rainfall and there were reports of widespread flooding across the whole of England. A contractor who had been insured with us for decades was undertaking the construction of a new swimming pool in Aylesbury. All the foundations and a plant room full of machinery, pumps and the like were now under four feet of contaminated water. I appointed a loss adjuster, who I knew and respected, to look at and deal with the claim. He reported back to say that the damage could be greater than £1m and that the loss was due to the heavy rainfall the whole of England was experiencing. A local stream had overflowed and ran right through the building site. He said there was no recovery – the loss was attributed simply to storm damage.

On the face of it, the adjuster's explanation seemed plausible. Indeed, we had many other claims across the country, but I was puzzled. Aylesbury was on my patch and I knew it had a flood prevention scheme, so how come my building site was (apparently) the only place in Aylesbury to get flooded? I decided a site visit was needed.

I turned up and met the site agent sitting forlornly in his site cabin in a pond of water. The water was not draining away. I thought this was odd as nowhere adjacent to the site seemed to be waterlogged. I gathered that the loss adjuster had not physically been to the site but had called the agent on the phone and had spoken to him for about 20 minutes and based on that sent me a long report which gave the impression of a site visit, but without actually saying so. I was singularly unimpressed. I decided to take a walk.

Water of course flows downhill. Outside of the building site, there was a lane that ran parallel to a stream, so I followed the lane to a main road and walked a little way along. I could see that the stream flowed under a bridge (or culvert) under the main road. The water on the upstream side was deep, about fifteen feet wide, and filled with debris and muddy water. It was this muddy water that had backed up and was flooding the building site. I crossed over the main road to see the other, downstream, side of the stream and there I saw only a tiny trickle of water flowing. The stream at this point was about three feet wide at most and there was no debris to be seen.

On my walk back to the site there was an old man tending his garden. I stopped for a chat. I asked him about the flood and he told me that the meadow (on which the swimming pool was being built) was, historically, a floodplain. The name of the road was Osiers Way and Osiers were men who weaved willow into baskets... willow grows best when it is close to water, so why build on a known floodplain? He added that the stream frequently backed up and this was not the first time it had overflowed, but was the most serious.

I could see the beginnings of a recovery action but was unsure as to who to blame. Culverts have to be maintained and kept clear of debris for the very reason that if blockages occur, not only can it be difficult to remove them, but flooding can occur when the river or stream backs up. Well, that is what happened here... but who is to blame? Also, who commissioned a construction project on a known floodplain? The Local Authority may be in the frame, perhaps the National Rivers Authority or even perhaps the Highway Authority. I was unsure, but someone had to have a responsibility. I'd have to think about it.

Meantime I was off to metaphorically 'kick the arse' of the adjuster who'd lied to me.

A scaffolder had fallen from the scaffold he was erecting inside a building in Stevenage that was to undergo extensive repairs following a fire. He'd suffered a broken ankle. The massive building was nearing completion when a fire broke out on the roof and the subsequent smoke and extinguishment water damage was to add the better part of a year to the completion date. All the parties were unhappy and wanted the repairs to commence without any delay and to use as many personnel as possible to accelerate the completion date. We were already paying out hundreds of thousands of pounds for the fire damage, and now a serious accident.

The accident happened during the clean-up phase immediately after the fire. An internal scaffold needed to be erected to extend 5 storeys to the glass-sloped ceiling cum roof before the repairs to the damage could begin. I arrived at the site and was shown where the accident had happened. I was told that the reason the man had fallen was due to the scaffold plank he was standing on had snapped. This is unusual but can happen if the boards are part-sawn or have not been checked for damage. Anyway, the board was available and I took it with me for safekeeping in the car. The allegations against us though were frankly bizarre. The claimant said that he lost his balance on the scaffold due to the glass being swept from the roof down onto him. As the scaffold was incomplete (he was erecting it with his crew at the time) there were no safety rails etc. There was no mention of a defective board, but given that the board was supplied by his employers, that would have been an EL claim against his employers rather than a PL claim against the main contractors. EL was another insurer, PL was us.

I inquired about the falling glass and was informed that broken glass was being swept over the edge of an atrium. The glass was a special safety glass that shattered into tiny, relatively dull fragments when broken. However, the atrium was about 100 feet away from where the scaffolder fell. Gravity, it was said, could not get glass to fall 100 feet sideways. 'What about the wind' I asked, given that the building was now open to the elements following the fire, could the wind have blown glass that far? No one thought it plausible, I had the broken plank, and that was the cause.

I denied liability, offering an alternative explanation, namely the defective scaffold plank, and drew in the scaffolders as a second defendant, but the claimant stuck by the falling glass story. With no alternative cause being pleaded the matter went to trial... at Croydon County Court of all places, just a few hundred yards from my old office at AIU.

I met my team just outside the court doors and was

looking at the court list when I noted, wide-eyed, that the judge was Tim. I had instructed Tim when he was a 'senior junior' barrister* (he was my barrister on the crane collapse matter) and he had later been elevated to QC and now was a practising judge.

[* Barristers come in two flavours – Junior and Queen's/King's Counsel or QC/KC. A barrister may practice, or be called to the Bar, for one or forty-one years and still be a 'junior' but those with more years are known colloquially as 'senior juniors' and sometimes have more experience than those who are elevated to the rank of QC/KC who may be younger and less experienced. Once at QC/KC level, there is nowhere else to go, except to be offered by the Lord Chancellors Dept to re-train as a Judge. The pay of judges is considerably lower than the potential earnings of a QC/KC, but the job comes with many perks, including a pension. Oh, and since the death of HM Queen Elizabeth II, QCs became KCs the very next day.]

As I had investigated the claim and was offering an alternative theory to the accident, I was considered a witness and was there to give evidence. I wasn't looking forward to that prospect, but the breaking board was far more plausible than the drifting glass story.

I approached my team and said that I had to say I knew the judge in the case. I'd even had a social lunch with him at another solicitor's house the previous year. My barrister, a junior called Francis, said that he would mention this as soon as the trial opened.

The court was hardly packed as there were only three parties and there was no one in the public gallery.

Naturally, each party came with a barrister, a solicitor, a junior solicitor and a trainee (to take all the notes), plus the parties who were to give evidence...like me.

The court was ordered to stand by the Clerk and in strode Tim resplendent in his wig and gown. After bowing we sat and Francis immediately got to his feet.

'If it may please your honour, I am requested to bring to your honour's attention, that a key witness in the case of D1 [he means defendant one, my insured – the scaffolders are called D2] Mr Trevor Cottington is known to your honour.'

Tim looked over his half-moon glasses and looked behind where Francis was standing. 'Oh yes. Indeed, I do know Mr Cottington well, in fact, I have in the past had many instructions from him. Of course,' he added gravely 'if anyone here thinks I shall find fear or favour on his behalf I shall happily recuse myself and call for an adjournment and allow another judge to hear the case at a later date...' and he trailed off.

The claimant's barrister rose and said, in a rather oily manner, that he was sure the judge would hear the matter completely impartially and raised no objection to the case proceeding.

At this point, D2's barrister, Neil, rose to his feet and said that he too did not object and as far as D2 was concerned they were prepared to allow my statement to be taken as given and would not be cross-examining me anyway. (This was a turn-up for the books, I thought.)

'In that case,' continued Tim 'as there are no objections from the parties, we shall proceed.'

It is always the case that in trials the claimant is heard

first, then the defendant(s).

The claimant kept rigidly to his story about the falling glass and said that there had been complaints about it too (news to me, I thought). Francis did his best in cross-examination, but the claimant maintained that the board must have broken when it crashed onto the ground, not by breaking first causing him to fall. He would not be swayed.

Neil then twisted the knife by saying that the case now only rested on who the judge believed, the evidence of the claimant, who if he was to be believed had no case against D2, but to assist the court he said that D2 had come to terms with the claimant for commercial reasons and now was claiming that settlement against D1. (Ah, now I understand what you have done, you slimy git, you are asking the judge to believe the claimant, or me. I now know I'm going to lose. I was fuming.)

I have truncated events but that is the essence. While Tim retired 'to consider the matter', I was chatting to Francis about my flooding problem in Aylesbury. I wondered aloud if he had any thoughts? I said that I needed some advice on the matter and had recently seen a similar case involving flooding called 'Bybrook Barn' or something like that, but before I could continue my thoughts, Neil turned to me and said 'Bybrook Barn? Bybrook Barn? That was my case. I won it!' I turned to Francis and jokingly said 'You're fired, I'll instruct Neil.' At that point, the clerk returned and we all rose to hear Tim deliver his decision. Judgement for the claimant against D1. D1's claim against D2 fails and D1 to pay D2's costs in addition. I'd been done up like a kipper.

You win some, you lose some... but I may have said that before.

To be fair to Neil, he has invited me to a sumptuous Christmas lunch every year since, for which I am very grateful, even though he never fails to remind me of the time he beat me in Croydon County Court.

Chapter Twenty

MEDIATIONS AND SUCHLIKE

Mediations became all the rage in the late 1990s and early 2000s and were, I believe, originally conceived in the USA as a way of resolving a dispute with, effectively, a referee or mediator as they are known.

In the USA the mediator suggests to the parties settlement values of a case and presses them to come to a decision. In the UK we are, as one might expect, a little more reserved. Mediators merely suggest to parties that settlement parameters may be between x and y leaving them to work out the strengths and weaknesses of their cases and then to gradually coax the parties to make offers and counteroffers. I have participated in dozens of mediations and one of the key attributes is that everything discussed there is strictly confidential. This will make it difficult, if not impossible to give the names of parties, so I will use broad spectrum names, places and parties.

The format of UK mediations is generally the same. The parties gather in a multi-roomed building and set up camp. The mediator has his room and this tends to be the biggest room. The largest mediation I attended had probably 35-40 people in the room and, as will become apparent, maybe only five were really needed. The mediator will introduce themselves to each party in turn, and get the names (everyone uses first names as it is said that it makes things less confrontational) and positions of the parties (I tend to say that 'I'm the chequebook'). As the mediator has read all the parties 'position papers' pre-meeting, they ask whether we think the case can be settled? We say it could, provided that such and such party moderates their demands. The mediator will then go to the other party's rooms and do the same and generally by 11 a.m. we will all be called into the main meeting room for what is known as the plenary session. Here each team, starting with the claimant, will read out their position paper, add a few extra points and say what they are seeking – nearly always the amount they are suing for. The other parties then do the same. This is, to my mind, totally pointless as we have all read and re-read the position papers and not once in all my years have I, or anyone else, said something like 'Oh, now I have heard that, it changes EVERYTHING, awfully sorry …how much do you want?'

Lunch is provided at around 12.30 and it is not normally until 2 p.m. that offers begin to be made. If all goes well, a settlement is thrashed out by around 6 p.m., but I have known some go on to 10 p.m. or later and some even last days. I think in overview settlements are agreed due to a mixture of boredom and tiredness.

That is how they are supposed to proceed, but my first one in 1998 came as a bit of a surprise.

We insured a small housebuilding company that owned a large slice of land near Swindon. Unfortunately, they could not afford to build on it as they were strapped for cash and interest rates were high. A major housebuilding developer had the finance and the 'name' but crucially needed land and a local firm to build the houses. A deal between the two was made, basically 'on the back of a cigarette packet' that our insured would provide the land for free, they would build the houses and the developer would sell them, provide the finance and all profits split 50/50. It seemed a simple enough deal. In the end, 200 houses were built without any problem and both parties were very happy with the profits they made, which ran into a few million pounds each.

About five or six years later a single house suffered cracking caused, rather strangely, by land heave rather than subsidence, due to defective foundations. The developers paid for all the repairs themselves and without any warning sued our insured for about £200,000 being the cost of repairs and other losses. Our insured, the builders, were genuinely upset about the litigation as it came after the parties had enjoyed a good relationship from the start. However, they were in a difficult position both with the litigation and their insurance coverage.

Builders cannot get insurance for the repairs to their bad work – materials or workmanship. What they are covered for is the consequential damage following bad workmanship or materials. A simple example would be a builder constructing a wall using poor mortar. The wall collapses crushing a row of parked cars. The insurance would pay for the damage to the cars, but not for the rebuilding of the wall.

In this housebuilding case to repair the foundations the whole house needed to be demolished, so it was arguable as to whether the whole house was defective, or just the foundations that were not covered. The developer couldn't care less which party would be paying, the insurers or the builder... but the builders had no money.

With the profits they had made from the housing development, they had purchased several plots of land at the height of the property boom. They now found themselves with a land bank but no cash with which to develop them. The sale of any of the land would not only take time but may not be sufficient to pay the claim. The only asset they had was any proceeds they could squeeze out of me from their policy.

I was called to a meeting at a small solicitor practice, close to where I lived and nowhere near Swindon, who was not representing either party. I was greeted by Robert who said he was the mediator. (The 'what' I wondered?) Fiona was from the big law firm against us along with her client, Clive, from the developers. I was with my insured, Mike and my loss adjuster Martin.

Robert explained that this was a mediation and would be confidential etc. Fiona then went on to make her case and said that there could be no doubt about Mike's liability here – they made a bad house and Clive had paid for the repairs, please hand over £200,000 plus legal costs.

I was completely unprepared for this and said that in effect we had been ambushed. I did not know this was supposed to be a mediation, wasn't entirely sure what a mediation was... but we were here and prepared to talk and listen but I said that there were issues to overcome. Firstly, Mike's firm had not been given the chance to repair the house. Had they done so they would not be claiming any profit, costs would be minimised and Martin had guessed the true cost of repair might be £100,000. Secondly, there was absolutely no need for Fiona to become involved at all. The dispute could have been resolved between Mike and

304

Clive amicably and only if they fell out was it necessary to get solicitors involved, so Fiona could sing for her costs. Thirdly, Mike's only real financial asset was what our policy may, or may not, cover... but it was nothing like £100,000.

Fiona restated her case and said that unless they got £200,000 they would continue the action against Mike's firm and strip their assets.

It was at this point that I am slightly ashamed to say I 'lost it'.

'Clive,' I said rather angrily 'I don't know if you realise but Mike here has no assets – his firm has nothing in the way of cash. You can waste more money with Fiona but she is pissing in the wind... best explain that one to her Robert... as the only resource Mike has is a very limited amount that may be recoverable from my insurance, which at the very top end might be £25,000. Go ahead and get a judgment in default and push Mike's firm into liquidation but if you do that you won't even get my £25,000 because that will go into the Liquidator's pot and you will be just one of dozens of creditors who might get back a penny in the pound. Your call.'

It has always been my habit to speak to the parties who are out of pocket rather than their lawyers, who have zero interest in commerciality. I have held many settlement meetings and mediations without lawyers as they just get in the way of commercial resolution.

Robert called for a break and Mike asked if he could speak to Clive privately. So, Mike and Clive went off for a chat for about 25 minutes and came back and said that he thinks a deal could be achieved if I threw in £25,000. I confirmed that my contribution was on the table. I asked how he got to a settlement?

Mike explained that it was true they had no cash, but they had land and Clive didn't... so Clive accepted a proposal that Mike would give a smallish plot of land to Clive and between them they would build some more houses but instead of splitting profits 50/50, it would be 75/25, with Clive taking the larger share and would chuck in my £25,000 as an on-account payment.

And the deal was done all in a couple of hours too! Lawyers added nothing to the resolution.

Meantime, Neil had accepted my instructions on the Aylesbury flood loss. Letters of claim had gone to the Local Authority, The Dept of Environment and the Highways Authority. Each blamed the other for failing to clear the debris from the culvert. However, someone had cleared the debris and there was a film of debris removal. Apart from tree trunks, branches and leaves, there were old bicycles, a supermarket trolley (from a firm long since out of business) and of all things a Betamax video recorder and the accumulated debris filled a couple of skips. The stream now ran, or rather trickled, unhindered.

The loss had been presented at around £2m plus costs, overall perhaps about £2.5m, but if the claim went to trial the costs would easily push it to £3m.

Typical of the civil servants we were forced to waste time and money by making alterations to the names of the defendants. The DoE had changed its name to DEFRA (Department for Environment, Food and Rural Affairs), but finally one of them accepted that they were the correct defendant, and we proceeded to a mediation.

The plenary session was quick. We said it was obvious that the culvert had not been maintained for years, or at all, as the defendant had no records of ever cleaning it out, so we thought they had no defence to liability. As to our claim, we were comfortable with our numbers, but if they had a sensible proposal, we would 'listen'.

We were back in our room by 11 a.m. and there we stayed for five long and tedious hours.

It turned out that the Government had promoted mediation as a way of settling disputes and reducing the burden on the courts, but as a body the Government, or more accurately, a department had not mediated anything and had no experience in doing so. Our mediator explained to us that he was having to teach civil servants to 'haggle' but they seemed unable to grasp the concept. He said that they were happy to pay a judgement of £3m as in their eyes that was a 'bill or invoice' but until they had a bill, they could not pay anything. Also, in their opinion, if we were prepared to take less than £2.5m we did not have faith in our case and so they should pay nothing at all. It was also explained that anything over a certain figure had to be approved by the minister, at that time John Prescott.

It was coming up to 5 p.m. and I said that if we were to get a deal, we had to put something on the table that could be accepted by 5.30 p.m. by which time we thought civil servants would wish to end their day. I suggested £2.25m all-in and at 5.27 p.m. they accepted.

It transpired I was the first person ever to mediate with the Government.

I was also the first person to mediate a claim, in this case, a personal injury claim in Jersey. The facts of the accident were boring, a fall on a building site, but the claimant said he was unable to get any work solely because of his back injury.

The court practices and procedures in Jersey are, frankly, weird and difficult to understand.

The mediator was a solicitor from Leeds and I flew over from London with my counsel, Stephen. We were to meet with Caroline, our Jersey solicitor, just after lunch and the mediation was scheduled for the following morning. The meeting with Caroline went well and we were finished by about 3.30 p.m. and were expecting a dinner invitation, but nothing was said. Sadly, Caroline indicated she had another appointment and would see us in the morning.

Stephen and I left the office and wondered what to do. Stephen announced that maybe we ought to go for a beer as it was his birthday. I said no, shame on that, we needed to do something memorable... so I took him to Jersey Zoo!

We arrived rather late, something like an hour and a half before the zoo closed and I negotiated a two-for-the-price-of-one deal at the entrance. It's a lovely zoo, not that I saw much and vowed to return someday.

The following day we had the mediation and it was a case where liability was in dispute as well as quantum. I was puzzled by a long gap in the claimant's work history. Aged 16 he left school and found a job as an apprentice butcher. Then there was an unexplained gap from the age of 17 until he was in his late 20s when he took a job on a building site where he had an accident injuring his back. After much persuasion the answer came back that the claimant had been convicted of murder and that explained the 'ten-year gap' in the work history... and that, I added, was surely why he found it difficult to get another job. It was not because of the injury; it was because of the murder conviction.

After a long day, we got a deal that satisfied everyone and Stephen zoomed off to the airport to get back to London, but I and the mediator had a flight booked for the following morning. I suggested to the mediator that as we were staying in the same hotel we might as well have dinner together. He agreed and he was a good dinner companion. When we got the bill, I said that I would take care of it, but he was aghast. He said that it would compromise his impartiality and insisted on paying exactly half, right down to the last penny.

I have seen Stephen on many occasions since then where he has been both for and against me and he always reminds me of the time I took him to the zoo on his birthday!

Controlling a mediation is difficult for anyone especially where there are a lot of parties, each represented by solicitors and counsel... and all think they are right.

One eight-party action I was involved in had four claimants and four defendants. The lead defendant was me and I believed that we had a full recovery against any, or all, of the three parties behind me as it were – imagine an hourglass – I was the pinch point in the middle. I was liable to the four above but hoped to get all the sand down to the three below. The claim was tedious, so I will avoid mentioning it, but with eight parties the costs and expenses of all was, as ever, eye-watering. The mediation was getting to mid-afternoon and I said to the mediator that to try to save time and costs I would settle with the parties above and then squeeze what I could out of the ones below. Two of the three were prepared to offer something, but the third, represented by a snooty barrister said that he wanted to attend any settlement discussions I was having, but his client was not prepared to offer anything. I said 'Listen, mate, if you go to an orgy, join in the fun. You can't just sit on the sideline and just watch. If you are not prepared to offer anything then 'fuck off' back to your room and sit on the naughty chair and I'll talk to you later.' I was, as you can imagine, rather irritated at this point. The barrister turned and left without a word. My solicitor then said to me 'you do realise that you've just told a QC to 'fuck off'?' 'Yeah, well, he was getting on my nerves, but I expect he's heard worse.'

It took me an hour or so, but I had 'hard' numbers out of the claimants that I could now put to the guilty three. Two made sensible offers but the snooty third made no offer. I warned them that they were going to be facing another claim in Contribution and it would be sizable, but they were having none of it. In the event, I had to drop it due to a lack of witnesses and I was pretty cross about it too.

Months later I was at another conference in chambers I knew well. Sitting across the table was a chap who looked very familiar, but I simply could not place him. After an hour or so the penny dropped... it was Snooty QC! And he was on my side this time. Very embarrassing for us both I think.

A mediation of thirty or so was in progress and I had told everyone that although the start time was 8.30 a.m. at an office very close to Cannon Street, my train would not get in until 8.30 a.m. so I would be a few minutes delayed. (Yes 'delayed', remember?)

I entered the room and there was just one empty seat, mine clearly, but I had to walk round half the table to get there. I made some quip about everyone carrying on as doubtless they were just reading out their position papers and I'd read those and would catch up quickly enough. On the opposite side of the table sat a lady solicitor I knew well. I was the claimant this time so fairly relaxed about the whole matter. I caught her eye and mouthed 'New hair? Nice'. She blushed and looked down and scribbled some notes as if she were paying attention too. She glanced up and once again I mouthed 'Have you lost weight? Looking good' and winked conspiratorially. (I'll do almost anything to put off the opposition!). As the session ended the mediator asked if there were any questions. I said I had none, but added that as my train home was at 5.35 p.m. I was leaving at 5.30 p.m. to get it, so the defendants better get their chequebooks out in good time.

It got to 5 p.m. and still no sensible offer from the defendants, so I did not think that they were taking my time guillotine seriously. At 5.20 p.m. I rejected a low offer and made my final counter offer and ten minutes later I was out the door. Halfway across Cannon Street, my phone rang and I was told that they had accepted my deal. I am sure that if I had stayed, they would have pressed for a further round of offers. I do not mind a horse trade, but not hamsters.

Another mediation had more-or-less concluded and the only thing outstanding was £250 which happened to be the other side's policy excess and they were adamant that they would not pay it. My guy knew the director of the other side well, they did loads of business together, and this was, in reality, an insurer-to-insurer dispute, but policy excesses can scupper deals. My guy said in a broad Irish accent 'Pat, do you still bet on the horses?'

'I do' came the response.

'Tell you what, I'll flip you for it. Heads you pay me the £250, tails and you keep it'.

'Done'.

The coin was tossed and it came down 'tails'. Pat then offered to buy my guy a beer! All parties left happy, which is the best outcome.

Usually, all parties leave a mediation thinking they have either paid too much or accepted too little, but I suppose that works out just the same. In striving to keep matters professional, and knowing that in most cases the issue between the parties is almost always about money and that we meet the same parties time and again (the insurance market being smaller year on year) I have said it is worthwhile remembering that some days you are the statue, some days the pigeon.

Chapter Twenty-One

I'VE JUST REMEMBERED...

A lady had an accident and suffered a broken wrist. We did not think we were liable but the judge disagreed and awarded her £4500. However, the claimant did not think that £4500 was enough and, unusually, decided to appeal. This was my first Court of Appeal action and in reality, it was only about money, liability could not be Appealed.

At the time, £4500 was still a lot for a broken wrist, the settlement range was £2500-3500. She had some minor other losses but as far as we were concerned this was a good deal. However, in the notice of Appeal, she said her life was 'ruined' and she could not do any basic domestic tasks, such as shopping and picking up her grandchildren to give them hugs and wanted £50,000 to settle.

As the hearing was her Appeal on quantum, we were permitted to serve new evidence... and I got some surveillance on her. The hearing was back in the day when you could undertake 'trial by ambush'. The claimant went first, hobbling into court (rather theatrically for a broken wrist) and took the stand. She gave the judges her tale of woe and how she could not do anything and they seemed genuinely accepting of her story. Then our turn came.

Our private investigator was sworn in and then he wheeled in a portable TV and video recorder and saying nothing simply hit the 'play' button. The video lasted a good half hour and showed the claimant leaning over the freezer counter at Iceland supermarket and with her 'bad' hand picking up a frozen chicken and putting it into her shopping cart. At the checkout, she again used her 'bad' hand to put everything onto the conveyor belt and then to pack it into her shopping bag, which she again carried in her 'bad' hand. The film then cuts to her arriving at what must have been her daughter's house and two children come running to 'granny' and she picks them up with both hands. The video ended and again saying nothing further the investigator left the stand.

The lead Appeal judge called the claimant immediately back to the stand and asked what she had to say about what the court had just seen. She answered the immortal phrase 'Must have got me on a good day m'lord!' Her award was reduced from £4500 to £2500 but she was ordered to pay the defence costs of the Appeal, so she got nothing. Ah, shame.

I had to visit one firm of union solicitors in Southampton with grim regularity and our meetings were usually quite adversarial. We would argue over liability, quantum, costs... just about anything. One hot summer day, the sun was high, the tarmac was melting and I did not have an air-conditioned car, so was rather sticky. I thought that my opponent, being in a stuffy office would be ill at ease too, so I went into the meeting bearing gifts – to be precise an ice cream each. It occurred to me that anyone being offered an ice cream on a hot day is unlikely to refuse (he didn't) and it is difficult arguing with someone whilst licking an ice cream. It worked as we were very relaxed and when it came to speaking about the files he said, 'Look, I want £5000 on this one, £2500 on that... if you are going to deny this other one, I'll accept it, but on the last three I'll take a nominal £1000 on them, providing you are not silly about costs.'

'£5000? Wow. I'll tell you what, all the others are agreed, but let's not muck about, it's not five thousand is it? I thought three?'

'Meet me at four thou and we have a deal, OK?'

'OK, done.'

'Bloody hot day isn't it? Thanks for the ice cream by the way, nice touch. See the footie last night?'

We spent another thirty minutes talking inconsequential chit-chat. I knew he'd not forget the ice cream and at our future meetings we had got to the point of hardly bothering to argue the niceties of liability and quantum, he just said what he wanted on each case and if they were sensible, I'd agree.

A strange claim came in for a woman who had been hit on the head at a pop concert by, of all things, a football. The main act was a singer of some repute and I believe had a trial for Glasgow Rovers or some other Scottish team and he peppered his act by booting footballs into the crowd, which usually resulted in a scrum of people trying to get at a football as a souvenir. Let's call the singer Rod. Well, Rod kicked a football into the crowd and it hit this woman right on her forehead. She claimed whiplash as a result and brought a claim for damages.

I commissioned a medical report from a doctor in Harley Street and his report said words to the effect: 'I examined this middle-aged lady in my consulting rooms today. She was 4'8" tall and weighed 13s 5lb (187lb). She is by definition clinically obese. She explained the circumstances of the accident and said she had a whiplash injury. On examination, she had so much subcutaneous fat on her neck that I was unable to manipulate her neck at all. I could not understand how, absent any flexion, she could have had a whiplash-type injury. Footballers head footballs all the time and none to my knowledge ever get whiplash from the action.'

Just to add injury to injury, on leaving the consulting room, she fell down the stone stairs of the offices and broke her arm!

I sent the report to the other side and then gave them a call a few days later.

'I take it you have read the report?'

'I have. Not flattering is it?'

'No... and not worth diddly-squat.'

'Look, all she really wanted was a 'sorry' from Rod and maybe a signed album or two.'

'Well, I can get you those if that'll resolve it?' There was a shortish pause and then he said rather sceptically,

'You're going to sign them though, aren't you?' (He'd seen right through me then!)

'Look, she doesn't know Rod's handwriting and neither do you...so who'd know? But I'll give you £500 and she can buy his complete collection and still have a chunk left over. Deal?'

'Deal.'

Sadly, a lady in the front passenger seat of a car had gone through a windscreen suffering terrible facial injuries. She was not wearing a seat belt so 25% would come off her damages come what may. My driver was at fault for the accident though. The lady passenger had plastic surgery and the time came for a meeting with her solicitor. I had insisted that professional 'before and after' photos were available so that I could see the extent of the alleged scarring.

I sat in the solicitor's office and he handed me a bundle of photos. Maybe it was for the shock value but the first were of her in her hospital bed post-accident. There were ugly stitches all over her face, her eyes were blackened and she did look like a horror film. I was then handed a batch of her wedding photos, where it was agreed she was bound to look her best, and then a further batch of her now, six months post plastic surgery.

I flicked from the two piles. OK, she has made a good recovery. There were a few pock-marks on a cheek, but I thought they added character and were easily masked by makeup... but the nose was completely different. She'd had rhinoplasty and before the operation, she had a very prominent 'Roman' nose (she looked like a parrot, OK?) but now... well, it was a petite 'button' nose and made her look rather attractive I thought. I was about to say my piece but the solicitor could quite clearly read my mind.

'I know what you are going to say: 'She looks better now than before'. I'm not having it OK? She went through a windscreen and suffered months of agony and operations and this woman (holding up the wedding day photo) my client's husband married... and now he is married to someone who looks quite different.'

We argued for a bit and finally agreed on an amount for damages, shook hands and a settlement was agreed. I was just leaving the office and I turned and asked, 'Just between us, do you agree she looks more attractive now than before?'

He wearily sighed and said, 'I do, but I just can't tell her that!'

Some thirty or so years before the tragic Grenfell Tower disaster in London, I was involved in an almost identical matter in Egypt.

A rather grand hotel in Cairo had, of all things, a large BBQ situated in a tent adjacent to the hotel itself. In case you misread that, I repeat and emphasise... a bloody *BBQ in a tent*. I cannot imagine who thought that was a good idea, but someone did and the BBQ evenings were very popular.

Cooking was over large charcoal braziers and doubtless, there were a lot of meats being cooked, when suddenly there was a fat flare-up on the charcoal and the tent caught fire. A quick-thinking Filipino waiter grabbed an ice bucket full of ice and enthusiastically threw it over the flaring charcoal, but the fire had already taken hold. The waiter along with all the guests in the tent ran for their lives. The flames had by now reached the sides of the hotel which were covered in industrial aluminium cladding (with a sandwich of flammable insulation) and they too caught fire, right up to the roof. Tragically there were many fatalities and injuries in the hotel.

The following morning the Egyptian Police began their investigation into the fire and, naturally, wished to interview all staff present and verify their actions. The waiter was interviewed. He cooperated fully explaining what he had seen and done. He considered himself to be an 'almost hero' as he thought he might have stopped the fire. The Police then went and looked at the braziers, and finding no ice there, said that the waiter must be lying and arrested him! It did not seem to occur to the Egyptian Police that putting ice onto burning charcoal might cause the ice to melt. The poor chap languished in a cell for a few days until local lawyers arranged for his release, on bail, pending additional investigation and the machinations of the Egyptian judicial system. I am not sure what I would have done had I been the waiter, but he wasted no time at all and fled the country, never to be seen again.

'Oh, and make sure you wear clean socks.'

'I'm sorry, what did you say?' I was on the phone with a contractor to arrange an inspection at a house in the wonderfully named Brown Candover, a sleepy hamlet fairly close to Basingstoke. 'Clean socks...why?'

'Oh, you will be going inside the place and the carpets are snow-white and the owner insists no shoes are worn, see you tomorrow at 3 p.m.' and with that, he hung up.

The claim was boring, a simple plumbing leak and there was to be a joint (ha ha) inspection between the main contractor (who I represented) and a plumbing subcontractor and his loss adjuster. The property was huge and owned by the heiress of a brewing empire. According to my insured, the house had been gutted and all that had

320

remained were the four walls. The 'refurbishment' of the house was more than £5m and had taken years. The owners were now in residence and they had discovered that there was a plumbing leak in one of the many rooms on the ground floor and the repair costs were said to be significant.

The room in question may have been a massive dining room, but at that time it was empty of furniture so the function was not obvious. The room had a 'musty' smell and was unusually humid. There were no carpets and the floorboards were of reclaimed oak and each was of a different width and had been screwed down with the screw heads hidden beneath dowels. The plumbers maintained that if there was a leak, it was because their pipe had been damaged by the carpenters laying the floor and screwing or nailing into a pipe. The carpenters denied it. The obvious course of action then was to take up the floorboards and have a look, hopefully proving who was to blame, and so that is why we were all there.

We stood there in our clean socks as a carpenter carefully lifted a floorboard to be met by an arc of water gently spraying into the air. However, the hole in the pipe was nowhere near a screw and nor was it at a joint. On close inspection, we could see that there was a tiny pinhole in the copper pipe. Another board was lifted and sure enough, there was a further pinhole and then another.

'That's copper pipe from Poland,' said my man, pointing an accusing finger at the plumber. 'They make crap pipe and you were told not to use it.' The plumber shuffled his feet staring at the floor, avoiding eye contact with anyone.

'Well,' I said, indicating my remarks to the plumber's adjuster, 'that's as clear as can be. I presume you will take over the claim?'

'You do the repairs, send us the bills and we will consider it' he answered, rather ungraciously.

'I don't think the cost of redecorations in here will be too great, after all, it's only painted in magnolia on lining paper.'

'Actually, you are quite wrong' interjected my man, 'take a closer look. You will see that the paintwork is in fact a special 'designer' paint and the interior designer insisted that only my best men, with the finest new brushes, painted the walls. One stroke down and one stroke horizontally. Look closely and you will see the paint looks a bit like tartan. Oh, and that is not lining paper either. It's specially made and cost about £100 a roll. Any creases in the paper mean the whole room has to be redone because they will never get a colour match between the old and new paint. My guess is the whole room will need to be stripped back and redone. You won't see much change out of £50k.' (and we didn't... but eventually I got the whole lot back from the plumbers).

The meeting ended and my man wondered if I would like to take a look at the kitchen? I said that would be good, and we padded in our socks to the kitchen. It was huge. The ground floor of my house was smaller. 'Come next door,' said my man with a beckoning finger, and we walked into another kitchen.

'This one is just for BBQs,' he said, his hand sweeping over rows of grills about twelve feet long.

'Bloody hell. This is bigger than my kitchen at home!' I said rather awed.

'Come see this then' he said and we went down a flight of steps to a massive steel door with a wheel on the front, like you see on bank vaults. The door swung slowly open on massive hinges. The door must have been eighteen inches in thickness. Inside was a lobby, then a room on one side packed to the ceiling with tinned and dried food on massive shelving. A fairly large, fully equipped kitchen was opposite. The kitchen too was bigger than mine at home. In the centre was a lounge area where there were sofas and armchairs and I could see board games and toys on shelving. A TV hung on the wall and there was a cabinet full of VHS films. A very large bathroom and fully equipped bedrooms finished the accommodation, apart from... an underground swimming pool.

'What is this place?' I asked, my jaw dropping open.

'Nuclear bunker' he answered 'for when the balloon goes up. Fully equipped with its own power supply, water filtration etcetera, enough to last three years apparently.'

'Crikey. How the other half live eh? Seems to me to be a huge waste of money...' but he cut me off.

'Don't think of it like that. They are spending their money. This job has kept me and my lads in work for three years and the money they pay us for all this work is, in turn, turnover, for which you get paid our premiums. If they were just keeping it in the bank, I'd agree with you – doing nothing with money is a waste, but they are spending it, so think on.' Put like that I did feel admonished and sort of had a grudging admiration for the client.

We padded our way back to the servants' entrance where we had come in, only to be passed by three children in school uniform, all wearing shoes I noted, tearing past and then a barking dog chasing on behind. I was about to say something about the carpet and the children and dogs when he said 'Yeah, I know...it's one rule for us and another for them!'

I knew Colin had a phobia of wasps. Every time one was in the office he would go screaming and flapping like a girly. What I didn't know was that he had another phobia too.

At the side of the Hammersmith flyover on the A4 road was a new building designed to look like Noah's Ark. It was called 'The Ark' so I suppose that fits. The building was designed and constructed by Danish firms, but they had a water leak that had damaged the ceiling. The affected ceiling though, made of a particular wood, was in an atrium area and the floor-to-ceiling was about four or five storeys high. The damage was a white streaking across the ceiling and Colin and I were there to discuss and agree on a method of repair. The contractor hoped that using special narrow 'cherry pickers' with a basket on the top, men with cloths and a cleaning solution should be able to clean the damage. Sourcing the cherry pickers was going to be a problem though. The equipment needed to be narrow to get through the doors, otherwise it meant scaffolding the whole atrium. Anyway, the site manager assured us it could be done in that way, even though he predicted that working at that height in a bouncy cradle might result in some giddiness or seasickness.

We had finished our discussion and the site manager asked us if we would like to have a look at the view and I said 'Why not?' So, off we went, up in a lift to the 5th floor or so and then through a door and up a long spiral staircase. When we came outside, we were in, what I took to be like a ship's conning tower, and in front of us was a shortish glass-floored walkway to an open-air crow's nest. The site manager walked ahead, I followed then turned around and momentarily could not see Colin following. He was flat on the floor, spread-eagled and trembling. He mumbled 'I'm terrified of heights' and shuffling on his stomach he started to push himself backwards to the tower where he felt more secure. I enjoyed the view, both of London and to my shame, of Colin's discomfiture. I couldn't wait to tell the rest of the office.

To be fair to Colin, he did tell me that on one job he had to go onto a roof and once up there, again sat cross-legged on the flat roof whilst a huge Irish site agent went and fetched him the damaged items he was there to inspect, helped him up and carried his briefcase for him back to the ground.

But of all the things Colin did that affected me, was the time he had to go to Pentonville prison to deal with some construction issue, an injury probably, for renovation work... and got himself locked in. He was given a visitor's pass, and was told that he had to be finished by a particular time as there was to be a shift change and also because it was lunchtime, no one goes in or out until 2.30 p.m. Of course, Colin overran his meeting and was locked in for two hours or so, which in turn meant he would be late getting back to Reading, and he was in my company car. I was always puzzled how he managed to do so many miles (not that I was bothered) on all his calls. He explained that he went everywhere from the M25. So, if he was going from say Reading to Guildford, he would not go cross-country, no he would drive towards London on the M4, pick up the M25, go south and then down the A3, basically going two sides of a very acute triangle. Madness. Why did he do that? His only explanation was that was what he always did.

Did I mention my inability to understand electricity? It is not as if I don't understand the basics, I do. I know how it is made, spinning magnets at high speed around copper coils, but I do not know why that makes electricity. Do the magnets or copper coils wear out? If not, why not? I also do not understand why electricity goes down wires, copper or otherwise, on its own. Water needs gravity or a pump to make it flow down or uphill, but electricity does it on its own without being pushed, pulled or sucked. And don't get me started on alternating current, electricity whizzing backwards and forwards along a wire at a zillion miles an hour. Why? Transformers change one high voltage down to a lower one. I sort of follow the need for that, but in my head, a transformer is like a big tube of toothpaste. Lots of stuff is squeezed into the transformer (high-voltage toothpaste) and out of a smaller hole comes a thin ribbon of low-voltage toothpaste. But is there a big wodge of electricity backing up? And if so, where is it? Maybe this is payback from being sent out of Mr Biswas's physics classes for nearly every lesson from when I was 13-14 back in Grammar School?

Mechanics: Understood. Light: Understood... broadly. Gravity: I thought I understood, but now I am not so sure. The principles of flight: Understood, air flowing over wings giving 'lift' and all. Hmm, hang on a minute...but why can the same plane fly upside down? Or on its side? Maybe not understood then. Electricity: Not a scooby-do. So, with that background, you can imagine how thrilled I was to be handling claims for transformers.

New Zealand's South Island has a lot of rivers which run in deep gorges, ideal for dams and using the plentiful supply of water to drive turbines to make electricity. However, the population of the South Island is smaller than the North Island, which is where the electricity demand is greater, so it needs to get there by very long cables indeed. At the power plant in the South Island, the electric current needs to go through a transformer before it goes down the cables to the North. The people at the NZ power company are wise. Rather than order one transformer, they ordered three. One to run, one as a backup in case of a failure and a third in case of failure of #2 when #1 was undergoing maintenance. Very sensible in my view.

Now transformers are, for their size, weighty bits of kit. Even the one I had for my train set was surprisingly heavy for its size. The NZ ones were about the size of a smallish house and each weighed about 200 tons. Within the transformer, to keep it cool was about 100 tons of oil. [Ah, that explains the maintenance bit – oil degrades at high temperatures – so it needs replacing from time to time.]

The three transformers were taken by ship from Sweden to NZ where each was placed on a multi-wheeled low loader and slowly driven to the top of a mountain where they were to be installed. Why they needed to be on the top of a mountain was never explained. Maybe they liked the view, or is it that electricity does go faster downhill? Anyway, I digress. Once in place, they were filled with oil and amid some fanfare, the switch to #1 was flicked on. (Doubtlessly it was more complicated than that, but I hope you get my drift). I imagine there was a great humming as the transformer did its thing and then the engineers noticed that there were bubbles of gas coming from the oil. The gas was tested and found to be hydrogen. Hydrogen is explosive, so fearing a 'big bang' the NZ Power chaps switched over to #2. It started to gas as well... and so did #3, but not as badly. No one could figure out why the transformers were gassing and the only way to find out was to strip one down. Meantime, with fingers crossed they ran with #3 and prayed that #1 and #2 could be fixed easily. In case you have forgotten, they were on the top of a mountain, hundreds of miles from the nearest 'clean room' in which an inspection could be done, and the kit was the size of a house. So, they decided to build a 'clean room' on the top of a mountain.

The oil was considered contaminated and it had to be disposed of. As NZ is a very environmentally conscious country it needed to be taken to a plant that could deal with it. In the North Island of course. A very long way away. Not forgetting that the oil needed to be replaced an order was placed for 100 tons of the stuff. (Yes, I know they probably needed 300 tons, but there was nowhere to store that much on top of a mountain).

The clean room was built and the #1 transformer was stripped down. The engineers could not see anything wrong with it, no loose connections or anything, so after a thorough check, tightening up all the nuts and bolts and making sure there were no loose items left inside, #1 was refilled with oil. It had taken about three months to do the strip down and rebuild. Then #3 was switched off and #1 was brought back into service. It immediately started to gas again, so they immediately switched back to slightly gassy #3. I believe at this point NZ Power were more than a little cross. They said that they had ordered three non-gassing transformers and three non-gassing transformers they wanted. The manufacturer said that they would take #1 back to Sweden for a more detailed investigation and repair if necessary. This would take about 8 weeks by ship, another 8 weeks to strip down and repair and another 8 weeks to bring it back. In all 24 weeks or roughly 6 months. Meantime NZ Power would have to run with #3 and pray that nothing went wrong or the lights would dim in NZ. The Power company reluctantly agreed.

Six months later #1 arrived back at the quayside in Wellington for the long drive to the top of the mountain. In lifting the transformer off the ship, the crane dropped it heavily on the quayside, causing who knows what damage. NZ Power, now frightfully cross, said that although the transformer was designed to withstand earthquake tremors (common in NZ) it was not designed to be dropped. So, back #1 went to Sweden for another strip down... and another 6 months of delay.

Meantime #3 hummed and bubbled away.

The manufacturers decided they needed another 6 months to sort out the problem, which had already taken a year, so they decided to build a #4 transformer in parallel to fix #1. They would send #4 as soon as it was ready then exchange it for #2 and send back #1 when it was fixed. As to #3, they prayed that NZ Power would just live with the gassing.

The claim was presented to us on a style of policy that was new to me – a Product Guarantee Policy. I had never seen one of those before (or since) because after this claim we never wrote them again. I had to travel to central Sweden in winter to settle the matter with the insured. I met with a team of people, all eager to squeeze the last kroner out of me.

Sven, the lead negotiator, was a short, sweaty, and plump lawyer with a habit of thumping the table with his fist to make a point. Next to him was Titty, another lawyer, a tall slim lady who nodded furiously at everything that Sven was saying. I later learned that Sven and Titty were married. Their surnames were different, but that is because it is not usual in Scandinavia for the wife to take the husband's surname, they often hyphenate it or she keeps her maiden name. Back in the meeting room, there were about ten against me and my lawyer.

It was agreed that the dockside damage was on a marine policy (which we did not write) but the problem was one of 'damage'. The transformers worked just fine... they just gassed... but is that 'damage'? The policy was subject to Swedish law, hence my attending with a local lawyer, my friend Artur. Sven argued that gassing was damage, Artur said it was arguable, and there was no Swedish law on the point. In court, the matter was an all-or-nothing case and a good 3-4 years of legal wrangling before a judgment. Meantime the claim was tens of millions of kroner and was still not finalised. The number 1 transformer had still not gone back to NZ.

My argument as to damage was, I thought, simple enough. Imagine you purchased a car and driving it found that it had an annoying squeak. Would that be 'damage'? Would that problem be enough to entitle you to reject the car? No, in my view. Suppose the manufacturer has taken back the car, stripped it down and still cannot identify where the squeak is coming from, maybe a discounted price would suffice? Sven argued, with Titty nodding furiously, that hydrogen gassing was not like a squeak, hydrogen gassing could cause an explosion. But it hadn't for two years and may never cause an explosion or anything at all. We were of course entrenched in our respective positions.

I needed to break the deadlock and made the point that neither of us wanted a long, drawn-out fight. It was not good for business and besides the manufacturers did not want it publicly and internationally known that they made duff transformers... so maybe a compromise was in order? It was. A deal was done.

As to whether the transformers on top of the mountain are still active and gassing away, I have no idea!

A power station in the UK had a transformer explosion. The shockwave was so great that the transformer, which weighed a paltry 120 tons, shot sideways about three feet. The transformer was critical to electricity supply and our policy covered both damage and business interruption loss or loss of profits. The claim was considerable and although I was not the 'lead' on the policy, the whole market was invited to a big meeting at the power station to understand the issues and hopefully agree a way forward.

It was a hot summer's day and I entered the meeting room where there must have been about thirty seats around a massive boardroom table. All the seats filled up and I think there were still one or two standing. In light of the large number of people present, a chairman determined the agenda for the meeting. The session started with a presentation from the electrical engineers, who described the situation. Following this, the floor was opened for questions and discussion.

The engineers began their presentation and within minutes I was completely at a loss trying to understand red phases, blue phases and yellow phases. In my mind the shutters came down and I became more interested in the pictures on the walls. I did try to understand what was being said, truly I did, I even wrote copious notes, but they meant nothing to me on readback. After two hours or so the engineers finished their presentation and sat down. At this point, the chairman enquired if there were any questions? If there were, he said, please state your name and company and to whom your question is directed. To keep matters in order he suggested that he start at the top end of the table and go around clockwise. I was sitting at about 7 o'clock. Between 7 o'clock and 11 o'clock were all the insurers. I could not believe it but no one had any questions, not one, not even a tiny query... and then it got to me.

'Trevor Cottington, from CIGNA Insurance. Just one question, actually just for the engineers. My question is this: why did the transformer suddenly go... 'bang'?'

There were a couple of sniggers to my left at about 9 o'clock, but the Chairman looked sort of horrified and said after a pause 'Sorry, but that, Mr Cottington is precisely what we have been discussing in detail for the last two hours or so.'

'Yeah, I know that but why, in layman's terms, did it go... 'BANG'?' I said 'bang' louder in case they didn't hear me the first time.

The Chairman gave me a small smile and then said in an exasperated tone, 'We simply don't know.'

'Oh, thanks. Just wanted to make sure I understood.' And there was a collective sigh of relief from those between 8 o'clock and 11. I knew full well that they hadn't understood either but were doubtless too afraid or embarrassed to ask. I never am. I can't be expected to know the ins and outs of all industries so I ask questions in innocence and with impunity.

The damage to the transformer was such that it could not be repaired and a new one needed to be found. The experts scoured the globe for a spare redundant transformer. A new one would take six to nine months to make, assuming that a manufacturer had the capacity in their schedule to fit us in, but we expected that all manufacturers had full order books.

The scrap value of the transformer was about £200,000. A brand spanking new one, if one could be made, was about £1m maybe £1.5m. Meantime the loss of electricity production was costing about £1m a week, so we were facing a massive loss of profits claim.

The insured said that they had found two transformers on 'Craigslist' (a global site for classified equipment). One was in Texas and was similar, but not identical and would need a lot of work done to configure it to UK specifications. The price and repair costs were estimated at £1-2m. It would also take about 12 weeks to get to the UK and a further 6 weeks for repairs. The second, an identical one, was in Scotland at a redundant power station where it had been mothballed for around five years. It would take two weeks to transport to the site and maybe a further two weeks for tinkering. The CEO of the insured had called his counterpart at 'Thistlepower', or whoever they were, and offered to buy it. The price was a staggering £10m.

When faced with numbers like that it does make one slightly blasé, but the mathematics were simple enough for all to understand. Buy the USA one and it might cost £2m + £18m of loss of profits, so roughly £20m. The Scottish one, £10m + about £4m loss of profits, so £14m; or a new one at £1.5m and loss of profits of £35m, so £36.5m.When put like that it was, as they say, a no-brainer... get the Scottish one, but we knew the Celtic swine had us bent over a barrel and was stuffing us full of free-range haggis.

It was suggested that the CEO do a bit of haggling. He did and got the price down to a mere £7.5m.

What I did not know about electricity production is that the power plants sell their electricity in advance of actually making it on the 'futures market'. (eh?) You see, the power requirements of the country are known and predictable. There is no point in making electricity during the night when we are asleep and only the streetlights are on, but Saturday evening and Sunday lunchtime are peak times, and so are Christmas Day and New Year's Eve, so that is when it pays to sell your power to the grid. Thus, the power companies bid for the 24-hour slots in advance of actually generating the stuff. It all seemed a dark science to me, but that is how it was, and is, done.

When it came to the loss of profits claim, that too is a dark art. There are savings to be accounted for, but sometimes increased costs too and to calculate all that requires the assistance of the mythical beast known as a forensic accountant. I have known several forensic accountants in my time. I cannot say they make maths 'fun' but it never ceases to amaze me that two accountants, faced with the same spreadsheets, always come up with different conclusions.

I did say that as we had taken a premium based on predicted profits of, say £1m a week, then as the transformer will be down for four weeks, why not just agree £4m? It would make matters so much simpler and take away all the arguments... but no one was having it. It took many weeks of calculations and tens of thousands of pounds in fees before we finally agreed on the claim at £4m anyway.

I was called upon to deal with a loss at an oil refinery in Corinth, Greece. An extremely large pressurised gas container called a Horton sphere – basically a large steel ball on legs, the whole thing about the size of a three-storey house, had failed. Pressure vessels need to be tested for structural strength every few years and to do this it is filled with water, which is heavier than liquid gas. A Lloyd's surveyor was attending as the gas sphere was being filled with water. He was standing inside the bund holding his clipboard, making some notes when suddenly there was a very loud cracking sound. The bottom of the sphere fell out, and a huge amount of water rushed across the ground, sweeping the surveyor away and smashing him against the bund wall, breaking one of his legs. I believe he made a claim for his injury, but it was rather difficult to establish that anyone was at fault. Anyway, I was there after the broken sphere had been removed, and I was going to examine the replacement to see if the claim could be settled.

I'd flown to Athens and went by taxi to my hotel, the taxi driver keeping up a steady commentary about (I think) the traffic, which was awful. He could have been talking about the state of his marriage, politics, football, or anything really, but his one-sided conversation was all in Greek and I don't speak a word of it, so I just nodded and made the occasional hmm of agreement. I had arrived late and although my room had a nice view of the Parthenon, which was all lit up for the tourists, I spent the evening in my room with a room-service meal and watched CNN News on the TV as that was the only English language thing to view. I said previously how boring some international travel is and this one certainly ticked that box. The following morning the broker and local loss adjuster met me at the hotel and we drove the hour or so to the refinery at Corinth. It was a swelteringly hot day and I had wisely removed my tie as by the time we reached the refinery my suit was clinging to me like a wet limpet to a rock.

The car pulled up outside a security office in a cloud of pale orange dust. A burly security guard came out of the office and twisting his hand in the air, gave our driver the international signal to turn off the engine. The guard looked like a member of the military in his dusty khaki uniform and massive peaked hat and there around his rather large girth was a massive revolver tucked into a leather holster. The guard exchanged a few words with the broker, who spoke Greek, and we all were required to follow the guard to the office to sign in and hand over our passports. The guard reached under his desk and produced a pair of pliers, a small circle of wire mesh and a piece of wire. Proceeding to the rear of the car he bent down and carefully placed the mesh over the end of the exhaust pipe and secured it with the wire. It was explained to me that this was a fire precaution. In the event of a gas or petroleum leak, a backfire from the car could cause an explosion, the mesh acting like a 'Davy Lamp' on a miner's lantern. This seemed a sensible precaution and I nodded sagely. We climbed back into the car and off we went for a short ride to the sphere.

On turning a corner, there in front of me was the massive new Horton sphere. The whole thing was surrounded by dozens of orange propane cylinders and a maze of tubing. Flames from the propane were curling around the sphere during the heat treatment of the steel. The flames must have risen a good ten to twenty feet over the top of the sphere which glowed a dull red. From where we stood the heat was rather like standing beside an open oven door just as the Sunday roast was being taken out. Turning to the broker and smiling I pointed to the flames and then to the little piece of mesh on the exhaust tailpipe and said that if there was a source of ignition of anything at the refinery that day, I was pretty damn sure that the car would not be to blame. The broker rolled his eyes and shrugged his shoulders and agreed with me, but said 'Rules are rules' ...which I suppose they are.

Although the sphere had not finished the commissioning, the insured were happy enough to agree on a settlement and we concluded the claim. After collecting our passports from the security office, the broker drove me back to the airport. From my trip to the Czech Republic, I returned with a bottle of the local national drink, slivovitz (a plum brandy) so at the duty-free at Athens airport what could be better than a litre bottle of ouzo? The answer is drain cleaner... because both bottles went down the sink... they were awful.

Chapter Twenty-Two

ALL PLAY AND NO WORK

I have been extremely fortunate in my career to have been invited to hundreds of excellent lunches and dinners, horse race meetings, go-kart racing, driving events, football matches and concerts as well as the Olympic Games in 2012. I cannot thank my hosts enough, though it occurs to me that the millions of pounds in fees the company had paid them over the years may have softened the financial blow somewhat.

Back in my days at the Reading office, one event stands out in my memory. To attract more business, the branch manager organized a Race Day at Newbury Race Course. I was not only invited, but also asked if I would like to bring two guests. I chose to invite a solicitor and a loss adjuster. I have never been much of a gambler, but a free day out including a pub lunch, meant that even I could justify a fiver on each race. In the unlikely event that I won anything I'd regard that as winnings, but still only keep to my maximum stake. I can read 'form' and I understand 'odds'. I think there is a perfect analogy between underwriting and writing a risk, and being one of those chaps standing on a box with an umbrella shouting out odds at a race track, or turf accountant as they are more properly known. The only difference between the two disciplines that I can see, is that the turf accountant knows whether he has made a profit on the 2.30 race at Haydock Park by 2.35 that day, whereas the underwriter may not know for years. The turf accountant will also lay off large bets with another turf accountant so that he does not get such a big hit should the big bet succeed. In my game that is called reinsurance, but operates in exactly the same way.

But back to the day at the races. There were seven races that day, all over fences. I find flat racing rather boring by comparison, but standing by a fence when a herd of horses comes thundering by, the ground trembling beneath your feet, is rather thrilling. It also makes me thankful that I am not a jockey, as falling off a ton of muscle at speed, as others are trying to trample you to death, is not what I would want to call 'a living'.

I had not won a thing and had big hopes for the 6th race. The horses set off at speed and at the first fence, there was a faller. The jockey got up but the horse, sadly, did not. We saw the sight of a tractor and trailer plus a couple of jeeps drive to the spot, a curtain screen was raised and the poor horse was euthanised. I didn't win of course. Whilst waiting for the 7th race, where there was a field of fifteen 'novices' to take to the start, we saw some show-off in the middle of the course start to taxi his single-engine aeroplane. I turned to my colleagues and said 'Aren't planes supposed to take off into the wind? It looks like that bloke is taking off down-wind.' The little aeroplane, revving noisily down the grassy strip and with grace and elegance that was a marvel to behold, left the ground, made a shallow turn to the left, flipped over and crashed upside down with a thump... right into the middle of the racetrack. An ambulance, fire truck and other vehicles all roared to the scene. 'Hey,' I exclaimed, 'we've got the full team here to deal with that – loss adjuster, solicitor and insurers!' My mirth though was offset by the fact that the last race was abandoned, which was a pity as I was sure my horse, 'Norfolk and Chance', was a sure-fire winner at 100-1. Instead, we did what all sensible people do at moments like that, go to the pub and drown our sorrows.

One of the nicest guys I met in the legal profession was Shane. He worked for a major London firm that specialised in dealing with insurance disputes. I had masses of dealings with the firm ever since my days at AIU and got to know dozens of their lawyers over the decades, but if there was one to wear the crown for entertainment, it was Shane. He was a master storyteller and knew just about every decent restaurant in London and possibly the world. A gourmet and oenophilia (wine connoisseur to you and me) and generous to a fault, a lunch with Shane was one where it was inadvisable to return to the office. Standing over six feet tall he looked like Holbein's picture of Henry VIII.

In 1998 it was the World Cup and Shane had bagged four tickets to see a match in Bordeaux. He kindly invited me and the game was hopefully one where we would see England face someone, provided that they won their group. The itinerary was a mid-afternoon drive from London to Paris, via the Channel Tunnel, an overnight in a chateau on the outskirts of Paris, then after breakfast, another drive to Bordeaux, see the game, back to the chateau and the following morning return to London. So, in reality only one and a half days out of the office. It all seemed splendid and I gratefully accepted the invite.

Typically, England did not win their group and so the match we were going to see was Romania vs Croatia. None of our troupe could care less who won, but it was to be an experience and I was still looking forward to it. The others in our troupe were Niraj (a lawyer working in Shane's firm) and another insurer called Mike. We were driving in Niraj's brand-new BMW convertible and the weather was warm and dry, so the roof was down. Sitting in the back with Mike we could not hear anyone say anything, even each other, so conversation was a little stilted. On the Paris ring road with Shane map reading, I mentioned (loudly) that we seemed to have passed the same turn-off a couple of times, each from a different direction and so handing me the map (those Scouting years paying off at last) I finally got us to the chateau about an hour later than planned.

Luckily, we were not too late for dinner, but it meant eating now and going to our rooms later. The food was fantastic and Shane pushed the boat out with wine and liqueurs, though I thought it best, what with a long drive in the morning, to hold off. Shane and Niraj didn't though and finally, being the last in the restaurant, we said our bon-nuits and collecting our bags went up to our rooms. Shane handed Niraj a key to his room and then announced that there were just two rooms, but separate beds and hoped that we did not mind sharing. I can't think that we had much of a choice, but I was to share with Shane, leaving Niraj and Mike in the adjoining room.

The room was huge and there were two large single beds, so at least I was not having déjà vu from the Loss Adjusters Dinner all those years ago. We each did our night time ablutions and I slipped into bed. Shane got into his and I swear that the moment his head hit the pillow, he was asleep, snoring loudly. Over the subsequent years I have tried to describe Shane's snoring and the best I have come up with is this: try to imagine a warthog with sinus trouble being gang-raped by a gorilla who is dragging a hammer down a sheet of corrugated iron. I am convinced that the windows were rattling. I did not sleep a wink, all night. At one point I contemplated gathering my bedclothes and sleeping in the corridor, or the bath, but courage failed me.

I suppose I must have dropped off momentarily, as my phone alarm woke me and wearily, I swung my legs out and sat on the side of the bed. I was about to grab a quick shower when Shane asked 'Mind if I use the loo first?' I figured he was a chap of 'a certain age' and prostates being prostates...so I said 'Sure.' The sight of Shane in his massive Y-fronts has been indelibly etched on my retinas forever, but worse was to come. A few minutes later he came out of the bathroom and said it was OK for me to go now. I grabbed my wash bag and with some enthusiasm for a shower, I strode into the bathroom only to be met by an assault to the nasal senses. It wasn't just a wee he'd had, it was worse, far worse. The vast quantity of rich food, the wine and liqueurs had achieved their natural transit in record time and now I was suffering them too. I could barely breathe, my eyes stung and holding what was left of my breath, I frantically tried to get the tiny bathroom window open. It didn't budge a millimetre. There was nothing more I could do, I had to take a breath. I now have some appreciation for those poor soldiers on the Western

Front during a gas attack. OK, this didn't kill me, but it was damn close. I turned on the shower full blast and did my best to shower holding my breath. I hoped the steam would dilute or even alleviate the smell. If it did, I didn't notice, because by now my olfactory senses had been damaged, so I believed, beyond redemption. Oh, to be able to smell freshly cut grass, flowers, burning rubber, anything, in fact, yes, anything at all would be a blessing.

I dressed in record time and plodded down to the breakfast room. Mike was alone at a table so I joined him.

Over a very pleasant breakfast, Mike said that Niraj snored all night too and so, like me, he was exhausted from a lack of sleep. We vowed that as neither of us snored, we would share a room when we returned that evening.

The drive to Bordeaux was long and tedious. Shane was convinced that Niraj was driving too slowly, whereas Niraj maintained that as his car was brand new it needed running in, carefully. They swapped driving from time to time, Niraj driving fast but sensibly, Shane flooring the accelerator and driving at maximum revs.

We got to the game just before kick-off and according to Google, Croatia won 1-0 with a penalty. The game was utterly forgettable.

No sooner had the final whistle been blown than we were back in the car for the return trip to Paris. It was thought that by driving fast we might make the England vs Argentina game on the TV at the chateau. However, we were on the outskirts of Paris and the game was about to start, so we decided to catch the game at a 'Bar Sportif'. The Bar was dingy, but packed with men and the menu hardly haute cuisine (steak sandwiches and fries) but there were beers aplenty and the game was on the wide-screen TV.

We soon realised that the French were supporting Argentina as they scored after just 6 minutes and the place erupted with cheers, except at our table. A few minutes later England equalised and four Brits cheered on their own, getting filthy looks from the Frenchies. We hurled good-natured insults to each other as the match progressed, though knew things were bad when Beckham got sent off for petulantly back-kicking an Argie. The game finished and went into extra time and then a penalty shoot-out which, of course, England spectacularly lost 4-3, much to the cheers and jeers of our French hosts. As we were leaving, I could not resist one last dig and shouted back that but for us Brits they'd all be speaking German...at which point Shane wisely grabbed me by the shoulder and we hot-footed it to the car, leaving the place in a shower of gravel with the BMW wheels spinning.

At the chateau, we were too late for any night-cap and frankly, I was too exhausted for any more drink so Mike and I went to our room, where I am pleased to say, I had an uninterrupted night's sleep, even though I was now in Niraj's bedsheets... but I didn't care.

About a month later I bumped into Niraj and after chatting about our experiences I asked how was the car? It was at the dealer's, apparently for a new gearbox...

Nick and Bill are two other lawyers I have had dealings with over the years and are also from the same firm as Shane. Nick is a slight chap, very fit and younger than me, but unusually for a man of his stature, has a

345

throat like a drain. I can just about match him in quantity, but if the gauntlet were thrown down, doubtless he would win every time. Bill is an Aussie and whilst he tries to match us pint for pint, he insists on lager, which Nick and I maintain simply doesn't count. We enjoy fabulous Christmas lunches with Neil (now a QC/KC) and another guest or two and we have to write the rest of the day off as by the end, visually, there appears to be two of everything. I look forward to these lunches immensely and only missed one when due to a snowflake landing on a railway line just outside of Weston-Super-Mare the trains from Hastings were cancelled and I could not get to London.

The Olympics were coming to London in 2012 and tickets for all events sold out in moments. I am not terribly interested in athletics and never really watch it on TV, but one event was going to be at the Olympics for the first time. A sport of considerable skill and athleticism, involving tactics and stamina with the contestants wearing specialist clothing. I refer of course to the ladies' beach volleyball... Nick had got three tickets and he and Bill invited me to join them for what looked like a fun afternoon of tense action watching finely honed tanned athletes at the peak of their craft.

The event was at Horse Guards Parade in St James's Park and we were to watch an early evening event. I was rather hoping to be within sweat-flicking distance of the action, but it turned out that our seats were way up in the stands. We sat with our beers (Heineken – overpriced and horrible, but Bill seemed to like it) and waited patiently for the action. A hush descended over the crowd and to cheers and applause four bronzed and muscular blokes strode to the sandy 'beach'. 'Er, those are men Nick,' I said somewhat disappointedly. 'So it would seem' he answered and added, 'I think the ladies must come on later.' Without any further ado, it was time to go and get some more beers and honest to God... it was a hell of a trek for three bottles of beer.

We did see the ladies play, but they were an awfully long way away, but at least I can say I have been to the Olympics and not everyone can say that.

Chapter Twenty-Three

IT'S ALL CHANGE

My time in London was coming to an end as the bean counters had decided that having the construction claims in London and all other claims in the regions was not cost-effective and ought to be centralised.

I happened to be working in the Reading office one Friday doing some paperwork, when the new Claims Manager, Graham (ex of Birmingham office but now transferred to Maidstone) came in for a meeting with Colin and Sarah. Graham suggested I leave immediately and take home whatever I was doing. I guessed what was coming, so hastily gathering up my files I left without saying good-bye.

Colin and Sarah were offered redundancy or a move to the Maidstone office. They took the cash. Colin ended up working for a recruitment company and Sarah at a broker.

The whole of the field operation that I enjoyed and was a part of was being cast to the winds. It was not a good time.

Back in London, another experiment had run its course as well. I do not know who thought it was a good idea, but someone obviously did, and the grand idea was to have a centre of excellence in London covering all claims on construction policies written out of Europe. The thought was that we could employ someone who was multi-lingual and they would handle the claims under our guidance. Dominic was recruited for the job, a Belgian who spoke French, Flemish, and German and had a smattering of Dutch and Spanish too. The one language he didn't have any understanding of was 'insurance'.

We soon came across differing practices and procedures from each country. Moreover, the French brokers didn't want their claims dealt with in London and as technicians, we did not know the laws of each country and soon fell foul of some rule or another. Evidently, no one had given any thought to how we were to communicate. Our secretary could not type foreign letters on an English keyboard, having no 'accents' 'umlauts' etc, so Dominic had to type them. Of course, we could not then read what he had written, so everything had to be typed twice, once in the local language and then in English. If a mistake were made then the whole thing had to be retyped (twice) and in the event of a linguistic dispute, the original language had to prevail, which we could not read. It made everything much slower and was a nightmare.

I do not know what they paid Dominic, but whatever the lad spent his salary on, deodorant was not on his shopping list. The lad had B.O. We even had complaints that his odour was being carried in the air conditioning throughout the building. We tackled him about it, gently at first, but Dominic maintained that his 'natural' scent was a turn-on for the female of the species. Not the English ones, Dominic. I was tasked by Chris to 'say something'.

'Dominic,' I said firmly, 'you stink. There is no easy way of saying this but you are stinking out the building, there have been complaints. No excuses. Don't care what you do outside of work, but here, in the office, you put on underarm deodorant. End of discussion, OK?'

'Oh,' he answered somewhat bashfully, 'I did not know this was a problem. It isn't in Belgium. (I bet it was mate!) But I will do as you ask.' And he did. Sometimes only a very direct approach will work.

By 1997 the company was going through a major cost-cutting exercise and Dominic along with others were 'let go'. Our team were to be relocated from London to Maidstone. This gave some of our team real issues with travel as Karl for one had moved from Maidstone to Essex as the travel was easier, and now he was being asked to move back again.

In my case, there was no option of commuting from South Oxfordshire to Maidstone, only a house move would do, or take redundancy. The company offered to pay for the house move, my salary was to remain the same, and I could keep my company car and have my own parking space in Maidstone so it seemed a reasonable deal. Karon and I discussed the pros and cons and as our children were at an age where moving schools would not be a problem, we agreed I could take the plunge and move the family to Kent.

We chose the children's school first, then found a house a few hundred metres from the school in a village about 16 miles south of Maidstone and so a relatively easy commute.

There was a slight hiccup with our house purchase in that the sellers were the Estate of the deceased owner. However, the old boy had died leaving his property to his wife who had pre-deceased him, so her probate needed to be reopened and his got complicated too... and he was a 'name' at Lloyds, one would have thought that he'd got his affairs in order. By January 1998 we had moved in.

During the previous four months or so I had been staying in a hotel for three nights (M-T-W) returning on Thursdays (to go for my swimming lesson, even though the hotel had a pool) and working from Reading on Fridays or commuting back to Maidstone just for the day. It was exhausting really and played havoc with my waistline. I put on a stone and went up a waist size. Well, three-course dinners and fried breakfasts were largely to blame.

In Maidstone, our team carried on largely as before but it soon became apparent that there were several anomalies. For example, I had negotiated rates with solicitors that were more favourable than the teams in Maidstone. That was plainly daft, but was a consequence of having two different claims teams working under two different managers. One of the first actions I was asked to do was to trim the legal panel from whatever it was down to just six firms. In the end, we settled on eight as being the most practicable, but saying goodbye to old friends at firms was very hard on the soul.

I was still going over to Scandinavia and trying to manage the team. In time Karl and David both left.

It was 1999 and for the whole year, the talk had been about the 'millennium bug' and the catastrophes that would occur when all electronic timepieces turned from 12.59.59 to 00.00.00 on 31.12.1999 and the equipment on which they were working, suddenly stopped working. Computer 'experts' were busily reprogramming and checking equipment to make sure that they were not going to crash at midnight on 31st December, but I thought that this was a lot of hooey and said so.

As early as 1998, underwriters had been planning and implementing a Y2K exclusion clause for all renewals. However, had I been asked, I would have recommended including the risk, as I believed the world would not suddenly stop on 31st December. In the event, aeroplanes did not fall out of the sky and it was a total non-event. I recall that our office in Stockholm found that their landlord's electronic key pass did not operate, so could not access the office to see if everything was working (it was) and that certain taxi meters, also in Sweden, failed to work after midnight. But I do not think that the taxi drivers failed to get paid by their passengers.

In early January I began teasing brokers about our cracking new Y3K exclusion clause. 'Absolutely watertight,' I said, 'had a team of lawyers drafting it over Christmas.' One or two even asked to see it... before the penny dropped.

The other major event in 1999 happened almost without our noticing as no rumours were circulating and there was nothing in the press, but overnight the company I was working for was purchased by ACE.

ACE was set up in Bermuda in 1985 with a financial centre in The Cayman Islands and grew rapidly writing excess casualty business and other high-level business. They were by all accounts extremely profitable and had a desire to become a global name and brand. The easiest way of achieving that was to buy a company that had an existing global presence and CIGNA fitted that bill. It also helped that CIGNA were not terribly profitable. So, armed with a lot of cash ACE bought the international and domestic property and casualty business of CIGNA and overnight went from being a bit-player to one of the top 15 or so insurance carriers in the world. Overnight the employee count for ACE went from around 400 to 40,000.

We had been summoned to London to hear the announcement and the new management team stood on stage and gave us a pep talk of how the new company would be going from strength to strength, blah, blah, blah ...and of course, there would be 'changes'. I heard that as redundancies. The presentation was not as skilfully done as I would have expected. I had no idea who any of the speakers were as they did not introduce themselves and although questions from the floor were requested, I decided that my question of 'Sorry, who are you?' might lead to the proverbial 'early bath' for yours truly.

There were huge swathes of people who were 'let go' mainly in the USA. One of the things we were told was that as we were now rebranded, anything with a CIGNA name on it had to go into the bin – paper, pens, mugs, the lot. ACE wanted to clear the decks and the bin turned into a skip as historic documents were merrily tossed away. I thought this was foolish and would come back to haunt us, but obeyed. Mind you, it is amazing how much paper you squirrel away in the belief that it will come in useful one day, so a general clear out was somewhat cathartic. We were all given a bottle of quality champagne with which to celebrate the new company, so things were not all bad.

It was during 2000 that I think a lot of time was being devoted to the new office environment. We were to be going paperless. I had also been promoted to Casualty Claims Manager and now was in charge of a team of about twenty.

The problems of man management are not lost on me, but for the most part, it is not my strongest suit. I had inherited a motley crew. Some were excellent technicians who desired advancement, others were good technicians but had no real interest in advancement and others were just plodders. There were one or two hanging on by the skin of their teeth.

I mentioned before the teams PACT and SECT (Chapter 12) and now they were thrown together with my construction team. Trying to make a cohesive team out of them was not going to be easy. Firstly, the PACT/SECT manager, a nice guy called Neil (who used to be the claims superintendent in Birmingham) took an internal move back to Birmingham, but as his replacement, I figured I was bound to be resented by his old teams.

One of the first things I did was to try and ensure that there was some parity over salaries as there was a huge disparity between the new hires and the 'old soldiers'. It seemed there was no reward for loyalty and that the only way to get a pay rise was to leave and find a new job with another, rival, company. This appears to be the case even today. By my calculation, all the staff who had five or more years with the company were paid 20% less than new hires. I also figured I needed at least seven new hires to manage the increasing volume of business. In the event I was given a budget to try to even up the pay gap and allowed to employ five new heads. It was a start.

Whilst I was on a recruitment hunt the paperless project was gathering speed. The process was called Apollo. There was a claims chap (Robert) giving input and at our weekly management meeting, he would give us updates on how the matter was progressing. At the beginning this was interesting but after weeks and weeks of listening to him frankly droning on about the problems, I said that this was wasting our time. If we had input into the project, I could have understood the need to hear about the issues, but we didn't, so I asked to be excused. Robert was a nice chap, but if he had a fault, in my eyes, it was that he saw everything as black and white, and was a stickler for procedures. A year or so before, a large claim I was handling required a big payment. The matter was co-insured and all the co-insurers had sent us their cheques for their shares payable to us. I wanted to send out one cheque for the 100% amount, but Robert refused to honour the payment request because, until they were cleared, the co-insurance cheques 'might bounce'. I was livid, the co-insurers were major multinational insurance companies!

One of my new team was indeed a very old soldier. Don was in his 60s, 'old school' and very set in his ways but quite a 'character'. He specialised in motor and although that book was waning, he had, extremely reluctantly it must be said, taken on standard PL work. If there was one thing in which Don excelled, it was his telephone manner. A familiar exchange might go as follows:

'Good morning claims department, Don speaking, how can I help? ... hmm, yes of course I can ... how much? ... £5,000? ... not a problem at all, I'll get on to it straight away ... and you ... nice to speak to you too' and then he would hang up and mutter under his breath, 'fucking solicitors. If he thinks I'm fucking paying that today he's got another fucking think coming. Wanker.' He was great fun to listen to, but it was fair to say that his customer service skills needed some improvement. Unfortunately, Don would not embrace change. His whole life was geared to a routine that he never changed. He had a tortuous journey into the office by rail which meant he was the only person who was allowed to work 8 – 4 each day, and on the dot of 4 p.m., he was out the door. Despite his poor customer service skills his knowledge of motor claims was unparalleled and I liked him. In all the time I knew him, he never had a day off sick. But the change from paper to paperless was going to be too much for Don and he told me that as soon as we went paperless, he was retiring and he didn't want any retirement 'do' either. As Don had been with the company for decades, I said that it would be disappointing for his colleagues not to have a farewell party, so against his wishes we did throw a party and secretly I think he was pleased.

As the move towards a paperless world progressed, normal claims were still coming in thick and fast. I admit to being somewhat of a control freak and I made it my business to see all new claims just to ensure that they were being allocated to the right kind of handler.

Nevertheless, a few of the claims made me pick up the phone...

'Hello, yes my name is Trevor and I work for ACE and I have your letter of 16th addressed to the Only-a-Pound shop. You are complaining that the item your client purchased is not of durable quality and broke within days. Yeah, it cost a pound. Just a pound. How durable do you expect an item to be that cost just a pound? I'll send you a pound in compensation. OK?'

We insured a supermarket chain that, like most big businesses, expected us to respond to letters where compensation was claimed, even if the claimant was a 'nutter' and the claim had no merit at all, rather like this one:

"Dear Sirs, I am writing to claim compensation from your supermarket firm. Last Saturday I purchased a six-pack of your own brand Bakewell tarts. Imagine my horror and disgust when on opening the packet I found that all the cherries were OFF CENTRE and did not look anything like the picture on the box. My son's 1st Birthday party was absolutely RUINED as a result and I await your cheque for an appropriate level of compensation".

There had been a national recall of a very well-known brand of cola beverage that had become accidentally tainted by carbon dioxide that itself contained traces of benzene. Now benzene is carcinogenic and harmful to health. Before the Food Standards Agency got all cross, the manufacturers wisely had arranged a recall, removed the cola from all stockists and poured the whole lot down the drain. However, some had been sold and doubtlessly consumed. According to our food scientists, to run the risk of developing cancer from benzene-infused cola, you would have to have drunk a swimming pool's worth in 24 hours. A bit unlikely methinks. The alternative, said the scientist, would be to eat a charred sausage that had been cooked on a BBQ as that would have the same carcinogenic properties.

The cola firm sent us a most peculiar letter of claim from a customer. The man claimed compensation for his shoes that had rotted after he had spilt the benzene cola on the floor. He said he had walked through it, and now his shoes were falling apart. My suspicions were raised as the letter was written in crayon in a spiral pattern around the edges of paper he had torn out of the medical notes from the mental institution in which he was incarcerated. (I kid you not). And the cola firm wanted us to write back to him (again, I kid you not).

There was some sniggering in the back of the office by the filing cabinets and some of the younger chaps were passing around photos. I went to see what was causing them mirth. It turned out that a female support garment manufacturer we insured had made strapless bra cups that had an adhesive layer under the cup that was, well, a little too adhesive. Upon removal of the cup, it was also taking off a layer of skin. Nasty... especially for the more well-endowed ladies. It was these photos that the chaps were passing around. I told them to stop being so laddish, gathered up all the claims and handed them to Michaela. She was one of the claim handlers who had seemingly been written off by previous managers as someone who would never advance and was only capable of dealing with menial, routine processing. I like to give people a chance to develop and so in handing the files to Michaela I explained that I thought that sensitive cases like these should be dealt with by someone 'more properly qualified'. She still looked puzzled and said 'But why me?' I leaned down and whispered conspiratorially 'Cos you are a woman with big boobs and understand these things, those jerks don't.' Michaela did go on to greater things a couple of years later.

Email is so ubiquitous now that it comes as a surprise to some that there was a time before email. We had computers on our desks, but the monitors were small and as far as email was concerned, we could only email internally. Then a technological crack appeared – we could email brokers... and the crack widened to our solicitors and loss adjusters...then the floodgates sprang open and we could send and receive to all. It may come as a further surprise that we even went on training courses about how to send emails. One of the things I remember is that email should be seen as the electronic equivalent of a letter or a phone call.

'If you wouldn't send a copy of a letter to someone or you wouldn't call them, don't 'cc' them in' was the advice. When I look at the email traffic now, it seems that if I don't copy in the person in charge of ordering toilet rolls in the Puerto Rico office, I have somehow failed to properly communicate. It is a ridiculous situation and I blame Bill Gates.

With open communication can come miscommunication. It seemed that 'someone' in the company had been using email for non-business use (they had been talking about American Football matches apparently, so were probably in the USA) and in consequence, our IT department had been instructed to monitor all email traffic and if anyone used 'inappropriate words' then the offender would be reported to Human Resources and disciplinary action would follow. That sounded like a plan, but a bad plan to my mind as there was no list of what words were considered 'inappropriate'. I suppose all profanity was rightly on the list, but the way around that was to use an asterisk, so that would beat the f*cking Email Police I thought.

Almost immediately, I was contacted by IT as someone in the team had offended and I was required to take action. The offending word was... 'football'. And the offender had used it repeatedly! I duly contacted HR and said that as we insured the Rugby Football League it was somewhat difficult not to use the word. 'Football' duly came off the list.

I had travelled to see a solicitor in Glasgow and we had enjoyed a really good dinner together and he complained about his weight and breathlessness. I suggested that he give up drinking for a while and cigarettes for good. The following day in a routine email he added a P.S. 'taken your advice, I've given up the booze and fags.' I replied straight away with 'well done' and in a millisecond a message appeared on screen saying that I had been reported to HR for using an inappropriate word, the word was 'fags'. Once again, I said to HR that I had not

360

used an inappropriate word, all I had done was reply 'well done' and 'fags' is not inappropriate in the UK anyway. So, fags came off the list.

The solicitors in charge of handling a large number of claims for a major store that had sold faulty leather chairs and sofas, created a spreadsheet containing all the claims. The list included approximately 4300 claims. Originally, the furniture manufacturing was located in a hot and dry part of India. However, later the manufacturing was shifted to an area of China where the labour was cheaper, but the climate was wet and humid. So, to prevent mould from growing on the leather, a tea bag of chemicals was stapled to the frames of the furniture. The chemical crystals evaporated and the fumes killed mould, so all was thought to be well and good. The trouble was that the chemical also could cause skin rashes, and so it proved. Anyone sitting on the leather with their bare skin touching the leather could get a rash. There was even a claim within the list for a poor dog that lost its fur. For reasons that I found baffling, one of our reinsurers had asked to be sent a complete and detailed list of all of the claims. I simply attached the spreadsheet to an email in response and said 'Herewith spreadsheet of claims as requested'. A millisecond later I was once again being reported for using inappropriate language, specifically this time 'bloody' and 'pussy'.

I did not recall a claim for a cat, just the dog, but I supposed a feline was possibly among the claims, so I did a word search. Under one claim, the injury was described as a "*suppurating bloody wound that went pussy*". Oh, for f*ck's sake, I wanted to reply, but instead off I went to HR for the third time. For once they did not have a sense of humour failure and agreed that this was all getting a bit silly.

'Are you the manager?' an irate caller enquired.

'I am. What's the problem?' I calmly answered.

'It's Tony here from Bloggs Brokers and I've sent in an urgent new claim by email but I've had no answer.'

'Hmm, that's not like us Tony, let me see what I can find on the system'. At this time, we have gone completely paperless and we were encouraging brokers to submit new matters via email. Previously, hard copies (or what we used to call "post") had to be scanned and sent to the file handler for action, which took an extra day or two. I took the policy reference and name but despite all searches, there was no sign of the claim.

'OK,' said Tony, 'give me your email address and I'll send it to you. It's got an attachment and as it's a photograph it may take a while to get through your server. I'll give you a bell in five minutes, OK?'

Five minutes later Tony called but I said I'd not received any email from him. I carefully respelled my name and address and Tony said, exasperated, that he would send it once more. The email still did not arrive. I decided to call the email Police. When I finally got through to someone, they confirmed that all of the emails Tony had sent had been 'quarantined' (by which they meant deleted) by the system, because the email contained pornographic images. I said that was the claim! A disgruntled employee had sabotaged a print run of a children's magazine with a very pornographic image... and we insured the printers. I had to get Tony to send the email again and this time the email came through and we dealt with the claim.

Do we still have email Police? I've no bollocking idea.

It took a good six months or so before the Apollo system was bedded in. There were numerous bugs to fix and an 'upgrade' almost every month but I came to like it. Not everyone could cope with having to type their correspondence and some suffered, myself included, with arm and neck aches – or 'repetitive strain injury' or RSI as it is known. One of the issues was the perceived need to see a whole A4 piece of paper on screen (the incoming letter), plus another A4 piece of paper on the opposite side of the screen (the reply). To accommodate this the VDU screens, we were given were massive and took up 90% of our desk space.

Flat monitors were in their infancy at the time and were considered too expensive anyway, so we had to put up with these monster screens. The upshot of this was that users were too close to the screens, so some developed eye strain with resultant headaches and some developed RSI in their wrists from all the mouse activity. Some of the team could not cope at all and resigned. One even brought an action against the company and for my part, I thought she had a case; no thought whatsoever had been given to the ergonomics and design of the office.

During this time, I was spending most of my time interviewing and 'selling' the benefits of a paperless office to interviewees who were equally sceptical about the benefits as we were the vanguard in a paperless office system. The other problem with recruitment in Maidstone is the catchment area. Anyone who was career-minded commuted to London. Public transport to Maidstone by train was poor, so most drove to work and the parking cost was high, even if convenient (a multi-storey car park was directly opposite) and there were only a couple of other small insurance companies represented in Maidstone from whom we could poach staff. Outside of Kent County Council and the Police, ACE were the biggest employers in the town.

I noticed that my vision was suffering. My optician could find nothing wrong with my prescription, but I was still getting blurred vision in one eye. Persuaded by The Sainted Karon, as she was to be known, I went to see my GP. He diagnosed stress and, although I didn't need reminding, that stress can bring about death, and that can be fatal... he suggested I should be going for regular walks and take up a hobby or evening class, provided that there was no exam at the end. That is when and why I got Freya the dog and took up watercolour painting as a hobby. As to the pain in my right forearm, he suggested physiotherapy.

The physio-terrorist (as I fondly called her) was a very nice lady named Sue. I was able to visit her on my way home from the office, where I had been working long hours: from 8 am to 7:30 pm most days. I described my working environment and with my shirt off, Sue began to manipulate my neck. Pointing out that it was my arm that was the problem, Sue said that once she had finished unknotting my neck, which was rigid, she would start on my arm. She applied electrodes to pads which were then stuck onto my neck and back and turned on a tensing machine. As the electric shock hit me, I immediately admitted to being Osama Bin Laden, but after a while the sensation was soothing and I started to relax and even turned the dial up a notch or two. I left that session about an inch taller. Sue said my posture was dreadful, I needed to sit up straighter, get a proper chair at the office and if possible, a different type of mouse and keyboard. Yes, mum.

I reported my concerns to HR and I was provided with a more suitable chair and after a couple of tries with other rodents, settled on a smashing one called a 'roller mouse'. Not only do I find it brilliant, it's quicker and easy to use. However, colleagues accustomed to a standard mouse find it puzzling and confusing, and so stay clear of my workstation!

Sitting directly in front of me was a new recruit called Sean. He was a real Jack-the-lad and good fun. He had taken to calling me Boss or Guvnor which I didn't mind. However, sitting directly in front of me meant that I could see what he was doing most of the day. He was far more computer savvy than me (most people are) and I could see that at any one time, he had loads of windows open when he needed only two – Apollo and email. His excuse was that his brother sent him messages all the time and he was looking at those. I told him to keep his private stuff to lunchtime and left it at that.

One afternoon there was a commotion coming from Sean's desk. He had clicked on a message from his brother and suddenly from the speaker came the sound of a man shouting.

"QUICK CALL A MANAGER, I'M WATCHING INTERNET PORN AND I CAN'T TURN IT OFF! QUICK CALL A MANAGER, I'M WATCHING INTERNET PORN AND I CAN'T TURN IT OFF! QUICK CALL A MANAGER, I'M WATCHING INTERNET PORN AND I CAN'T TURN IT OFF!"

And sure enough, there on his screen was an extremely pornographic image. Sean was busy clicking and pressing every button on his screen to try and remove the image and sound but to no avail. Finally, he just unplugged it.

I was partly able to see the funny side but said this had to stop – now. I told him to tell his brother to lay off the jokes or I would get the email Police to block all his communications or HR would become involved and he risked a formal complaint.

I still liked to get my hands metaphorically dirty and do some proper claims work, actually see people, and try and resolve claims. A contractor had been appointed to relay new gas mains in a residential street. The homeowners had been told that their gas supply would be cut off for a few days at most whilst the new main was being laid and the houses reconnected. Trenches had been dug and all pipework identified. Once the reconnections had been completed the gas supply was turned back on. The following morning after reconnection, Ernie was in his kitchen and he had filled his electric kettle to make a cup of tea. On flicking the 'on' switch there was an almighty explosion and Ernie's house simply disappeared. He was standing in the remains of his house, no walls or roof remaining... and there wasn't a scratch on him.

What had happened was that in the past his house had been laid with a gas pipe but it had corroded and a new one had been installed. During the reconnection process the contractor had connected both the 'new' pipe as well as the old corroded one, which had no end-stop. Gas was pouring out of the corroded pipe into the understairs cupboard, filling the downstairs with gas whilst Ernie was upstairs asleep in his bed. Although natural gas has an extremely pungent smell, poor Ernie had long ago lost his sense of smell and didn't notice it when he went to make the cup of tea that morning. The simple act of turning on the kettle must have generated some kind of spark and 'kaboom'. Ernie was at the epicentre of the explosion and so didn't hear a bang; his entire house simply disappeared around him. The debris went in every direction and damaged houses in neighbouring streets and dozens of cars were impacted too. Luckily and amazingly, no one was hurt. The logistics of dealing with claims from dozens of home and vehicle owners (and their insurers) was a nightmare, but obviously the contractors were to blame, so we settled all the claims. The HSE were none too pleased either and I think the contractor was smacked with a hefty fine.

Whilst filling vacancies I took on a few temporary team members, two of which came from Independent Insurance who were based in Edenbridge. We had been hearing a lot of unsettling stories about the 'Indy' as they were known. They were renowned for undercutting the market on rates, basically buying in business and then when the claims came in were slow in paying, assuming they paid at all. Their reserving practices were fraudulent, as was later proven.

I had a claim on with the Indy involving a scaffold collapse in Edinburgh. Our insured were the main contractors and the Indy insured the scaffolders. A liability split had been agreed upon, but part of that deal was that we would settle the claims and then ask Indy for their 50%. This works well when you trust the other side, and here I had an agreement, in this case, an exchange of letters to that effect.

Having settled the final aspect of the claim I was looking to Indy to honour their 50%, no mean amount either, about £250,000, but small beer to most insurance companies. I waited and waited. Reminders were sent but I received no reply.

I mentioned to Rosie, the ex-Indy person I'd hired and someone I liked and trusted, about the difficulty. She explained that unless I had a judgment, as a third party where only a promise had been made, there would be little chance of getting paid. She went on to explain that every month the Indy put aside a chunk of cash to pay claims. Out of that, they would pay 1st party claims (basically property losses) then some expenses, then judgments and then third-party claims, assuming there was anything left in the pot that is. She said that the chances of us ever getting to the top of the pile were pretty remote.

She thought though that if I sent a carefully worded letter to certain people, it might provoke a reaction and move us up the pecking order. I didn't think there was anything to lose by trying, so I said let's give it a go.

Rosie drafted the letter and I sent it to all the people she suggested, both in hard copy and by email.

The following morning all hell broke loose. I was telephoned by their head of claims saying that what I had written was disgraceful and they would send a bank transfer that day. They did too. And what did my letter say?

'Do you have sufficient funds to pay this claim?'

That's all it took. I was very grateful.

There were two addenda to that story. The first is a 'tee hee hee'. The agreement I mentioned was finalized while the Indy claims representative and I were at the Fatal Accident Enquiry in Edinburgh. There was little doubt that the scaffolders (insured by the Indy) were largely to blame, but to avoid further fuss, the Indy chap offered to split the claim 50/50 provided that, as we insured the main contractors, we dealt with all the losses first. I accepted and he put it in writing. Had the claims person at Indy read the contract properly, or at all, they would have seen that my contractor had agreed to indemnify all people coming onto the site (a single project policy). Still, they couldn't have read it... so they screwed themselves over for two hundred and fifty thousand smackeroos. I didn't see a penny of course.

No sooner had the bank transfer arrived, I found myself attending the British Insurance Awards held at the Royal Albert Hall in London as a guest of a firm of solicitors the following day. Another 'black tie' event, but to keep in with the new corporate colours, I was wearing a rather fetching lime green bow tie.

Those evenings can be dull, but it all depends on who was compering. It might have been Dara O'Briain, Jonathan Ross or Jeremy Clarkson, or someone boring, the numerous categories seem to go on forever and make it a long night. It takes stamina to get to the end and, trust me, it also requires copious amounts of wine to keep you awake. I was very awake. It came to 'Insurer of the Year' which in our books is 'the big one', the one everyone is waiting for. The nominees were read out and with some fanfare, the gold envelope was solemnly opened by the Editor of the 'Post Magazine' (the journal for insurers) and the winner's name was slowly drawn out. 'And the winner is...(pause) for their creativity and professionalism the judges have given the award this year to... (bigger pause) Independent Insurance!' No sooner had the last syllable left the editor's lips than 'someone' (OK, it was me) at our table let out a huge 'Hah, joke!!' just before the applause started. Michael Bright, the chief exec of Indy wobbled up to the stage to get his trophy as the applause continued. I stayed resolutely silent.

A few weeks later Indy went bust. From being worth £1bn the company was now worth nothing. All 2000 employees lost their jobs and pensions and tens of thousands of policyholders were left to re-buy insurance mid-term. Michael Not-So-Bright-After-All eventually got seven years for fraud. Nowhere near long enough some might say.

I am forever indebted to Rosie for her sound advice. She went on to become a senior manager at another insurer and rightly did very well.

Back in the factory, my #2 was probably Peter. We worked together in London and I got to know him well. He was keen, a good technician and very conscientious. He looked after the claims for a theme park we insured (the one where the girl cut her finger) and he was a very smart dresser. I'd sent him on a routine claim for an accident on the log flume at the park. It was out of season and the park was shut to visitors and the flume had been drained. (Did you know that the water in the flumes has a chemical retardant added to stop foaming? If they didn't, little sods would squirt washing-up liquid into the water to see the whole thing become a foamy and slippery mess). Anyway, Peter arrived and needed to take a photo of some mechanism or other that was at the top of a flume. A member of staff was with him and he thought he had all the photo angles he needed, but one more from inside the dry flume would be really helpful... or so he thought.

Climbing carefully over the edge of the flume so as not to stain his trousers, he turned and squatted to take the snap when suddenly the grip from the soles of his shoes on the green slime of the bottom of the flume caused him to gradually slide. In his panic, he tried to grip the side of the flume, but it was too late, down he went on his backside, arms flailing, his Armani suit getting liberally covered in stinky green slime until he came to a natural stop somewhere on the flume. The lady who was with him ran down the steps to assist him back over the flume edge and, passing the matter off as if this sort of thing happened every day, Peter thanked the lady and went back to his car.

How do I know all that? At a client meeting, I was asked if Peter was still with us? I said he was, but why were they asking? The representative of the client was actually the lady who rescued Peter and she said she had struggled in vain not to laugh at his misfortune, but no sooner than Peter had left she fell to her knees, crying with laughter. She was even more disappointed that the CCTV was switched off. So was I, as I'd have loved to have seen it.

The office was undergoing renovations because of years of complaints about the summer heat. Air conditioning was being installed, causing the department to relocate to different floors on a frequent basis. Although we were essentially paperless, we still sent out letters in the post, so we had printers and a large stationery cupboard - actually rows of racking in a separate room. Just two or three secretaries remained, the formidable Sue who was the matriarch and had been there for decades, Trena and Michelle, whose jobs were to type any long reports we had and organise travel for us. The stationery domain was theirs too and each time we moved floors along came the boxes and boxes of printer toner cartridges and the like.

I had my own printer and one day I needed a new toner cartridge. In taking one from the shelf I noticed that there were about a dozen others on the shelf. We had moved these time and time again, but they never seemed to be needed. Being nosey I then asked the ladies to which printers those toners belonged as from the 'use by' dates they were long past being viable, in some cases five years out of date. It turned out, not so surprisingly, that the printers to which the toners were designed had long since been replaced by newer models and all the toners were obsolete...but no one dared to throw them away as they were 'expensive when purchased'. In a secret pact with the ladies, I put all the redundant toners into my car and sold the lot on eBay and with the proceeds we all went out for a slap-up Chinese lunch. It was better than putting them in a skip.

I had to go to Montreal for a market meeting. Although the flight was over 8 hours in duration (the threshold for going business class) Sue had said I had to travel economy as the claims department was on a budget squeeze. My fellow coinsurers on the plane were all at the 'pointy end' arriving fresh and relaxed. I left the plane feeling exhausted and irritable because there was a crying child nearby who had decided to express its displeasure by wailing for most of the flight. Our group collected our bags from the carousel and we figured it would be sensible to share a taxi. We each gave the name of our hotels, two were 'downtown' but I was not. No, to save a few dollars on the hotel room rate, I was staying at a hotel in somewhere called Laval. Of course, I had no idea where that was, though the taxi driver had a beaming grin as we set off. The driver said he would drop me off last and I had agreed with the others to meet up in half an hour for a beer or two and discuss the case. My companions were dropped off at their hotels and then an hour later I was at my hotel in

Laval. It was about 20 miles away through murderous traffic and across a toll bridge to boot, which I had to pay for. So, I paid the taxi fare, went to my room, showered, unpacked and got another taxi back downtown. After a very short meeting (just the one beer, as I was 90 minutes delayed) I got another taxi back to Laval. The next day another taxi back downtown... and so it went on for three days. The room saving – about CAD$50 per night. The taxi fares came to over CAD$400. I was livid about this so-called cost saving and from that time I largely managed my own travel arrangements. I did have an evening to myself though and went to see a play. I got the last ticket and was against a wall. Yeah, international travel is so much fun.

One of the things I was encouraged to do was to try to get my team professionally qualified. I was unqualified myself, so it would be a bit hypocritical of me to insist others sit exams when I hadn't. There was a new organisation called the Society of Claims Technicians and unlike the Chartered Insurance Institute where the CII syllabus covered claims, underwriting, broking and a host of disciplines, the SCT was just claims focused.

I sat the exams and was one of the first to ever gain Associateship, which gave me letters after my name of ASCT. I later was elevated to Fellowship and was for a brief time, FSCT. Then the Society was absorbed into the CII and my qualification was transferred to DipCII – or 'dipsy' as we call it.

By now I had recruited the five extra claims handlers and I thought the department was running smoothly. The stupidly big monitors had been replaced with flat screens and backlogs were manageable, even reducing. Our old paper files had been scanned and were now able to be viewed. Even Apollo was playing nicely when I got an email from my manager, Alan, about a new recruit starting in our department on Monday called Darryl. Alan said that he thought we had everyone we needed? I replied that we were indeed fully staffed and I'd not interviewed anyone for months so HR must have got the wrong 'Trevor' (it was possible) and the wrong department. Alan said he would follow it up.

That afternoon I got an urgent call from HR to attend a meeting...

Chapter Twenty-Four

A CHANGE IS AS GOOD AS A REST

That afternoon I was ushered into a small meeting room with Graham, Alan and Gaile from HR.

It was explained that changes were being announced and I was going to move to a new position of Executive Loss Adjuster (ELA) and this Darryl character was going to be taking my position as Casualty Claims Manager. I could not quite take in what I was being told and must have sat there rather stunned as I do not recall saying anything.

The ELA position meant that I was only going to look at technical claims (which suited me) and as I was still going to be reporting to Alan, there was no real change. I would be dropping all the managerial tasks (recruitment, holiday rotas, dealing with discipline, complaints, training and development etc none of which I liked) so it was sold to me on a win/win basis.

I wasn't happy though. I knew who had done this to me but not the 'why'.

I decided to take legal advice. My solicitor said that technically I had been made redundant and could claim constructive dismissal, but to make a claim for that I would have to leave. Of course, the thought of having no salary, and a possible legal fight, whilst paying a mortgage and general expenses, did not sit easily, even though I was told I would probably win. The other side of the coin was that my sideways move did not involve any salary loss, just loss of face. Could I cope with that? I guessed I would have to.

Not once have I ever blamed Darryl for what happened to me at that time and, when he arrived, he set about organising things his way. He made a case for the extra two people I had previously requested and this time it was approved and he set about recruiting straight away... he needed to, as within a couple of months of him taking charge about five of the team resigned. Whether they would have left anyway I do not know, but it made me have a teeny bit of schadenfreude.

As an ELA I was working with another Alan (just to add to the confusion) although both were known by nicknames. Alan #2 was known as Gambo, so to avoid confusion, that is how I will refer to him.

I had taken my portfolio of claims with me so I had plenty to do and meetings to attend. Gambo and I were to split the new matters evenly, which meant I probably took 80% of them. It was intended that we only handled big claims, over $500,000 or anything particularly complicated. A lot of our work was in the USA and Canada, dealing with cases that were being handled by our people there, but from time to time we became directly involved. It was Gambo who was handling 'Billy' which is why I took it back under my wing.

From time to time, I still went out to investigate the odd claim, one of which I took on simply because it happened close to where I lived.

A couple were camping at a site close to the beauty spot of Bewl Water where there is a large reservoir, actually a flooded valley, but as that does not feature in the tale, it can be ignored. According to the Letter of Claim a faulty gas canister on a gas light had exploded and two people were badly burned... as we insured the manufacturers of the canister, we needed to get the facts.

The facts were, according to the owner of the campsite, rather different to the story provided by the solicitors. The campsite was within walking distance of a pub and late one warm and humid summer's evening the pair came back from the pub, presumably, as the courts would say, worse for drink. The chap found that his gas lantern cylinder was nearly empty, so he removed it and attempted to fit another. Being dark, it must have been a fiddly process and he failed to get it fully clipped on, so he tossed the cylinder to one side. He had two more spare cylinders (as they also fitted their small gas stove) but the second was also found to be 'faulty' and that too discarded onto the ground. He managed to get his third one connected, then turned on the lamp and struck a match. Kaboom!!

The two discarded cylinders were full of butane, which is heavier than air and so he and his partner were physically sitting in a pool of highly flammable gas spreading around their feet as the butane boiled inexorably out of the tiny punctures on the discarded canisters. The commotion caused other campers to come to their aid and a 999 call was made. The fire was out in moments, but the two sorry campers both had flash burns.

I was shaking my head about all this but asked the campsite owner how he knew the story. He said that after the fire the two injured campers went to hospital by ambulance and he inspected their, now charred, grassy pitch by torchlight. He said he had found three empty gas canisters and... (and this I found incredible) he had taken them away for safekeeping and had put them on a shelf in his barn 'as he expected that at some time someone would come to investigate!' They had, and it was me, so signing a receipt I took the canisters away. They were scorched and a bit rusty now, but to my eye, the puncture marks on the top of each looked the same. I could not see any fault with the canisters. I suppose there might be a fault with the lamp though, but again I doubted that as those things are pretty robust.

I contacted the claimant's solicitors and told them that I had the canisters and, unbelievably, they suggested that we pay for the forensic investigation. Damned cheek. I said that metaphorically they were pointing a gun at me and wanted me to not only give them the ammunition but pay for it as well? Not a hope. I said I would send them the canisters if they wished, but added I did not think there was any case to answer and the matter, if pursued, would be robustly defended. I never heard from them again.

If there was a problem with dealing with claims in the USA it is that for those who do not know the United States of America is, I am sorry to say, anything but 'united'. They may as well be fifty different countries as laws, practices and procedures frequently differ from state to state. Some are seemingly pro-defendant (precious few actually) but most are pro-claimant. And why? Because of their jury system. No other country in the world has a jury system for civil matters for trifling claims. The first a defendant company gets to hear about a claim is when a set of impenetrably worded pleadings lands with a thump on the desk. Some of the pleadings go on for hundreds of pages with constant repetition and conclude not with an amount that the plaintiff seeks, but the plaintiff 'demands trial by jury'. Like that helps. What is more, due to a constitution that has not been brought into the 19th, let alone the 20th or 21st, century you could request a trial by jury for any monetary amount over $15.00; basically, the cost of a cinema ticket. Utterly ridiculous. There are more lawyers in the State of New York than in the whole of Japan. Countries do not get rich by suing each other, only attorneys get rich. And why are Americans so litigious? After decades of handling their claims, my only conclusion is greed. That is it, just greed. Attorneys frequently take 50% of all the awarded damages, so it pays them to rack up the value of a case before an unwitting jury. It certainly has nothing to do with truth or justice.

I cannot help though but admire the creativity of plaintiff attorneys who bring claims for things which in other countries would be laughed out of court.

The 'angel's share' is a phrase that comes from whisky manufacture. As whisky or bourbon takes a long time to mature in oak barrels, a tiny amount evaporates through the wooden barrels, so after seven years of maturing, instead of the hundred gallons of spirit that went into the barrel, only ninety-nine remain. One gallon has evaporated away... the angel's share.

The problem with the angel's share is that the vapour, whilst smelling pleasant enough, settles on property and algae love the stuff as it is, for them, food. Algae grow on surfaces, sometimes causing a black mould.

Although there is no scientific proof, attorneys also allege that the vapour is harmful to health, ignoring the irony that drinking the stuff can be even more harmful, so they gather together a class action and sue the local distilleries. It costs hundreds of thousands of dollars to defend these spurious actions and this is exactly what the attorneys realise. It costs more sometimes to defend these cases than pay them, even though the case has no merit whatsoever.

One day a bunch of attorneys made the trip from the USA to Scotland and went about knocking on houses door-to-door around several distilleries trying to get locals to sign up for a class action. I don't think they fully realized that even in Scotland, which still has a jury system for injury cases, the level of damages would be inconsequential. According to what we read in the local press an attorney knocked on the door of a house and was met by a burly Scotsman. The attorney explained the harm of the angel's share commenting on the mould growth on the windows and paintwork of his house and how if he signed up for the class action, he could get extensive damages. The Scotsman apparently licked his finger and with his wet finger wiped away a streak of mould 'And you can get me damages for that? Away with you, that's natural pal, there's mould everywhere, the climate is damp – it's Scotland! Also, if you think for one moment, I am going to sue my employer, who's the only employer around here, for something as trivial as that and that causes them to shut the distillery down and put me out of a job, for something that a wee wipe with a J-cloth with a squirt of Jif will remove... you can f*ck off you pr*ck'.

So, the attorneys packed their bags and left... but still brought the actions in the USA. I do not know what happened as 'mould claims' were excluded by our policy.

Another class action was brought for welding fumes. This time the allegation was that manganese in welding rod fumes led to welders developing Parkinson's disease...but only in America. British, Dutch, Japanese and Norwegian welders, along with every other country in the world seemed largely immune to Parkinson's disease from welding fumes. I say 'largely' because about 1% of them did develop it. But there again so did 1% of nurses, air-traffic controllers and even lawyers... or put another way, 1% of the population. Insurers spent tens of millions of dollars defending these actions until the action was struck out. Why? The answer was that the doctor who had seen a great number of the plaintiffs for a medical examination had diagnosed manganese-induced Parkinson's disease in all of them. It seems from the number of people he saw daily, that he was able to both see, examine and come up with a diagnosis in as little as five minutes per patient. Even the judge thought that this was an abuse of the process and struck out all the plaintiffs seen by that doctor, which were most of them and of the few that remained, even the plaintiff attorneys didn't see the crock of gold they were expecting and gave up. It took about ten years though and as I said, wasted millions of dollars defending them.

Under US food standards, sourdough bread by law can only contain just three ingredients – flour, water and a starter of fermented yeast. I think maybe a pinch of salt is allowed too, but that is it. Enterprising attorneys have been bringing actions against big bakeries and supermarkets on the basis that some sourdough bread has added ingredients such as pectin and the odd flavour enhancer... and as those ingredients are not in the sourdough bread recipe, the bakers cannot call it sourdough bread and because they have labelled it as sourdough bread, consumers have been mis-sold the product and so misled, the bakers have had 'unjust enrichment' (profits) which they must now pay back to their customers. Oh, please. Really? Mis-sold?

California has its own rules (a code) for insurers' behaviour and strangely I do not think they are too bad. Treating customers fairly and making interim payments are good things. But the code relies heavily on the US Postal system communicating with policyholders/plaintiffs etc. At one training session I attended I asked the panel that in geological terms and timescales, California suffers a major earthquake every 100 years or so, the last being in 1906. We were now way past that and although there are tremors frequently, if California suffered one on the same scale as 1906 (around 3000 fatalities – and no high-rise buildings), with a greater infrastructure and population today than in 1906, the devastation would be significant... there would be no roads, electricity, telephone and other utilities would be cut off; but somehow the US Postal Service would still function. How come? I was met with a sea of bemused and blank faces. Maybe no one had given that any thought. Surely not?

But it is not all doom and gloom. The latest I heard was that juries are now so used to the media soundbite that long speeches by attorneys are falling out of favour. According to some companies that monitor jury behaviours, the average attention span of a juror is around 5-10 minutes; about the same time as a TV show in between advertisements. Most jurors have not read a book in the last five years and some have never read a book at all. As a lot of jurors will have seen TV shows where a whole murder case is resolved in an hour, they sort of expect the same in reality. If a trial goes on for more than a couple of days it is often thought that by the end, they will have forgotten the facts.

I was still seeing my old brokers and policyholders from time to time and one Friday I was paying a boozy lunchtime visit to a loyal policyholder (who had been insured with us for decades) near Letchworth with Joe, an underwriter when whilst waiting at the station for a train, I got a call on my phone. It was not good news.

'Trevor, this is Roland (the head of claims) I understand you are out of the office at the moment. You are not to come back today and I am to read you the following statement. The claims operation in Maidstone is being transferred to Glasgow. All staff are under the threat of redundancy or relocation, but there are some exceptions – you, Alan, Gambo and Darryl, plus a few others are to be relocated to London...' he might have said something else but at that point, a train went by and I could not hear.

'You OK Trevor?' said Joe, 'you're as white as a sheet mate. What's happened?'

'Not sure Joe' I replied, my mouth was dry and I was feeling rather dizzy, 'but from what I gather, the claims operation is being relocated to Glasgow. Nearly everyone is being laid off, but I'm being relocated to London. I'll give the office a bell and find out more.' At that point, our train arrived and although I called the office on numerous numbers the lines were all dead.

When I got home, I relayed what little I knew to Karon. Being unable to speak to anyone, possibly until Monday, made for a dreadful weekend.

On Monday I got in at my usual time and was taken into a meeting room for an explanation. It seems that the bean counters had been at it again and had persuaded the company that a relocation to Glasgow for not just claims, but the whole Maidstone operation, was economical. It was thought that some would relocate from claims (just two did) and as salaries were lower in Glasgow and there were several insurance companies to poach from, in consequence, recruitment would be easy. The Scottish Government were also giving a huge financial incentive for new employers and as it was not just claims relocating, but the whole of Maidstone office, the cash would more than offset the redundancy costs. There had been numerous secret meetings over the preceding weeks, and possibly months, but the news of a move to Glasgow had leaked out to the press and so a crisis meeting had been held the previous Friday. The team were all told what was happening, but no questions would be answered and everyone was told to go home. The switchboard was turned off and that explained why I could not get through to anyone. It seemed that the announcement had been handled very badly.

It was thought the senior staff would have no issue about working in London. We would get a salary increase to cover the cost of train and parking and as all other terms would remain the same, we still had jobs to go to, what was the problem? The move to London would not take place for about 3-4 months, meantime it was business as usual.

The mood in the office was incredibly sombre as might be expected. Tears had turned to anger and quite a few decided to 'work to rule' and even if they were at their desks, did not start until 9 a.m. and were out the door on the dot of 5 p.m. I didn't blame them. As the weeks went by, I was amazed by the sheer professionalism of those that remained. They cared more about their work than the company cared about them.

Of the newer recruits, the amount of redundancy they were likely to receive was peanuts, so a lot left as soon as they found other positions. This of course meant additional work for those that remained and overtime was offered to try to keep on top of the work (not that any came to me I might add).

It was not a good time.

Gambo took redundancy and his position was filled by Richard one of the senior adjusters. Richard and I were to report to Darryl and in turn, he was to report to Alan.

Back   to   London   then.   Déjà   vu.

Chapter Twenty-Five

DÉJÀ VU ALL OVER AGAIN AND AGAIN

I live reasonably close to one station but it has fewer services to London than the next nearest. I tried both services for comparison but eventually settled on the nearer one.

I now needed to be on a train at 07.11 and that meant getting up at six. It was going to be a struggle, but I had to do it. Fortunately, the company were fairly relaxed about timekeeping and as I only ever took a 30-minute lunch break, I was able to leave the office at 4.45 p.m. to be sure of getting my train at 5.01 p.m. and that would get me home for around 6.30 p.m. It was still a long day and I was permitted to work at the ghost office of Maidstone on Thursdays to enable me to get to my art class at 7 p.m. I kept to that routine for a few years until newer technology allowed us to work from home via a secure computer link.

The spiralling cost of rail travel and parking however did not keep up with annual pay increases. Nevertheless, I was happy(ish) with my lot.

Richard and I split the work 50/50 alphabetically and we both kept key clients. Our initial offices were in the 'lower ground floor' or basement and we sat adjacent to a team who were handling engineering and energy claims (just what I used to do when I was in London the first time around). I did not mind being in the basement as I euphemistically thought we, in claims, 'were the

388

foundations upon which the company rested' which made me smile.

Meantime, Darryl spent a great deal of time in Glasgow both in training and recruitment and although the bean counters had thought that recruitment would be cheap, quick and easy, of course in practice it was anything but. For one, to lure people away from other firms, you need to offer salaries and terms that are greater than those they currently enjoy. A lot had notice periods of three months too, so the whole restaffing of the office took a lot longer than predicted... and yes, cost more.

Dealing with the larger claims and being in the same office as the underwriters had its benefits as well as causing the underwriters some consternation. Whenever I went up to their floor to get an answer to a query, they had learned that my visits were never likely to bring 'good news.' They would pop their heads up and down over the screens like worried meerkats, wondering if I had come to see them or, hopefully, some other poor sod. It was a game I liked to play... I would go past an underwriter who I could see had just breathed out a huge sigh of relief, and then I would spin around and say something like 'No it is you I want to see!' and their face would fall.

The strange thing about working in London, and the City in particular, is that go more than 500 yards from the office in any direction and 'there be dragons' ... because you'd be lost. Finding an office, a pub or a restaurant outside of your patch would be enough to bring you out in a cold sweat. Naturally, I managed to find a large number of watering holes between the office and the station and have enjoyed many an evening of beery loveliness with colleagues. Only once have I ever over-enjoyed myself to such an extent that I have fallen asleep on the last train and woken up an hour away in Ashford, much to Karon's annoyance.

In 2006 the company had recruited an American to write a new line of business that was expected to take off in the UK and Europe – Environmental Impairment Liability (EIL) and I was asked if I would take on dealing with all of the claims... at least for now. EIL is a strange beast in that it covers nearly all the things that general liability coverage excludes – such as gradual pollution and clean-up of own land. It's a sort of hybrid between property and liability cover and as I had dealt with both, I gladly accepted the challenge.

EIL gave me a lot to learn and I attended all the lectures I could about the subject. Before long, bearing in mind that few other companies were writing it anyway, we were the largest EIL carrier in the UK, possibly Europe. I am sorry to disappoint, but none of the claims I have dealt with are 'funny' but they have caused eyebrows to be raised.

The basic principle of EIL is that the polluter pays for the damage. This seems reasonable enough. If you spill something, clean it up. But what if you buy land and you find that someone else had spilled something, or buried it, leaving you as the owner with the legal liability for the clean-up, especially if the seller no longer exists? I'm afraid you are stuck with the cost.

A fire had been burning for days at a waste recycling plant we insured. Our loss adjuster had reported back that the insured company had leased a plot of land and had taken in old wood, shredded it, stacked it in heaps and then sold the chippings to a power station to be burned as fuel. The plant took money from the company depositing the wood and money from the power station buying the chippings. It seems like a licence to print money, doesn't it?

Except that you need a licence to store huge stacks of chippings. Wood, when wet, can get hot from bacterial action and decay, then steam, then smoulder and then burst into flames. This used to be called 'spontaneous combustion' but is now renamed 'chemically induced ignition' to make it less easily understood. The wood was a mixture of trees and MDF, chipboard and other timber, full of paint and varnish residues. Anyway, the licence to store quantities of chippings or other waste material is within the powers of the relevant Local Authority and at our insured's site they had a licence to store just 10,000 tons.

When the fire was reported the adjusters attended and took a whole series of photos and said that the clean-up cost was likely to exceed £1m. The policy limit was £1m and the brokers were over me like a rash to cough up the proceeds. The problem was that the insured was not telling the whole truth and as I pointed out the camera does not lie. The stacks of chippings were massive. The Authority had warned the insured about exceeding their licence and now the estimated storage was 42,000 tons. For a while, the sale of chippings was 45p a ton, but the market became over supplied and the price had fallen to 6p a ton. The insured offered the chippings at no cost, just the cost of transport, but the power station had declined the offer. It was now costing the insured more to transport the chippings to the power station than they would realise in selling. So, faced with no sales and a breach of licence, the fire was exceedingly 'fortuitous' in that we were expected to pay for the clean-up and get the insured out of a financial hole. Except it was not just one fire... there were several. This was arson.

A few weeks passed and the insured, who were described as 'from the travelling community', suddenly disappeared overnight, leaving the landowner with a bill of approaching £5m. The neighbours suffered months of smouldering smokey debris. And people think recycling is environmentally friendly?

A farmer was pulling a fuel bowser with his tractor and suddenly swerving to avoid a hedgehog on the farm track, tipped the bowser into a ditch, knocking off the fuel tap and spilling diesel. Cost of clean-up...£72,000. No news about the hedgehog though.

One icy winter's morning a herdsman was taking a herd of cows for milking and was just going past an above-ground circular galvanised steel lagoon of semi-liquid cow poo when one of the beasts must have bumped against the sides. A seam on the jointed steel sides, with a resounding 'crack', unzipped and the contents of the lagoon, some 2-300,000 gallons of liquid muck came rushing out. The herdsman was swept off his feet on a river of foul-smelling ordure, and sadly two cows drowned in the smelly deluge. The clean-up cost was over £100,000.

Using waste to generate methane and then using the methane to generate electricity seems, on the face of it, to be pretty environmentally 'green'. Waste-to-energy plants are popping up all over the UK, frequently on farms. The trouble is farmers are not generally engineers and as I have previously said, are not known for maintenance. Even static items, such as lagoon tanks, need checking from time to time and do not last forever.

A significant waste-to-energy plant has been installed at an agricultural college. The college was running an experiment to take in local farm waste along with food waste from the council collections and turn the mixture into methane. They then used the methane to generate 'free' electricity for the college and sell any surplus to the national grid. The college had two enormous holding tanks built for the storage of the waste and had a huge metal sphere where the bugs would chomp away on the debris for a few days generating the methane. When all the available methane had been derived from the waste the remaining gloop was clean and could be used as fertilizer. This all seemed easy enough.

The problem was (and is) that food waste is not just food. People put into their recycling bins not just waste food but sometimes plastic packaging, food labels, tin foil and plastic-coated paper. All of the non-biodegradable debris eventually either floats to the top in some cases or sinks to the bottom, creating crusty layers. Both need to be manually removed, but in my example, the layer at the top also had the unfortunate effect of blocking the safety valves. The person in charge of all this expensive equipment? A gardener. One day, there was suddenly a massive explosion, like a balloon popping, and thousands of gallons of muck flooded out and the explosion itself brought down most of the building. The repair costs were over £1m. The gardener went back to planting his daffodils and the college employed a qualified engineer to run the plant.

Things ticked over for years and whilst I did travel from time to time to countries to settle claims, most were pretty boring, to be honest. I had to go to Glasgow to give some training and assist up there with problem matters. I don't mind giving training sessions and the feedback I am given has usually been pretty positive. I'd like to think my semi-theatrical style has something to do with it and that I try to get some audience participation during the sessions.

One of the greatest problems in dealing with claims of a historical nature is trying to find the policy. This is particularly acute in handling disease claims. Typically claims for industrial diseases such as deafness, asbestosis or silicosis, are that the injured party, usually an employee, knows the period when they were employed but is unable to find the insurer on risk at the time.

The company they worked for may have changed its name or have gone into liquidation. It was for these reasons that the UK Govt. set up the Employers Liability Tracing Office (ELTO) and I was seconded onto a team as the claim department's representative. The team consisted of a couple of underwriting representatives, someone from IT, another from Systems and Data Analysis and a chairman. What we had to do was to find all historic policies that were not on the current computer system and upload them. I did say 'we' but the task was actually allocated to underwriters, but it soon became apparent that no underwriter knew the history of the company as well as an old-timer like me. The first thing we needed to do was ascertain the names of all the companies that now comprised ACE and when those companies became licenced to write EL risks. It turned out that INA obtained their licence in 1962.

We then arranged for our IT dept to interrogate the computer systems and come up with a list of all the policies. Their first effort came back with around 14,000 policies. I think my response was 'bollocks'. IT then showed a graph allocating the policies year by year. According to the graph, we wrote three policies in the 1960s, around fifteen in the early 1970s and then suddenly in 1977 two hundred and sixty-seven.

'You are not thinking about this' I said to the IT chap 'Why do you think we suddenly had an appetite for EL in 1977, but for the previous 15 years only wrote 270 policies or about one a month?'

'No idea' he answered 'but that is all we found.'

'I repeat, you are not thinking. The reason you are only finding policies from 1977 is that is when computers came into existence. OK, there may have been something before that, some steam and belt-driven data machine, but if there was such a contraption, it no longer exists. Those policies you have found are only there because in 1977 they were still live. There is no way historic policies would have been uploaded and I bet the only reason the older ones are there, is precisely because they had disease claims and old policies needed to be resurrected to the computer system.'

'What do we do then?' asked the Chairman.

'Find the archive store of the old policies which are in hard copy or the microfilms and upload them' I answered.

'But where is the archive?'

'My guess is Maidstone or Crawley. But where...I have no idea. I'm a claims guy, not an underwriter.'

To get to this point had taken the better part of three years. The ELTO people were undertaking regular audits of the action we were taking and the only person on the team who was there at the start was me. All the others had left, and the situation was reaching a critical point. If significant progress was not made, the company faced the risk of a substantial fine in the millions of pounds.

At last, a breakthrough. The archive had been found. It was, as I predicted, in a storage facility just outside of Maidstone in Aylesford. According to the facility people we had approximately 44,000 archive boxes, but few, if any were labelled. The only way to find out what was in them would be to take them out and physically look.

As an aside, I knew the old claims files were stored there and there was a list... but the list was on a computer system called Lotus 1-2-3, which was obsolete and no modern computer could run the program, oh and to make life even more fun the list was stored on a 6" floppy disc. It was highly likely then that any underwriting list would have been kept in the same fashion. The team spent a day at the facility and there was no other way to deal with this, each box would need to be opened and a new list of contents written. The microfilms had also been traced to a steel cabinet in Glasgow of all places. The next issue was finding a microfiche reader that still worked. We did and the last remaining spare light bulb was kept securely in a locked box.

The next thing to arrange was to get a team together to look at all the boxes. There was a great deal of dust on the boxes, but not as much as left by the remainder of the team who suddenly found more pressing matters to attend to. Going through 44,000 document crates and an unknown number of microfilms was going to be a major task.

The company had decided that they would allocate a sum of money to recruit five people to do the job, which was thought would take a year, possibly eighteen months. Four would do the physical job of going through the boxes, one would be the team leader and he had already been recruited. The work would be carried out in Brentwood, in Essex where the company now had an office. As the only person who knew the old systems, I was allocated the task of trainer. All we had to do now was recruit the four people who would go through the boxes...

My son Josh hoped for a music career. He and his partner Aleks were living in Essex, about 20 miles from Brentwood. Both had university degrees (Aleks had a Masters too). She was waitressing and he was working in a music instrument shop but both were on the lookout for other opportunities. They were both on minimum wage and needed money to get a deposit for a house and for that, they needed full-time employment. I wonder...?

I explained to Josh and Aleks that this was going to be the most boring job in the world. But the pay was around double the minimum wage and it might be the financial kick-start they needed. They both accepted the positions.

We are all on first-name terms in the office, which gave Josh difficulty. He resolved it by calling me 'Mr Dad' which I found rather endearing.

The boxes started to arrive from the archive and it soon became apparent that there was a great deal of junk being stored. I think the company were paying £10 a box per year for storage. Some of the boxes simply contained old newspapers, the contents of a long-departed employee's desk including pairs of shoes, out-of-date textbooks, old diaries etc. I was named and shamed by Josh as he found my old diaries ... well, it was important to know what I was doing in 1985. That information might come in handy someday, perhaps for a memoir?

When the team finally found a rich seam of policies in the boxes, the information then had to be uploaded to the ELTO website and there were no exceptions. Thus, a box of scheme policies for newsagents and GP surgeries from the

1960s was dutifully uploaded. I took a look at some of the policies and the premium charged was "2/6". 'What's this number?' someone asked.

'Oh, that's two and six. Two shillings and sixpence, or twelve and half pence in current money. These policies were in the pre-decimalisation currency which happened in 1971. It makes one wonder how anyone could possibly have a disease claim from working in a GP surgery in 1969 though.'

I think this phase of the ELTO project lasted two years. Aleks went off to get a 'proper job' with the Police, and Josh and one other remained and took on full-time positions in the hope of actually becoming trainee underwriters. I think Josh finally accepted that insurance is not as boring as he thought. It is, but he hasn't realised that yet.

One very hot summer's day in 2009 whilst sitting on an unairconditioned train that was stuck just outside London Bridge (signal failure apparently) I had read the Evening Standard from cover to cover. Perspiration had glued me to my seat. The crossword had been completed as had the sudoku and I had taken to reading the small ads when a banner at the foot of the paper caught my eye... the 'Annual Beer Festival at Earls Court'. It was the following week. I found the website and there were tickets available and an offer to buy nine, get a tenth free. I emailed nine business friends and all were up for it, so I bought ten tickets for the following Friday.

The Friday came around quickly enough and we all met at Monument tube station at 3 p.m. for the journey to Earl's Court. The area inside was vast and approximately 200 or so beers to choose from. How would I manage? We decided that the sensible thing would be to buy half pints, that way we would have greater choices. The venue was packed with men, many all dressed in the uniform of the day – T-shirts (not quite hiding the beer gut underneath), shorts, long socks and sandals. Oh, and a hat and a bushy beard. We were all in suits. The female of the species seemed a rarity too. From a distant part of the venue there was a massive cheer and a Mexican wave of cheering followed around the stadium. Someone had dropped a glass. As the afternoon continued there seemed to be a lot more of that happening. Not sure why. The revelry was all good-humoured and we soon settled into an afternoon and early evening of beery appreciation.

We were probably about six halves in, barely wetting the whistle, to be honest, when Erik (a Californian attorney working in London) announced he was hungry. I volunteered to go and get some suitable supplies. There were a great many choices. Nothing coloured green I noted,
mainly shades of beige – pork pies, pasties, crisps, burgers (beef, pork and, weirdly, ostrich) or scotch eggs etc; I settled on freshly made pork scratchings. I bought about four big bags of the delicacy, which smelt heavenly. I offered round the bags to share and Erik asked 'What is it?'

'Er... pork scratchings Erik. A real English delicacy. Try one they're great!'

Erik daintily prized one of the warm, curly brown treats from the bag and held it up to the light between his thumb and forefinger examining it closely. 'But it's got hair on it!' he exclaimed.

'Oh, just eat it Erik, they're really good you know.' Meantime the others in the group were tucking in with gusto. With some trepidation, Erik put one into his mouth and began chewing. His face lit up. 'Oh, they're great' he said, chewing away and grabbing a few more from the bag 'I've got to take some of these home.' And with that, he turned on his heel and disappeared for a few minutes returning with two more bags 'for later'. Now, Erik was a health nut. In fact, I think all he ate were nuts and seeds, so I warned him not to take a cholesterol test for a few weeks to get it out of his system, but by now he was getting glassy-eyed and probably wouldn't remember.

I think I left about 8 or 9 p.m. I got home, I remember that much, but do not remember the journey at all. My suit reeked of beer, pasties and perspiration. I figured that if there was a repeat performance next year, it would be jeans and T-shirts.

In 2010 our group of ten had turned into twenty and thirty in 2011. By 2017 I sort of recalled buying fifty tickets and I was attending not only on the Friday, but Wednesday too. The event had moved from Earl's Court to Olympia and due to Covid was cancelled in 2020 and 2021. Sadly, this means my commemorative beer glass collection will have gaps. Not that Karon will be in the least bit bothered – she complains that these valuable keepsakes take up far too much room and so have been consigned to boxes in the shed.

Karon also complained that my odd bottle of beer, 'takes up too much room'. At a solicitor's Christmas Party in 1997 we were all given a bottle of Festive Ale as a keepsake. A nice gesture. I kept mine in its original packaging in a slot on the wine rack for years where it gathered dust. One day, Karon was exasperated as there was no room on the wine rack for the £4.99 bottle of Tesco's Finest plonk she had just bought and told me to drink the beer as it was 'getting in the way'. By now the beer was 21 years old. Would it be drinkable? There was only one way to find out. So, taking the lid off I gently poured the golden ale into one of the glasses from the beer festival that escaped confinement to the shed; and took a sip. It was lovely. I was about three-quarters of the way into the pint when my curiosity was piqued and I googled the ale I was drinking, and I nearly choked. It was still available. Yes, at £180 a bottle!! I could have divorced her. Oh, dear God, what had I done? Was it a good beer? Yes. Was it £180 good? No, no, and thrice no. I should have done the sensible thing and sold it on eBay.

I mentioned that I had taken up painting and I dabble in watercolours, charcoal, ink, pencil and acrylics. I'm not very good, but I enjoy it. In one lesson (I have been taking lessons for over twenty years) my teacher gave us the subject of the 'qualities of light' and I was struggling to grasp this. [I suppose you are wondering what this has to do with insurance claims, but patience, I'm coming to that.]

I had noticed a picture in the insurance press of the BP Deepwater Horizon rig on fire. I had a major claim for the disaster. I contacted the publishers and they said the picture was not copyrighted, so I was free to copy it. The picture shows the rig on fire, on one side the sky is sunny, but on the other, the sky is black with smoke. Would this qualify as 'the quality of light'? Apparently, it would.

My first effort was in watercolour, but I was not happy with the result as the colours were too muted. My next effort was in acrylic and I happened to show it to a loss adjuster and she offered to buy it. Wow! I did another version, slightly larger and this one was snapped up by Erik, who has it framed on the wall in his office in California. I then did a third, on canvas this time and much bigger and sold that on eBay to another solicitor I knew.

I have subsequently painted Hastings Pier on fire too. My 'disaster period' then came to an end as no one has bought that one. Then again, most of my paintings are disastrous.

In January 2016 we received news of another merger/takeover. ACE was buying Chubb Corporation for $28.3bn in cash. Curiously and for reasons that have never really been properly explained, the deal stipulated that the new company be renamed... er, Chubb. Depending on whether you were an old Chubb employee or ACE employee you refer to this as either a merger or takeover. It was a takeover, pure and simple.

Thrusting two large firms together meant that there would be some casualties. There would bound to be duplications in all manner of departments from HR to

Finance and of course, claims. Those in middle to senior management were certain to be the most vulnerable and so it proved. Quite how or why some of the decisions were made was way above my pay grade, but Darryl now found himself facing redundancy as he was being replaced by Gary. Fortunately, Darryl was offered a position in Audit, which rather suited his style.

I liked Gary. He was very personable but he would, I think, be the first to admit that he was being elevated from running a team of six to sixty and that requires a very different skill-set. Further, and this came out very early on, the types of claims old Chubb had were very different to those at ACE. My settlement authority was greater than Gary's, which meant that although he was my de facto manager, he couldn't override my financial decisions (not that he would need to, my decisions are fine thank you very much). A large claim at old Chubb would have been £500,000+ but by now in ACE parlance, I didn't get out of bed unless the claim value had two commas in it... i.e., over £1,000,000. I used to quip that my initials TC meant 'two commas'.

I sat adjacent to Richard and was chatting to him one morning about a new matter where we were probably looking at a £2m exposure, when Gary popped his head over the partition and said, 'Did I hear that right, you have a £2m claim?'

'Yes Gary, I do. Why, what's the problem?'

'Well, I think I need to be involved! It's £2m after all.'

'Really? Not sure why Gary, this is well within my authority and I thought you'd be more interested in this £7.5m one... or maybe this one at £70m?'

'Oh my god, you have a £70m claim?!! You'd best tell me all about it.'

'OK, will do... but presumably you've sort of forgotten about the £2m one? I take it you now understand that these sorts of claims are fairly routine for us. Even this £70m one is nothing to get too excited about. It should be defendable and I have a pretty good handle on it anyway.'

I think Gary found that Richard and I were unmanageable and he was not happy about the move away from the Chubb imaging system called ECHO to the ACE one (Apollo) and he seemed to have a mental block about learning it. He then fell foul of missing a few important regulatory audit checks and was red-carded. I have met Gary once or twice since and he fully admitted to being a fish out of water. Still, he was a nice guy and I liked him.

Replacing Gary took the best part of a year and the team, now consisting of five ELA's, appeared to self-manage rather well. Chris (yes, another Chris) took Gary's place. He had only been with us for maybe two weeks when he suggested taking the team out for a celebratory lunch as he was having a 'big birthday'... he was turning 40. It took milliseconds for me to register it, but at that time he was just 39. My daughter was 30 which meant that not only was Chris younger than me (actually Darryl and Gary were too) but I was old enough to be his father! Good grief.

I am not making light of this, but there was such an opportunity for puns, that I simply could not resist using them at a meeting. Breast implants. We covered a clinic where the procedures were being carried out. I received many notifications although the main claims were against the manufacturers of the actual implants that were filled with industrial silicone rather than medical grade. There is clearly a serious side to this, not all cosmetic surgery is wanted and a lot of the claimants were women who had undergone mastectomies, so not funny at all.

On a serious insurance point though, if a woman had one surgery for one breast procedure that requires removal, that is one claim. But what if both breasts were operated on at the same time...is that one claim or two? And what if she had two separate operations, is that one claim or two? If one implant was OK and not leaking, but she elected to have both removed... would we only pay half? The point was important as the clinic had a significant policy excess of $250,000 per claim. Thus, each claim had either a $250,000 excess or $500,000 and there were a lot of claims, so the point ran into several million dollars. It was on these points that I was dragged kicking and screaming into a meeting for my views.

'It's a difficult one. These need careful handling. Of course, firstly on the one hand... but there again on the other...I don't know, I'd have to carefully weigh up the evidence, because, as you know, all are different. I'll just have to keep you abreast of developments...'

Amazingly, I wasn't taken to HR for a severe talking to.

Years ago, I was dealing with a tragic rape case in a hotel in London and the perpetrator had been caught and rightly sentenced to a good number of years at Her Majesty's pleasure (but not long enough I thought). The rapist was a well-dressed thief who simply wandered into a hotel intent on thieving whatever he could find to pay for his drug habit. While exploring the hotel, he came across an open door. Inside, he found a young female student whose roommate had gone out without taking her key, leaving the door open. The would-be thief changed his modus operandi and brutally raped the girl. He later raped others in the same manner, becoming known in the press as the 'South London Prowler'. A claim was made against the hotel alleging a lack of security, but it was my USA's management requests that I found laughable.

'Trevor, to defend the action we need evidence of how the guy got into the room. So, what we want you to do is this: go to the prison and get a statement from the guy that explains how he got into the room. We can then use that at trial.'

'Let me get this straight... You want me to go to a maximum-security prison and get a statement from a drug-addled convicted rapist in order to defend a civil action against a hotel? Obviously, he's going to tell the truth, isn't he? I mean, a court is bound to accept his word over that of his victim, especially as he denied everything in the criminal trial. And why would he want to cooperate anyway? There is nothing in it for him, is there? Sorry, I think you are nuts. I'm simply not doing it.' And I didn't. The victim sued her travel agent for damages, in the USA of course, and got a squillion-dollar settlement. The case was dropped against the hotel.

A construction company had a contract to put in a large storm sewer at a rather nice city 'tup North. Unfortunately, their subcontractors had made a mistake. The rather large hole they dug was a little too close to a nice row of terraced houses that each began cracking. The house closest to the hole had cracks so great the tenants could wave to their neighbour's next door and also in the street. The gable end was supported, and the challenge was how to handle not only six very upset homeowners but also how to carry out the repairs. The most badly affected house was owned by a Health Authority (HA) and was used as accommodation for nursing staff. So that repairs could be made, the HA would need to rehouse the nurses, pay for the repairs and claim the whole lot from the contractor. It was going to take months, if not a year, to do and we would have no control over the work. There had to be a solution.

I explained to my insured, the main contractor, that as they were first in the firing line, we would have to deal with the claims and then pass them to the subcontractors. This is known as 'pay and chase' and is not something that we like to do, but sometimes it is unavoidable. I suggested that if they had the cash, the most economical way would be to buy the HA house, do the repairs themselves (which we would pay for) and then sell the house. If the repairs were undertaken to a high standard, they would probably make a profit too. The trouble was it meant that we needed to get the HA to agree to sell it to the contractor and that the contractor had to have the available funds to buy the place. Fortunately, they did.

So, off I trotted 'tup North to meet with the HA. All the indications were that they were keen to sell if the price was right.

I went to see the HA with my insured and met with their Estates Manager, Charles. After doing the introductions which were good-natured, I apologised for the damage that had been caused. I then went on to surmise that the cash-strapped HA did not want a year of cash haemorrhaging away in the hope that we would not argue that the repairs could have been undertaken quicker and cheaper. I added that we would certainly wish to query quantum, so instead of creating an argument, I suggested that the property was sold and if the price were right, we would buy the house thus avoiding any nit-picking over repair costs. I did say that the property was not in the best decorative order, what with each room being a bedroom... which made it less attractive to a developer... it was only one house and developers usually like bigger places, the garden was all overgrown... the roof was dodgy due to the gable wall moving...and what's more the place was full of massive cracks! At that, Charles twigged what I was saying and said we had caused the cracks and the other damage in the first place! Waving my hand dismissively, I laughed that off and said that we would be reasonable and pay a fair market price and also pay the HA legal fees for the sale. The HA would have a chunk of cash, they would not have all the repair problems, and it was a win-win.

Charles could see the benefits and after a little modest haggling, a price was agreed. I gave a chunk of cash to the insured for the repairs and after repair, the insured did sell the property for a small profit.

The attitude of the sub-contractor insurers and their loss adjusters (who we used and knew well) nearly drove me to distraction. They queried everything and to make matters even more fun, denied liability outright. I know that in every contractor/sub-contractor dispute the main contractor usually has to take a 'hit' for his failure to properly supervise. It's a load of bull, but it's an argument that is difficult to defeat and seems common enough. Had the opposing adjuster made an offer of a 60/40 split I would have held out for 75/25 (with them taking the larger share) and would probably have settled on 67/33, but they denied outright! Well, this bull had seen a red flag. I decided not to sue them, as that would take too long. Instead, there is a method in construction disputes called Adjudication. It is not perfect, but is cheap and quick. The whole dispute has to be resolved by the Adjudicator in a matter of six weeks. Extensions of time are generally not allowed. There is no going back on the decision, unless the aggrieved party sues, and the whole procedure is thought of as rough and ready justice, which suited me just fine.

The opposing loss adjuster happened to mention during an earlier call (when we were still on speaking terms) that they were holidaying in India on a tour... and would be out of the country and uncontactable for a month from 1st October.

I then arranged for my solicitors to get the Notice of Adjudication ready and sneakily serve it on the opposition on 30th September. A shabby trick or good practice? Answers on a postcard please.

The opposition was very annoyed with me, particularly because the Adjudicator I had chosen, Paul, was a respected authority on construction disputes and had recently authored a book on the subject. Therefore, they couldn't object to the quality of the person I had chosen. They were up against the wall timewise and I graciously allowed them another two weeks to respond (Paul would probably have given it anyway, so I was not being overly generous). Paul apportioned the matter 80/20 (in my favour), and made them pay a significant interim payment too. I was delighted.

What happened next did not delight me though.

I fully expected that as the subcontractor had gone down 80%, their adjuster would take over the outstanding claims from all the other houses. I would have paid 20% of the expert and adjuster's fees too, but no, they said that as the main contractors we were contractually liable (true) and we would, in effect, have to 'pay and chase' and they would go through all the claims with a fine-toothed comb. Oh, and they would not pay any of my adjuster charges either as insurers cannot claim those. As to my requests for interim payments, they would not pay those as they were 'too small', but would roll them over to the final calculation. I was apoplectic but kept my cool for a few months.

Biding my time, I built up my case and this time, just before Christmas (ho-ho-ho!), sent in Adjudication #2.

This time I added in my legal, expert and adjuster fees as well as interest and Paul found for me on all accounts. Another large interim payment was awarded.

By the time that I settled the claims the opposing loss adjuster had passed the file to someone a little more realistic and although I threatened Adjudication #3, they paid me what I requested.

The conclusion?

Don't mess with me for one! I'm not unreasonable and am happy to negotiate, but do not brush me off. My insured were extremely happy with the outcome and have renewed with us ever since. As to the opposing adjuster, well their bloody-mindedness cost their insurer principals close to £500,000 and our business too. I have never used them again.

I said in my introduction that I would avoid mentioning any company names, but in the following tale, there is no option as there is only one organisation in the country that could be involved. Besides, apart from causing the accident, their handling of the aftermath reflects very well on them, so for that I give them credit.

The story begins one Friday in February 2007 when I happened to be in Glasgow in the company of a solicitor (he of the 'booze and fags' fame) at a 'Faculty Dinner' (the Law Society of Scotland) which was held in a very grand building in Glasgow city centre. The guest speaker was a very entertaining retired judge and he had concluded his speech when my solicitor leant over and whispered 'There's just been a train crash.' I turned on my phone and sure enough on the BBC news, there was a newsflash. The train involved happened to be one we insured and I was the emergency point of contact. Crikey, what could I do? The location of the crash was on the English/Scottish border, so not very far away. According to the newsflash, there was a derailment of a passenger train and reports of many casualties. It was past 11 p.m., I was in a dinner suit, pretty well oiled if the truth be known, so was unable to 'do anything' of a physical nature, but tried to call and email the contacts at the insured, but there was no answer. The following morning was a Saturday and once again I was unable to speak to anyone, so I decided to fly back down to London. To be honest, there was not a great deal I could have done. I was not authorised or trained to go 'trackside' and rail accidents are investigated by specialists from the HSE and the Rail Authorities, so I thought it best to wait until Monday when I was back in my office.

[Before I continue with this tale, one of the standard responses to any road accident involving vehicles is that one or other of the parties whacks in a written defence saying that 'so and so failed to swerve to avoid the collision'. Like I say, it's standard stuff. But when a car was driven down a railway embankment and ended up straddling the rail lines and causing one of the most serious rail accidents in the last 100 years, an unthinking barrister had placed in the defence that the claimant's train had 'failed to swerve to avoid the collision'. This spurious defence caused considerable mirth at the time and the tale was quickly passed around the claim community.

It is also industry practice that each rail company deals with their passenger claims first, settles them, and argues about liability later. It is a sensible way of dealing with claims and avoids any arguments over the victims having to prove negligence. It really cannot be any of the passengers' fault in causing a train crash, and as they are the innocent victims of someone's negligence their claims are settled by the train operators who fight over who was to blame later.]

On Monday I did make contact and was told that there would be a big meeting on Wednesday when it was expected that the HM Railway Inspectorate and Rail Accident Investigation Branch would have their preliminary conclusions as to the cause. In the interim the public relations department of our insured swung into overdrive and naturally enough the gentlemen of the press were all over the accident, reporting both fact and fiction. The driver of the train was hailed as a 'hero' by our insured, not that there was a single thing he could have done to avoid the accident.

I thought the manufacturers of the train itself ought to have received more recognition in that not a single window was broken in the crash (they were smashed from the inside or outside by the emergency services during the rescue of the passengers) and all of the carriages remained intact. I saw an article some many months later in one of Karon's glossy magazines, where a granny gave her true life story of the accident where she graphically explained how her face was dragged through the trackside gravel as the carriage slid along on its side. And there was a photo of her in her hospital bed, and there was not a scratch on her face. You can't always believe what you read in the papers.

So, back to the tale. On Wednesday I arrived at the Network Rail offices in Euston. It was now known that sadly there had been one fatality and about two dozen injuries, thankfully none very serious. As to the cause, again the RAIB had been very quick to publish a preliminary conclusion. I was accompanied by just one person from our insured and we were led into a massive meeting room, there had to be about forty people sitting around the table, with others standing. There were loss adjusters, lawyers, insurers and representatives from the RAIB. Introductions were made and the atmosphere was tense.

I decided to go on the offensive but in a kindly way. 'OK,' I began, clapping my hands together and with a big beaming smile on my face, 'which of you is going to be alleging that my train driver failed to swerve to avoid your defective points?' There was some slight sniggering from some of the attendees who surely knew the story to which I was alluding.

'Er, no one is going to say that Mr Cottington' responded the Chairman with a slight smile. 'In fact, based on the preliminary investigation, it is 99% certain that Network Rail or their contractors working on the line are responsible.'

'Thank you for that. But only 99%? OK, please explain then how that remaining 1% could ever be the responsibility of the train company?'

The chairman shuffled his papers nervously. 'What we are saying is that we will take over dealing with all of the claims and will deal with all of them to a conclusion.'

'So, 99% is 100% then? Nothing is going to be claimed against the train company? I must add that the company chairman is in the press as saying that all the victims will be treated compassionately and claims settled promptly. He will not accept, and neither will we, any delays in handling the claims. Can we have your assurance the claims will all be handled promptly and fairly?'

'Yes.'

'OK, thank you for the confirmation. Well, that's that then. I'll report back and close my file.' And with that, our tea and coffee largely untouched, we upped and left after probably twenty minutes, leaving the others to fight over who screwed up... spoiler alert: it was the contractors.

The accident had happened on the previous Friday, I opened the file on a Monday morning and two days later closed it for zero. I wish more settled as easily as that.

I defend cases in the main, protecting a policyholder's reputation and our earned premium. I have not lost sight though of the fact that at the end of any claim is an aggrieved person or company or person with horrific injuries. Sometimes things do get 'personal'. And nothing was more personal than when I became a claimant.

It all happened when my daughter purchased a flat in Northampton. The flat was in joint names as Hayley was unable to get a mortgage because, as a trainee solicitor, she was not considered to be in full-time employment. We set about redecorating the place. I severed a tendon in my right thumb when bashing some broken tiles into a box, a sharp tile flipped back and made the tiniest of cuts on the back of my right thumb. I hadn't even realised what I had

416

done at the time. However, all the work was completed and one Saturday afternoon in April, Hayley called and said that sewage was backing up out of her shower and toilet and was overflowing into the flat. The flat was on the ground floor and logic dictated that there must have been a blockage downstream for sewage to back up. The managing agents were no help whatsoever. They insisted that we get in a plumber and if the blockage was in a communal area, they would 'consider' reimbursing the plumber's charge. I tried to explain that the blockage had to be outside the flat as Hayley had not been there all day and water and sewage was coming backwards – the blockage had to be in a communal area. But it was no good, they were not listening.

I arranged for the local water company to come and look and they confirmed that the blockage was under the car park. They had rodding and jetting equipment with them but would only proceed if the managing agents gave the OK. The agents wouldn't. Why? Because the local water authority 'may not have insurance'. They did, we insured them, but that was not good enough. So, the damage continued and two days later the boneheads at the managing agents finally accepted that the blockage was indeed under the car park and it appeared to be a 'fat berg' mixed with paper towels, J cloths and discarded wet wipes.

Hayley's domestic insurers paid for the damage and alternative accommodation costs. Sadly, she never spent another night in the flat as she qualified as a solicitor before repairs were completed and moved jobs to Bristol. But I was aggrieved. Actually, we both were. The blockage was under the control of the agents and they exacerbated the damage due to their intransigence. We had a look at the lease and there was a clause relating to maintenance of the drains. The landlord/managing agents were responsible for that. I asked them for the records of drain maintenance, but they had none. They had never inspected the drains, ever.

The insurers of the agents appointed loss adjusters. We met at the flat and I got paid a compliment when the adjuster asked if I was '*the* Trevor Cottington'? I'm a definite article, not a mister. Apparently, I was well known and had a 'reputation'. (Hayley later said that I cast a long shadow.) I rather thought, in my naivety, that as one professional to another, we would have a fairly easy ride, but that was not the case. They said in their defence that they had a 'reactive maintenance regime' which I finally got them to admit meant that when something was broken, they'd fix it. But that is not maintenance I said, that is repair. No matter, they said, liability was denied.

Getting nowhere and without the support of our Insurance company, who thought that the claim was uneconomic for them to pursue, Hayley and I sued the bastards.

The first firm of solicitors the defendants appointed was a firm I knew. They dropped the file like a hot potato when they realised who was the claimant. The next firm appointed was based in Leicester and I did not know them. I was on the phone with them about a Direction's hearing (where the parties agree on a timetable, venue etc) one day when we discussed the Court venue. They hoped for Northampton as that is where the flat was and so were the defence witnesses. I said that we were claimants and we could choose the venue and as Hayley lived in Bristol and I was in Kent, we'd choose... Hastings. They said that this would mean a whole day out for them and their witnesses with possibly an overnight stay. I said that that would be a shame, but Hastings was a nice place, fish 'n' chips on the beach, ice creams... they'd love it. The thing was that we kept the claim below the small claims limit and this meant that apart from court fees there would be no claim for costs. The cost of them travelling and spending a day in Hastings meant that economically it was cheaper for them to settle than argue, so they sent us a cheque in settlement.

I repeat – don't mess with me, I'm a "The"!

There are the bizarre cases of course.

On the seventh floor of a hotel, a maid was pushing her cart of fresh linen, towels and toiletries down a corridor, when she noticed a reasonably dressed woman at the far end of the corridor, walking towards her, casually pushing the doors of other rooms. A door opened and the well-dressed woman went inside. The maid checked her list of rooms to be serviced and noticed that the room the woman had entered was to be cleaned, having previously been occupied by a pilot. The hotel was close to an airport and frequently used by crews on stop-overs. The maid went to the door and knocked, but there was no answer. She tried her pass key, but strangely it did not work either. She banged on the door again and said that if the door was not opened, she would call security. No answer, so security was summoned. It took a good 20 minutes to get the door opened, but when they went in, no one was inside. However, a window was open.

Meanwhile, outside of the hotel, waiting at a bus stop a man was suddenly hit on the head by a falling woman. Investigations revealed that the woman was a vagrant and was known to stalk hotels and student accommodation blocks in the hope of getting a bed for the day, some sleep and probably a free shower.

It seems that in her panic, the woman had tried to shuffle along the window ledge to avoid being caught once again, but the ledge was at a 45-degree angle and she lost her footing and fell. The woman was killed instantly. The man was rendered paraplegic. The man sued the hotel on the basis that the window should not have been capable of opening so far as to allow anyone to get out. The window catch was indeed faulty. We settled.

My working life was by now routinely handling rather boring claims. They are large, certainly, but none are so interesting as to be memoir-worthy. I suppose that is not entirely true. It depends on your point of view, I guess. A company we insured just fried the electrical system of a farm in the USA, the consequence of which was all the lighting and heating for their glass hot houses failed and their crop died. The claim was over $1m. The crop? Marijuana.

I seem to spend a great deal of time filling in spreadsheets for statistical purposes which I am convinced no one ever reads or learns from. In the days of paper and when we had an index-card system to record claims, we were once asked what the company could do to reduce the number of claims? One answer we gave was not to write any insured that began with the letter 'A' as we had more claims for insureds that started with 'A' than any other letter. It seemed a perfectly reasonable and statistically accurate answer to me. But did anyone listen or learn? I don't suppose they did for a moment.

The rest of my time is taken up with WOFT meetings (Waste of Flipping* Time) where I sit and listen to management with their views on a claim, who ask questions that are inane, historic or pointless and that never, ever, change the outcome. 'Trevor, the ship has hit an iceberg... can you let me know, asap, what colour were the deck chairs?'

(*other words beginning with 'F' can be substituted)

I have spoken about 'you win some, you lose some' but I think this narrative is pitifully low on wins. In April 2021 I achieved four successes in Courts of Appeal in four countries – France, USA, Japan and Saudi Arabia. The facts of each are of interest to me, but probably not to a wider audience. The French case was all to do with plastic boxes for microwave meals, the USA was terrorism in Israel, Japan an oil rig disaster, and trespass in Saudi. Like I said, boring. Collective savings? Far above $100m. My lawyers do take a lot of the credit for running the cases, but I'd like to think that I spotted the defences available in the first place.

I don't think I have become cynical about what I do, though I am increasingly concerned that automation of the claims process is not a 'good thing' overall. People buy insurance and people have and make claims. If I were the claimant, I'd like to deal with people who care, listen and empathise with me. Automated processes simply do not do that. 'Your call is in a queue and we are sorry for the delay but we are experiencing an unprecedented level of calls at the moment. Please stay on line. Your call is important to us and we will be with you as soon as possible'. There cannot be anyone who hasn't heard that, or a variation of the words, at some time or other. For how long will calls be at an unprecedented level?

The company recently introduced a whole process called CODE dealing with ownership of a problem and delivering excellence. I liked the principle and fully endorsed it, translating the acronym to Cottington Obviously Does Everything, which I thought was more fitting. In truth, email and the dozens of people who are now copied into everything means that few people take ownership of anything without some fear that they may be overstepping the mark...so they copy in others to try and take away any fallout. One document I send out, which used to go to about six recipients, now goes to over 150. Why? No idea, but I cannot believe all 150 read the damn thing or even need to see it. Just layer upon layer of arse protection, I guess.

Some years ago, a very loyal policyholder tried to get me on the phone. It was a Saturday in February and I was out walking the dog. When I got home my daughter said that my mobile phone was ringing constantly and on looking at the number of missed calls, I rightly guessed something was urgent, so I called the number. It was a contracts manager who explained that during the dismantlement of a tower crane, the operatives of the crane company had undone the bolts of the crane tower from bottom to top, not the other way around and the tower had toppled over and was now leaning at a crazy angle. The two operatives had been flung from the tower and had died in the fall. The Police and HSE were already on site and there was a further concern about the crane itself. If it fell it would flatten a school, so they were looking for permission to bring the crane down in a controlled explosion. Could I permit them to do that? The decision had to be now as in a couple of hours it would be dark and they could not do the demolition in the dark.

High winds were predicted and if the crane fell, well it would be a disaster. What should I do? I deal with liability claims and strictly speaking, this was a property claim. If the crane did flatten the school, then it would become a liability claim and a big one at that. I tried to contact the property claims manager, but I was unable to find their contact number on our web page – I was also unable to get hold of the adjusters nominated on the risk, so I did what I thought was right – I gave permission for the controlled explosion. It took three attempts and shattered a few windows before the crane came down safely, but the disaster was averted. I did not have the authority to do what I did, but who would have done anything different? On the following Monday, I bared my soul to the company management and expected some backlash, but thankfully and rightly, there was none.

Have I saved the best for last? It is certainly a strange case and if you are in the least offended by matters of a sexual nature, then best skip over the next story... but now you're are teeny bit intrigued, aren't you?

A letter of claim came in from a swanky hotel. The letter was long and graphic and involved a chap who I shall call Rupert. Now Rupert was engaged to Cecil and the two had decided that pre-wedding they would, over a long weekend go to a big city, stay in a 5* hotel, have fabulous meals, and do a bit of shopping in the boutiques. As a surprise, Cecil had arranged for a full body massage for himself and Rupert at the hotel. All was arranged and in one of the sumptuous massage rooms, Rupert disrobed as instructed and lay flat on the massage table, his nether regions wrapped in a fluffy white towel. Whilst lying there face down, smelling the jasmine and lotus flower perfumes the masseur oiled Rupert's back and began the massage on his shoulders and spine...and continued down the back of his legs, then gently lifting the towel, the masseur then continued on Rupert's buttocks. The masseur then instructed Rupert to roll onto his back. Rupert was by now somewhat 'aroused' and according to the letter of claim, was shocked and disgusted when the masseur took hold of his erect member and began slowly massaging that too...then orally. After five minutes or so of this unexpected 'treatment', Rupert shall we say 'arrived'. Then the masseur calmly patted him on the thigh and smiling, announced that the session had ended.

The letter of claim stated that Rupert was demanding damages for an unwanted and unwarranted assault. It was said that Cecil was completely unaware of the incident as Rupert did not want to think that he had been unfaithful to his fiancé and so had not mentioned it. Nevertheless, Rupert was certain that the upscale hotel would not want any publicity for this egregious act, so he indicated that he would accept just £10,000 in compensation and the matter would go away 'quietly'.

I contacted the hotel and wasn't so surprised to hear that the masseur had been 'let go' but had denied none of the allegations made against him, but did add that following the massage, Rupert had given him a £100 tip!

This was a matter that needed nipping in the bud and deciding on a suitable strategy, I phoned Rupert's solicitor. I said that all of the facts outlined in their letter of claim were indeed true, and nothing was denied, but did ask at what point during the massage did Rupert think that things had gone a little too far? When his penis was being rubbed or perhaps when he was enjoying oral sex for about five minutes? And why, if he felt he was the victim of an assault did he never say anything at the time, or on checking out, and why did 'thoroughly disgusted and ashamed' Rupert then leave the masseur a £100 tip?? I added that as the allegation was one of sexual assault, the Police needed to be involved and that would certainly involve interviews with Rupert and Cecil, but given that the masseur never denied the facts, the matter would be regarded as consensual. I added that liability was denied and if legal proceedings were issued, whilst it was true that the hotel would not wish that sort of publicity, such a story would be bound to be picked up by the press. Cecil would surely see it...and how would Rupert explain away the

£100 tip? The solicitor said he would 'take his client's instructions'. We never heard from him again. What a shame, I would have fun with that one!

The one thing that I can say is that there has never been a day when I have thrown a sickie because I found my job boring. Actually, I have not thrown a sickie ever, but I have found that doing what I do is interesting and certainly not boring.

I will miss it when I stop.

Epilogue

As I trundle to retirement, I do look back with a degree of fondness over my 45 years of dealing with claims. There can be few jobs where there is a culture of wining and dining ingrained in what we do. It may come as a surprise, but only once did I return to the office after a lunchtime of boozing and pretend to carry on working. I probably made a stupid decision or sent a letter I didn't mean to, so I never did it again. My management colleagues in Maidstone and London did, initially at least, invite me to their lunchtime beers, but I usually refused. Did that hold me back? Probably, as I never heard the gossip. Did I care? No. I was usually driving anyway that day and losing my licence would have been catastrophic for me and the family. If I do go out at lunchtime, I go out late, then make sure I do not come back and I make up the time later.

I have made a great number of friends and acquaintances over the years and although I do hope to keep in touch with them, I expect that in time I will become a footnote in the memory.

Josh is now a broker dealing with entertainment risks and Hayley is a solicitor specialising in insurance disputes. The apples have not fallen far from the tree.

Karon has listened to all my stories and for the most part, even thinks they are 'interesting' or maybe she's just feigning interest in the hope that I will eventually shut up. Many years ago, we agreed on a 'safe word' or 'words' to be more exact to prevent me from boring her. Imagine James Bond coming home and saying to Mrs B what a hard day he'd had. 'Darling, I've just jumped out of a light aircraft, with no parachute, landed in the snow, made skis out of tea trays, and slalomed down a mountainside all the while being pursued by snarling dogs and baddies firing machine guns, grabbed a heroine round the waist, jumped into a passing car, drove the car off a cliff into a shark-infested ocean only to be rescued by a waiting mini-submarine!' She might say 'you've got to be kidding me'... but instead Karon would simply say 'James Bond' and I know that this is the signal for me to stop talking.

Being a liability claims handler for most of my career inevitably means that I am going to be disliked by some people and hopefully liked by others. I was recently told that my nickname was 'Marmite' and if 50% of the people I have dealt with like me and what I do, then I think that has got to be seen as a success.

Money is the only thing we can give to an injured person in compensation. It's a rare day that I think that £x would compensate me for the loss of a leg, arm or loved one. I was chatting once to a young paralysed man and what he said he wanted most of all was to be able to stand in a pub, lean on a bar and buy his mates a round of beers again. A simple thing and something that he'd never be able to do again. I've always tried to empathise with the deserving claimant. I think it helps.

Actually, I have just recalled the time when...

'James Bond!'

'Yes Karon.'

I am not retiring, I am simply withdrawing, entirely without prejudice or course.

Afterword

I began writing this story of my insurance life in 2021 during one of the first Covid 'lockdowns' and have gradually added to it from time to time. But as you can see I hadn't retired when I wrote the 'epilogue', so strictly speaking I suppose it is not truly an epilogue, but that is pedantic and I'm not changing it now, so yah boo sucks to the pedants.

My departure from Chubb was a rather drawn-out affair. In March 2023, I was sitting with Chris (my manager) who was giving me my annual appraisal and, I hoped, a massive pay rise. It was not massive, but rather the norm for the time, and then I dropped the 'R' bombshell.

I had always made it known that I would give six months' notice of my proposed retirement date and I said that I would like to drop down to a three-day week and take retirement at the end of September. Although somewhat shocked by my announcement my proposal was eagerly accepted (rather too eagerly I thought) and by working a three-day week, I was immediately going to get a 40% pay cut. I was asked which three days I would work? I said Monday, Tuesday and Wednesday, but would only come into the office on Tuesdays, which was team meeting day, or whenever I had an external meeting. Again, this was agreed.

By agreeing to work M/T/W I was able to take advantage of all the bank holidays there were between now (it was the end of March) and the end of September. Oh, and in 2023 we were also given an extra day off for the King's Coronation. I also suggested that as most of my claims took many months or years to resolve, it would be pointless to take on new claims only to hand them over in 6 months. Again, this was also agreed.

As further luck would have it, a new recruit had arrived in the department as a transferee from Chubb USA. Apart from being way better looking than yours truly, she was also a qualified attorney so could knock spots off my USA knowledge of practice and procedure, so I immediately transferred all my USA claims to her. For ease of narrative, I will call her 'Mango' mainly because that is the nickname I gave her and luckily, she was not in the least offended and seems to be happy to use the moniker to me in any notes.

As the months went by my workload began to reduce as claims were settled. In the first couple of months, me being me, I tried to squeeze five days' work into three, but I soon learned to log off at just after 5 p.m. on a Wednesday and not look at my iPhone until Monday. I knew I had to wind down and soon got used to a four-day weekend. It was rather pleasant.

I had a stupid run-in with HR over my holiday entitlement. I had calculated that pro rata I was allowed over 6 months 50% of my annual leave. I was getting 27 days so I figured I was allowed 13 days. 'Oh no,' says the bonehead from HR, 'because you are considered part-time, you are only entitled to take a number of hours, not days.'

'How many hours?' I asked.

'Oh, 104 hours.'

Out with the calculator I tapped away and said 'But

104 hours is 13 days! And what about the 5 days I carried over from 2022?'

'As it is now April and you haven't used the 5 days, you will lose them.' Bastards. I asked another question:

'How many days of sickness have I taken in the last, say 10 or 20 years?' (I knew the answer was none).

'Er... our records do not go back that far, but from what I can see on screen, you haven't had any.'

'And my reward for 100% attendance and 38 years unblemished employment is that you remove my rolled over leave, which I could not take because we were under the cosh with new work and training of a new team member (that'd be Mango)?'

'Yes, I'm sorry, rules are rules and there are no exceptions.' (Again, bastards).

The very next day I took off sick. It was sort of true. I had just had dental surgery for the removal of a fractured molar root and was rather down in the dumps, but whilst I could have soldiered on, I thought 'sod them' and took a day as sick leave. I decided to take the 'robbed' days 'on the quiet' and not fill in the leave request on one of our many computer systems (we had 41). I think I took just 4 days... but I can't recall now whether I did or didn't. What I didn't do was take the 13 days of leave (sorry, 104 hours) and was paid for those instead, for which I was more than happy.

By June my leaving date was drawing nearer. It was 12 weeks away or in real terms 36 working days (or 288 HR hours), less bank holidays. I was asked by my manager about my plans for a 'do'. I mentioned that I celebrated my 60th birthday at the Wine Lodge, which was a Young's pub located in Fenchurch Street. Unfortunately, the pub had to close down due to a decline in sales caused by the COVID-19 pandemic. I thought about The Crosse Keys pub which was nearby, large and, for my benefit, the cheapest pub around (it's a 'Spoons pub) and I thought I could get a section cordoned off for the few people who would turn out. Then one of our firms of solicitors offered to host the event. I gave it a millisecond of thought and readily agreed!

As August turned to September the invites for the 'do' had gone out and it rather surprised me [a] how many people I knew and [b] how many were prepared to come to see me off and [c] how many I had forgotten to invite in the first place ...quite a few as it turned out. Although I was due to leave Chubb on 27th September, my actual 'do' was on Friday, October 6th. Our lovely friends at ASLEF had called a rail strike on the 5th and that meant the trains were likely to be screwy on the 6th and then the tube drivers were also due to strike, but on the 4th they called it off. I had been asked if I'd like to delay the party, but as I was scheduled to have a replacement knee operation in late October (which would put me on crutches for 6-8 weeks) I decided delay was not an option. So, the 'do' was definitely on. If only half of the acceptances turned up there would still be about 35-40 people there and I figured that would be just fine.

I had to visit Glasgow for a final farewell and training session. I decided that my friends and colleagues in Glasgow needed to hear my proposed farewell speech. I think it went down well, but there were a few passages I was unhappy about, so I decided to cut them for the main event. It wasn't that those passages were rude or anything, just rather Chubb-specific, and I didn't think they would translate too well for a mixed audience back in London.

In my last week at Chubb I had many invitations to a final lunch or dinner and without hesitation, I accepted them all, even if it meant having a boozy lunch and dinner on the same day! It's a tough life eh? Well, by now I had little or nothing to do work-wise and in that final week I wasn't even turning up until near lunchtime (what were they going to do? Fire me??). On the last day, I handed in my PC and phone to the IT guys and from that point onward there was nothing I could do... so went down to the pub. I knew I was going to have to sacrifice my iPhone and in preparation for that had invested in a new Google phone, but it is an Android (whatever that is) and I really couldn't work it. Anyway, the IT guys said my iPhone was obsolete and they were going to throw it away for recycling, and being a nice chap, I offered to recycle it for them. So, taking out the SIM card from the Android I poked it into the iPhone and was up and running again, but of course, I had lost all my contacts and more importantly the high score on one of the games.

And then to the 'do' itself. This was on floor 16 of the Walkie Talkie building in London and I'd been told there were 92 acceptances. Wow! I can't be sure but I think 85 showed up. I was thrilled. There were two rather lovely speeches from Chris and Trevor D before I picked up the mic and launched into my speech, which had been 2 to 3 years in the making. Karon had already 'red-penned' a lot of the more vitriolic comments much earlier and my Glasgow sanitised version was the one they got. There is no point in relaying it here as I think so much depended on the delivery on the night. I'd like to think I nailed it – certainly, there was a great deal of applause after I said 'and finally' and blew on a dog whistle and ended with the immortal line 'Well, I wanted to go out on a high note!'

I think I did.

People left some lovely comments on LinkedIn etc

Stacy M: It's come around quickly. You told us you would train us to be the best group of Casualty Adjusters in the country. I think you achieved that! Thank you

Bruce G: Congratulations Trevor - and best wishes for your retirement. You deserve it. They just don't make them like you any more !

Samantha S: "You can't unsee things"... that day in Wokingham will live with me forever! Enjoy your retirement with all your many skills and hobbies. [*she was referring to a video we saw about a surgical mesh inserted into a certain part of the female anatomy*]

Simon R: Quite an innings Mr Cottington! I've a lot to be thankful to you for, enjoy the retirement when it comes.

Arthur C: I wish you all the best for your retirement. It has been a pleasure knowing and working with you. You are probably the best claims handler in the world (or at least the best one I have come across)

Nicki S: Another legend lost from the market! We had so many laughs along the way, enjoy your well deserved retirement!

Helen W: What a day to retire! Thats my birthday - wishing you a wonderfully long & fulfilling retirement & sending you eternal gratitude for giving me a chance, which I hope you have never regretted

Jeremy B: Well TC - you've done a great shift and will leave a void in the market with the depth of experience and more importantly your character. I wish you health and happiness in your long deserved retirement and will catch up beforehand. Take a bow !

Simon S: It will be a great loss not having your guidance, experience, and counsel on our matter. I have worked in the insurance industry for 37 years with some very capable people and count you at the very top. You also bring your own style and character in a world of increasing harmonisation such that it has always been much more interesting (and productive) when you have been around.

Steve P : I really appreciated all of the years working with you! I remember the first time I went over to London – it was my first real trip EVER outside the US. When I sat down with you, all my anxieties went away when I realized you were doing the exact same thing we were in the US. You will sorely be missed in our industry.

Mark A: Forty six years by any measure is a huge achievement, but at the level and complexity you achieved, is worthy of the accolades bestowed upon you. Stories were abound, all very humorous.

Trevor D: Never predictable, always pushing the envelope and questioning the "norm", and testing "authority".

Hayley C: your use of apostrophes is appalling.

Nick W: Regrettably our paths only crossed a couple of times but you made each occasion amusing and memorable. One of my old colleagues also just reminded me of a letter you'd written to him slamming our coverage defence as "shallower than a worm's grave". You were probably right!!

Karishma P: Chubb will not be the same without you! A living Insurance Claims Adjuster Legend. Will miss our strategies and discussions and all the of the jokes and laughs we had along the way!

Mark A: Accounts managers hearts would miss a beat when your name appeared on their phone. Your wisdom and counsel are beyond compare.

Murray W: The longest eulogy ever.

About the Author

Trevor lives in rural Kent with his long-suffering wife, Karon, and a labrador or two. He is a keen, but terrible artist and/or gardener. He likes walking with the dogs, music, cooking and drinking beer.

After 46 years dealing with various types of insurance claims the experience has left him with an ever-increasing admiration as to how not only can someone injure themselves, but blame someone else for their own stupidity.

Printed in Great Britain
by Amazon